# FIRST DORCHESTER FAMILIES

Calvin W. Mowbray

HERITAGE BOOKS
2007

# HERITAGE BOOKS

*AN IMPRINT OF HERITAGE BOOKS, INC.*

## Books, CDs, and more—Worldwide

For our listing of thousands of titles see our website
at
www.HeritageBooks.com

Published 2007 by
HERITAGE BOOKS, INC.
Publishing Division
65 East Main Street
Westminster, Maryland 21157-5026

Other books by the author:
*Early Settlers of Dorchester County and Their Lands*

International Standard Book Number: 978-158549-199-5

# CONTENTS

# INTRODUCTION

This volume sets forth some genealogical sketches of the early settlers who obtained land in the area that eventually became Dorchester County. Most of the sketches contain, at least, information on the first and second Dorchester generations and in some instances that information is combined with some historical information about the family. It is unfortunate that most of the sketches had to be limited to the first and second generations because to have gone beyond that point would have greatly minimized the number of vignettes that could have been included in this volume.

This is not a work that "generally" editorializes about those families that are included herein; not is it a volume that attempts to aggrandize either the ancestry of those families or of the actual members thereof.

Every effort has been made to keep the vignettes as factual as possible.

It is of interest to note that many of the early land owners of Dorchester County were once inhabitants of Calvert County which in early Maryland included both sides of the Patuxent River. Raymond Staplefort and Henry Hooper owned adjoining tracts of land on Preston Creek in Calvert County; William Berry, Richard Preston, Anthony LeCompte, Hugh Hopewell and Robert Harwood were inhabitants of the Patuxent area; William Chapline, John Felton and Arthur Wright resided on the lower side of St. Leonards Creek. Francis Armstrong was a lieutenant in Captain Thomas Manning's Calvert County militia company; John Abington and William Dorrington were at one time commissioners of Calvert County. Francis Billingsley and Ismael Wright served at one time as Patuxent constables. All of these people became Dorchester County land owners. A survey of the origins of the early settlers of Dorchester County shows that better than sixty percent came from Calvert County.

It is, also, of interest to note that many of the geographical and place name of Dorchester County had their counterparts in Calvert County: Fishing Creek, Hunting Creek, Island Creek, Islington, Preston and Susquehanna Point are a few examples.

Some of the Calvert inhabitants who obtained land in Dorchester migrated to Dorchester, some remained in Calvert. Where the records are clear on this point the sketch is so noted. In any case, their relationship with matters Dorchester are shown in the vignette. The origin of the Dorchester settlers not from Calvert County, if shown by the records, is also noted in each sketch.

The list of early settlers of Dorchester County was compiled, in the main, from the patent records at the Hall of Records in Annapolis. The first 176 patentees were determined by starting with the earliest survey made for a patented tract in the area that became Dorchester County and then listing in chronological order according to dates of survey the first 176 tracts patented.

The patents obtained by the first 176 patentees covered the period 1659-1669.  Some transfers of land were made in that period of time and some of those transfers were recorded in either the Provincial Court Records or the Talbot County Court Records.  The grantees shown in those records have, also, been included in the list of 176 persons to first obtain land in Dorchester County.

The numerical order in which land was obtained in Dorchester County is shown in this volume by the number in parentheses after the family name at the heading of each sketch.  For example, (1) after Bentley indicates that the first patented tract surveyed in Dorchester County was for a Bentley.  The sketch will show in all cases the full name of the patentee.  The family names used in the headings are arranged in alphabetical order.

Shown herein, in addition to the list of those who settled in the period 1659-1669, are vignettes on some who settled between 1669 and 1683.  Those who settled in the latter period are designated with one (X) after the family name in the heading.  Also, shown herein are vignettes on some few who settled after 1683 and those are designated with a double (XX) after the family name in the heading.

Unfortunately there is a dearth of information on some of the early land-owners of Dorchester; some did not actually become inhabitants of the County and some of those who did, apparently for a variety of reasons, appeared only very sketchily in the records.  Never-the-less, those are listed herein.

It should be remembered that there are many variants to spelling of names in the old records of Maryland.  No attempt has been made herein to standardize all the many variants but in some few cases the generally accepted spelling has been substituted for some of the variants.

Finally, if any genealogical error is discovered herein or if any reader is in position to submit, without obligation, documented genealogical information on any of the early settlers listed herein where no substantial information is now shown, the author would be happy to receive such for future reprintings.

# EXPLANATIONS

Arch....Archives of Maryland

Calendar Year Change....Prior to January 1, 1752, the legal year
in England began on Annunciation Day, March 25th. The change to
Jan. 1st took place on that date in 1752, the change also applied
to the Colonies.  Hence, dates prior to 1752 between January 1st
and March 25th are sometimes written thus:  January 14, 1668/9,
that is 1669 according to present reckoning.  Some date are
written accordingly in this volume.

DLR....Dorchester Land Records.

F....Folio.

L....Liber.

Pat....Patent.

RR....Rent Rolls.

TLR....Talbot County Land Records.

Wills....Record of Wills at Hall of Records, Annapolis, Maryland.

ABRAHAM (26)

On March 4, 1662/3, a one hundred and fifty acre tract of land called "Ashburne" located at the head of Blackwater River was surveyed for Isaac Abraham of Calvert County (Pat. L7 F270). On March 21, 1663, another tract called "Marchland" was surveyed for him and it was located on the east side of Slaughter Creek.

On April 25, 1668, Abraham of Calvert County, planter, sold "Ashburne" to Robert Curtis. The records show that "Ashburne" began at the head of an old Indian field near the head of Blackwater Branch (TLR L1 F37). In November of that same year, he sold "Marshland" to Peter Sharpe of Talbot County (TLR L1 F63).

The will of Isaac Abraham dated October 14, 1674, and probated June 28, 1675, shows that he was at that time an inhabitant of Talbot County (Wills L2 F353). The will named wife, Elizabeth, who was the relict of Thomas Read (Arch. Vol. 41, p 379); a son, Jacob; and a daughter, Sarah Read. (Another daughter, Mary, was named in the will of widow, Elizabeth.)

There is nothing in the records to indicate that Isaac Abraham or any of his immediate family ever became inhabitants of Dorchester County.

Isaac Abraham did, however, leave a monument in Dorchester County by his acquisition and brief ownership of "Ashburne." This tract became a land-mark estate for its use by many prominent Dorchester families. Over the generations, such families as Curtis, Trevallion, Stewart, Manning and many, many others called it home.

AGG (148)

On January 29, 1669, James Selby sold a 100 acre tract of land called "Selby's Desire" to William Merchant and James Ogg (Agg) (DLR 1 OLD 9). The tract was located at the head of the Blackwater River adjoining the land of Isaac Abraham. Later Merchant and Agg purchased "Ipswitch," a 132 acre tract which was also located on the Blackwater. The record on this last purchase (DLR 3 OLD 44) shows that James Agg was a cordwainer. The two also acquired "Congum" and it too was located on the Blackwater.

Nothing further has been found in the records about James Agg.

ALDRIDGE (172)

On February 11, 1671, a 50 acre tract of land was surveyed for Henry Aldridge (Pat. L19 F111). The tract was named "Elsing" and it was located on the south side of Fishing Creek. Rent Roll Record L10 F382 contains the following note: "Given by Eldridge to James Busick's wife and in his possession."

In the ensuing years Henry Aldridge acquired a number of

additional tracts in the area including an adjoining tract called "Tadum" which was surveyed for him on August 12, 1679.

Henry Aldridge made a will dated November 26, 1690, which was probated April 20, 1695 (Wills 7, 176). In his will he devised "Elsing" and "Tadum" to his wife Mary and upon her death to Mary Stone, daughter of Rebecca Busick (before her marriage to Busick) and upon the death of Mary Stone to her mother Rebecca Busick.

Mary Aldridge, widow of Henry Aldridge, made a will dated November 28, 1697, which was probated March 8, 1699 (Wills 6,239). Mary Stone was named in that will so she was still living as of the date of the will.

It is readily apparent from the above facts that "Elsing" and "Tadum" did not come into the possession of Rebecca Busick and her husband, James Busick, until after November 28, 1697.

It should be noted that "Elsing" is the site on which "Old Trinity Church" is located and that James Busick is credited with donating the land on which it is located.

The question arises, "How could 'Old Trinity' have been erected before 1697?"

ALFORD (79)

On September 4, 1665, John Alford and William Wilson had a 200 acre tract of land surveyed; it was located on Tobacco Stick Creek and it was named "Musketta Quarter." In the next few years John Alford acquired several tracts of land in Dorchester County, some by patent, some by purchase. Apparently, his activities became centered in the Hunting Creek area when he obtained from John Richardson on August 7, 1679, five tracts of land in that area: "Fox Hill" 200 acres; "Wakefield" 300 acres; "Skipton" 200 acres; "Eldridge" 200 acres; and "Huntington" 400 acres.

In 1679 John Alford was named a justice for Dorchester County and he served in that capacity in 1680 and 1681.

John Alford made a will dated October 21, 1702, which was probated November 11, 1702 (Wills 11,243). In his will he named sons John, Matthias and Joseph; wife, Elizabeth.

It is interesting to note that William Wilson, a partner in 1665, was a witness to the will of 1702.

Dorchester Land Record 6 OLD 21 dated June 2, 1703, identifies Elizabeth as the wife of John Halpin and the widow of the late John Alford, Sr.

An Edward Alford made a will on February 28, 1741, which was probated May 17, 1742 (Wills L22, F501); in his will Edward named sons William, Edward, John and Thomas; wife, Mary.

Dorchester Land Record 8 OLD 291 dated March 28, 1728, contains the deposition of a John Alford, aged 70, who mentions his uncle, old John Alford, and young John Alford son of aforesaid John Alford. This deposition would indicate that the John Alford who patented "Musketta Quarter" had a brother who is not identified further in the records.

## ALLAN (XX)

The first Allan to appear in the Dorchester Land Records is Alexander Allan who acquired parts of "Jordan's Point" and "Worcester" in what is now the Hills Point area of Dorchester County. He acquired those tracts through his marriage to Priscilla Hill who had inherited them from her grandfather, Henry Hill.

Henry Hill Allan, son of Alexander and Priscilla, married Elizabeth Sherwood Botner on August 21, 1798. Elizabeth was the widow of John Botner and the daughter of Ann Asquith and Nicholas Sherwood. Elizabeth and Henry had the following children: (1) Alexander Allan, born August 5, 1779; (2) Mary Kempt Allan, born November 5, 1801, married John McNeal, June 22, 1819, St. Paul's, Baltimore; (3) Ann Asquith Allan, born March 23, 1803, married John W. McGrath, September 13, 1826, by Rev. Mr. Potts, Philadelphia; (4) Henry Hill Allan, born July 27, 1804; (5) Elizabeth Sherwood Allan, born August 16, 1806, married John Wilson Albright, October 15, 1829, St. Andrew's Episcopal Church, Philadelphia.

Elizabeth and John W. Albright had issue: George, Sarah, Elizabeth Sherwood, Theodore F., Virginia, Francis Janvier, Ann, Martha Janvier, Buena Vista and Henry Allan.

Elizabeth Allan, widow of Henry Hill Allan, resided in her last years with Elizabeth and John W. Albright in Philadelphia where she died on October 18, 1873, at age 98. She was interred in the family plot, Woodlands Cemetery, Philadelphia.

## ANDERSON (51)

On February 23, 1665, a 200 acre tract of land was surveyed for George Anderson. The tract was called "Saint Pulchers" and it was located on the Northwest Branch of the Transquaking River.

On December 16, 1669, George Anderson, tailor, of Calvert County sold to Alexander Draper of Somerset County the tract called "Saint Pulchers" (See Arch. of Md., Vol. 57, pages 479-480).

Rent Roll Record L10 F452 states, "No heirs to be found."

## ANDERTON (66)

John Anderton married Gertrude Smith, daughter of Thomas and Jane Smith of Kent Island (Arch. of Md., Vol. LVII, pages 246 and 249). Thomas and Jane Smith had two daughters, Gertrude and

Jane. Thomas Smith was executed for his part in Claiborne's Rebellion. Jane, his widow, married Philip Taylor by whom she had two children, Thomas and Sarah Taylor. After Philip died, Jane married William Eltonhead who was captured by the Puritans at the battle of Severn, court-martialed and executed.

On April 16, 1665, an 800 acre tract of land was surveyed for John Anderton. The tract was named "The Reserve" and it was located on the west side of the Nanticoke River. The tract was absorbed by the Nanticoke Indian Reservation.

It is interesting to note that "The Reserve" adjoined "Handsell," a tract patented by Thomas Taylor, half-brother of Gertrude the wife of John Anderton (see Taylor 50).

Talbot County Land Record, Liber 4, Folio 167, shows that John Anderton and Gertrude, his wife, had two sons, John and Francis.

John Anderton of St. Mary's County had on August 15, 1659, obtained by patent a 600 acre tract of land called "Anderton" in Talbot County. The tract was located on Tred Haven Creek at "Anderton's Point" (Pat. L4, F381). He was awarded 300 acres for transporting himself, Gertrude his wife, and Nicholas Garkey, his servant. Three hundred acres was assigned to him by Jane Eltonhead.

No further information has been found in the records on John, the son. The other son, Francis, married Mary Abraham, daughter of Isaac and Elizabeth Abraham and sister of Jacob Abraham. After Francis died, his widow, Mary, married William Scotten (DLR 8, OLD 447).

Francis Anderton made a will (Wills 13, 697) dated December 7, 1713, which was probated March 10, 1713/4; in his will he devised 295 acres of "Bath" and 50 acres of "Westward" including his dwelling plantation to his eldest son, John. He also named sons Francis and James; daughters Mary and Sarah; and wife, Mary.

James Anderton, son of Francis, died in 1730, and he named in his will (Wills 20, 29) his two sisters, Sarah Anderton and Mary Brown. His brother, John, was named executor.

Mary Anderton, daughter of Francis and Mary, married John Brown. Sarah, the other daughter of Francis and Mary, married Daniel Sullivan (see DLR 7 OLD 57-7 OLD 79-8 OLD 447-10 OLD 27).

Francis Anderton, son of Francis, made a will dated March 24, 1730 (Wills 20, 168) which was probated April 8, 1731. In it he named his sister, Sarah, and brother-in-law, John Brown.

APPLEGARTH (XX)

Members of the Applegarth family, apparently, did not become residents of Dorchester County until the late 1700's.

William Applegarth (1791-1826) was born in the Neck District and spent his entire life there engaged in farming. He died at 35 years of age. One of his brothers, Nathaniel Applegarth, who married Elizabeth Vickers July 30, 1810, was sheriff of Dorchester County from 1828 thru 1830.

John Applegarth (1814-1887) was born in the Neck District and his father, William, died when he, John, was about 12 years old. John moved to the Lakes District and operated a farm there until 1850 at which time he became a Deputy Sheriff and Assessor of Dorchester County.

Ann H. Tubman (1811-1889) who was born in Hooper Island married John S. Keene June 26, 1833 and after her first husband died, she married John Applegarth on August 31, 1840. Ann had the following children: Allie Keene, Emily A. Keene, and William F. Applegarth.

In 1855 John Applegarth, son of William, formed a partnership with a brother-in-law in the boot and shoe business in Baltimore; he returned to the Lakes District in 1859 where he retired in 1881. He moved to Virginia and died in 1887 at Martinsburgh.

A number of Applegarths appear in the marriage license records in the late 1700s, none of which have been identified with William and his brother, Nathaniel:

Robert Applegarth married Sally Thomas April 6, 1787.
William Applegarth married Nancy Busick September 24, 1791.
Philemon Applegarth married Nancy Howell August 10, 1793.
James Appelgarth married Amelia Beckwith January 31, 1799. Thomas Applegarth (1780-1851) of Ross Neck married Sarah Whitley December 13, 1802.

ARMSTRONG (15)

In 1657 Francis Armstrong immigrated to Calvert County. Five years later on April 17, 1662, a 400-acre tract of land was surveyed for him on James Island and it was called "Armstrong's Hog Pen" (Pat. L5 F284). In the succeeding years, several other tracts were surveyed for him in the Taylors Island area of what eventually became Dorchester County.

On April 15, 1664, Francis Armstrong, planter, of the Cliffs in Calvert County and his wife Frances, sold a 350 acre tract called "Sarke" to John Edmondson, merchant, of the Cliffs in Calvert County. "Sarke" was located between the lands of Andrew Cooke (Cooks Point) and Thomas Todd (Todds Point) (see Arch. of Md., Vol. 49, p 249).

On July 6, 1664, Francis Armstrong sold "Armstrong's Quarter" to John Taylor, planter of Calvert County; this tract, consisting of 200 acres, was located a little to the southward of James Island (Arch. of Md., Vol. 49, p 250).

On August 13, 1665, Francis and his wife sold "Armstrong's Folly" to William Killman. This tract of 400 acres was on the north side of James Island (TLR L1 F15).

It is interesting to note that in the early patent records of the Province, the bay between Cooks Point and Todds Point was designated as Armstrong's Bay.

Francis Armstrong left Calvert County and became an innholder in Talbot County. The records do not show that he ever resided in the area that became Dorchester County. His will dated February 18, 1668, and probated October 13, 1669, named two sons: Francis and Philemon, and a daughter Elizabeth.

## ASHCOM (127)

On April 29, 1669, a 200 acre tract of land called "Ashcom's Purchase" was surveyed for John Ashcom. The tract was located on Hungar River and it is what is known today as "Asquith Island."

John Ashcom, of Berkshire, England, immigrated to Calvert County in 1649 and was granted "Point Patience," a 300 acre tract for transporting himself, wife, four sons, and six servants. "Point Patience" is now part of the Patuxent Naval Base.

"Ashcom's Purchase" was devised by John to his son, Nathaniel, who in turn devised it to his son, John. There is nothing in the records to indicate that any of the Ashcom family ever became inhabitants of Dorchester County.

## ATKINS (109)

Patent Liber 11, Folio 442, shows that John Atkins, mariner, of Calvert County, was transported to the Province of Maryland in 1668.

On August 13, 1668, a 50 acre tract of land was surveyed for him; the tract was called "Return Point" and it was located on the west side of Hungar River.

Rent Roll Record, Liber 10, Folio 453 (1706) shows "No heirs to be found."

## BAXTER (39)

On March 3, 1664, a 150 acre tract of land was surveyed for Thomas Baxter; it was named "Cedar Point" and it was located on the north side of Island Bay (known today as Brannock Bay--Pat. L6 F256).

On May 3, 1699, Thomas Baxter of Stafford County, Virginia, sold "Cedar Point" to Edward Willoughby of Dorchester County (DLR 5 OLD 128).

No other reference has been found to indicate that Thomas Baxter was ever an inhabitant of Dorchester County.

BECKWITH (X)

The records show that Henry Beckwith was born in Virginia in the year 1619 and his father was William, who had migrated to Virginia in 1607 with Captain John Smith on the ship "Phoenix."

On November 7, 1671, Henry Beckwith and Arthur Wright acquired "Stewart's Place" which was located at the head od Stewart's Creek (now known as Beckwith Creek after Henry Beckwith and his family). "Stewart's Place" became the dwelling plantation of the Beckwith family.

On June 8, 1696, Henry Beckwith acquired from Thomas Skinner of Dorchester County a 50 acre tract of land called "Berry's Chance" (DLR 5 OLD 23). This tract was located at the head of Little Choptank River adjoining the land of Stephen Gary. In this land record Elizabeth is shown as the wife of Henry Beckwith and mother of Thomas Skinner, Jr. Elizabeth was the widow of Thomas Skinner, Sr.

In the next few years Henry Beckwith acquired a number of additional tracts of land, some in the same area, some in other parts of the county.

Henry and Elizabeth (Skinner) Beckwith had two sons, Henry II and Nehemiah Beckwith, and a daughter, Elizabeth.

Henry Beckwith II married Mary Warner, daughter of Magdalene and William Warner.

Nehemiah Beckwith married Frances Taylor on October 5, 1712, at Transquaking Meeting House (Third Haven Meeting Records).

Elizabeth, daughter of Henry and Elizabeth (Skinner) Beckwith, married Samuel Willoughby.

Nehemiah Beckwith and Frances (Taylor) Beckwith had two daughters, Elizabeth and Dorothy. Elizabeth married an Ennalls.

Henry Beckwith II and Mary (Warner) Beckwith had the following children:
    Nehemiah, who married Mary Thomas, daughter of William Thomas.
    Charles, who married Mary (last name unknown - See DLR 20 OLD 1).
    Henry, who married Anna Mowbray, daughter of William and Mary Mowbray.
    Elizabeth, who married John Taylor.
    Mary, who married John Vickers.
    Margaretta, who married Thomas Cooke.

Henry Beckwith II made a will dated January 4, 1755 (Wills 30, 190). He devised his dwelling plantation to his wife, Mary; to

son, Charles, "Refuse Neck" where Charles now lives and 150 acres
of "Stewart's Place" adjoining him; son Nehemiah Beckwith,
remainder of "Stewart's Place." He also named in his will
daughter, Mary, wife of John Vickers; daughter, Elizabeth, wife
of John Taylor; daughter, Margaret, wife of Thomas Cooke; and
son, Henry.

Mary (Warner) Beckwith, widow of Henry Beckwith II, made a will
dated October 21, 1756 (Wills 30, 610) in which she named the
following: sons Charles and Nehemiah; grandsons John Taylor,
Nehemiah Cooke, Edward Cooke; granddaughters Elizabeth Taylor,
Ann Cooke; daughter Mary Vickers and son-in-law Thomas Cooke.

BECKWITH (XX)
'George'

According to a Beckwith genealogy, William Beckwith was the first
Beckwith to settle in America. He came to Jamestown, Virginia,
in 1607 with Captain John Smith in the ship "Phoenix." William
had a brother named Thomas who remained in England but George,
the son of Thomas, immigrated to Calvert County, Maryland, in
1648.

George married, Frances, daughter of Nicholas Harvey. George
Beckwith returned to London where he died in 1676.

George Beckwith is referred to in Dorchester Land Record 4 OLD 44
dated December 7, 1681. In that Record it is noted that Charles
Beckwith was the son and heir of George.

BENTLEY (1)

The first tract of land surveyed in what eventually became
Dorchester County was surveyed on June 30, 1659, for Richard
Bentley (Pat. L4 F121). The tract was called "Michael Bentley"
and it consisted of 350 acres located on Hoopers Island. It
adjoined another tract called "Bentley" which was also surveyed
for Richard Bentley; the latter tract was surveyed on July 7,
1659. Today it is known as "Bentley Point."

Unfortunately, there seems to be no records to be found about
Richard Bentley other than the fact that he immigrated to the
Province in 1657.

The will of Andrew Insley, which was filed April 14, 1699 and
probated August 2, 1699 (Wills 6,291) shows that he owned the two
tracts as of the date of the will, and yet, there seems to be no
record as to how he acquired them. Andrew devised "Bentley Point"
along with some lands on Farm Creek near a place called Indian
Cabbins to his son James. He names a son, William, a daughter
Mary, son-in-law Michael Todd and Margaret, his wife. Andrew
named his wife, Elizabeth, executrix. Since his first wife was
named Margaret Jones (Early Settlers of Md. p250), he must have
married twice.

Rent Roll L10 F121 and Rent Roll L10 F343 both show that Richard Bentley was dead and that the tracts were taken up by others which would indicate that there was no official or legal transfer of these two tracts prior to his death and that he had no heirs.

It is, indeed, regrettable that so little is known about Richard Bentley, the individual who had the first tract of land surveyed in what eventually became Dorchester County.

## BERRY (22)

James and Elizabeth Berry immigrated from Virginia to Calvert County in 1652 with their three children: William, Richard and Benjamin.

William Berry, son of James and Elizabeth, was born in Northampton County, Virginia, about 1635. He first settled on a 900 acre tract of land which had been surveyed for his father and which was located on the north side of the Patuxent River, a few miles above the Preston homestead.

William Berry first married Naomi Preston, daughter of Richard Preston, and they had three children: William Berry, Jr., who married Naomi, daughter of Shadrach Whalley of Bucks County, Pa., on September 9, 1686; James Berry who married first Sarah, daughter of Henry and Elizabeth Wolchurch on April 14, 1686, and second Elizabeth, daughter of John and Frances Pitt on April 11, 1691; Rebecca Berry who married James Ridley on November 28, 1686.

William Berry, son of James and Elizabeth Berry, took as his second wife, Margaret, the widow of his brother-in-law Richard. Margaret was the daughter of Thomas Marsh. William and Margaret had one child, a son named Thomas.

On December 29, 1662, a 200 acre tract of land named "Berry's Chance" located at the head of the Little Choptank River and bordering Stephen Gary's land was surveyed for Wm. Berry (Pat. L5 F436). This tract was sold by Berry on March 20, 1668, to Thomas Skinner, planter, of Talbot County (Arch. of Md., Vol. 57, pages 286 and 287).

William Berry was a delegate to the Maryland Assembly from Calvert County and he was also a justice of that County. William and his family were prominent Quakers. At the time of his death in 1691, William was an inhabitant of Talbot County. There is nothing in the records to indicate that he ever became an inhabitant of Dorchester County. His descendants became prominent in the affairs of Talbot County.

## BLINKHORNE (83)

Patent L4 F216 shows that Robert Blinkhorne immigrated to the Province of Maryland in 1659 with his wife, Mary, and sons, John and Robert.

Three tracts of land were surveyed for Robert Blinkhorne in 1665 in what was to become Dorchester County: "Mathews Vineyard" 100 acres, "Blinkhorne's Desire" 400 acres, and "Blinkhorne's Point" 200 acres.

On November 28, 1673, Robert Blinkhorne, planter, of St. Leonard's Creek in Patuxent River in Calvert County and Bridgett, his wife, sold "Mathews Vineyard" to Richard Tubman (DLR 3 OLD 51). On July 16, 1681, Robert and Bridgett sold "Blinkhorne's Point" to William Walker (DLR 4 OLD 57).

Rent Roll Record L10 F352 shows that "Blinkhorne's Desire" which was located on Fowling Creek in what is now Caroline County was in the possession of the heirs of Robert Blinkhorne.

There is nothing in the records to indicate that Robert Blinkhorne or any of his family were ever inhabitants of Dorchester County.

BOYLSTON (47)

Certificate of Survey L9 F63 shows that a 300 acre tract of land called "Boylston's Neck" was surveyed for Thomas Boylston. The survey was made in January of 1665 and the tract was located on the west side of the Northwest Branch of the Nanticoke River about ten miles up the Branch.

On March 19, 1665/6 Thomas Boylston sold the tract to William Lewis (TLR L1 F12).

A tract called "Boylston's Neck" could not be located in the Rent Roll Records nor could any record of a patent be found on it. No further reference to Thomas Boylston could be found in the records.

BRADLEY (X)

Patent Record L18 F90 shows that Henry Bradley immigrated to Maryland in 1674 with his wife, Mary; and his sons, Richard, Henry and William; and Samuel his brother. Samuel died shortly thereafter leaving his estate to his brother Henry.

Henry Bradley had a 100 acre tract of land surveyed on September 3, 1674, called "Bradley's Lott." It was located at the head of the Transquaking River on the south side of Willis Dam adjoining a tract of land called "Francis Cottage." In that same year, he acquired by patent a 66 acre tract in the same area called "Bradley's Desire." He and Mary had three more children after their arrival in Dorchester County: John, Josiah and Mary.

The will of Henry Bradley was dated February 14, 1678, and probated July 1, 1679, in it he named his wife, Mary, and all six children.

Richard Bradley, son of Henry and Mary, married Alice Short, daughter of Christopher Short, and they had five sons and five daughters, all of whom were named in his will dated December 28, 1749 (Wills 27,293), along with his wife, Alice. His sons were Christopher Short Bradley, John, Richard, Samuel, and the youngest son, William. His daughters were Elizabeth McDaniel, Anna Cook, Sarah Mackeminey, Alice Cook, and the youngest Mary.

Henry Bradley, apparently, was a close friend of Bartholomew Ennalls for in his will Bartholomew made the following bequest: "I give and bequeath to John Bradley, one of the orphans of Henry Bradley, deceased, one cow when he comes of age."

BRAMBLE (106)

On March 6, 1668, a 100 acre tract of land was surveyed for Thomas Bramble. It was called "Middle Land" and it was located on Preston Creek of the Little Choptank River. On March 29, 1670, he had an adjoining 100 acres surveyed called "Bramble's Desire."

On May 8, 1689, Samuel Bramble of Dorchester County sold the 100 acre tract called "Middle Land" to John Draper. Since there had been no record of a transfer from Thomas Bramble to Samuel, it must be assumed that Samuel inherited the tract.

On September 16, 1690, Samuel Bramble registered his will in Dorchester Land Record 4 1/2 OLD 14; neither a wife nor any children were mentioned in the will.

BRANNOCK (150)

The first record of a Brannock in Dorchester County appears in Pat. L17, F76, which shows that Edmond Brannock immigrated with his wife, Jane, in 1666. Jane was probably the daughter of Alexander Roche since she was named in his will (Wills 1, 629).

A grant was received by Edmond Brannock for transporting himself and wife, Jane, on November 14, 1673 (Pat. L19, F4), for 100 acres called "Timber Neck" and it was located on Fishing Creek of the Little Choptank River.

In the meantime on December 2, 1669, Edmond Brannock had purchased from Robert Harwood of Talbot County a tract of land called "Harwood's Choice" which was also located in the same area (DLR 1 OLD 18). Subsequently, Edmond acquired a number of tracts in the Little Choptank River area and from part of those tracts originated the name "Brannock's Neck."

Edmond and Jane had the following children: Thomas, David, Edmond, John, Mary, Elizabeth, and Jane Jones. Edmond Brannock made a will dated September 1, 1701, and it was probated January 5, 1703 (Wills 3, 18).

David Brannock, son of immigrant Edmond Brannock, was living in South Carolina by 1734 (DLR 9 OLD 256).

John Brannock (1669-1741), son of Edmond and Jane, married Margaret (Beckwith) LeCompte, widow of Anthony LeCompte II. The step-children of John Brannock Sr. were: Nehemiah LeCompte, Anthony LeCompte and Margaret. His daughters, Ann, married (1) Robert Spedden, and (2) Joseph Pain; Elizabeth (1) Richard Fisher, and (2) John Baynard.

John Brannock, Sr., was an attorney and a planter; he served several terms as a delegate to the Maryland Assembly. He acquired by patent or purchase a number of tracts of land in the area of Brooks Creek. "Brannocks Bay" derived its name from him and his family. John Brannock, Sr., died in 1741; his will was dated April 8, 1741, and it was probated July 3, 1741 (Wills 22, 385). He named no sons in his will, although a John Brannock, Jr., was a witness to his will.

Margaret Brannock, widow of John Brannock, Sr., made a will dated October 13, 1751 (Wills 28, 324), and in it she named the following: Grandsons - John Spedden, Robert Spedden, Hugh Spedden and Joseph Pain; Granddaughter Mary LeCompte; Son Nehemiah LeCompte; daughters Margaret Matthews and Anne Pain; Joseph Pain, husband of Anne Pain, and granddaughter, Anne Pain.

Dorchester Land Record 2 OLD 133 of 1722 names John Brannock, Sr., and John Brannock, Jr. Not much is shown in the records about John Brannock, Jr.; he was not mentioned in the will of John Brannock, Sr., nor was he mentioned in the will of Margaret, the widow of John, Sr.

There was a John Brannock who made a will November 27, 1745 (Wills 25, 30). It is believed that this is the John Brannock that was referred to in the records as John Brannock, Jr. It is also believed that this John Brannock Jr. was not the son of John Brannock, Sr., but the son of Thomas Brannock, the brother of John Brannock, Sr. It is well to remember that at the time that these records were made the terms senior and junior did not necessarily mean "father and son," but were often used simply to distinguish an older person from a younger person of the same name. In his will (Wills 25,30) John Brannock named no wife or children, only brothers Edmond, Henry and Philemon and grandson Edmond, son of his brother Edmond. The names of these relatives in the will lend credence to the theory that this John Brannock was the son of Thomas and Frances Brannock.

Thomas Brannock, son of Edmond and Jane Brannock and brother of John Brannock and Edmond Brannock, married Frances Newton. Dorchester Land Record 12 OLD 136 dated November 8, 1743, shows that Thomas was born in 1675. He made a will dated January 28, 1744/5 (Wills 24,29). In his will he named the following children: John, Philemon, Henry, Thomas, William, Margaret who married Curtis Evans, Mary who married John Meekins; and he also named his wife, Frances. In his will he did not name a daughter, Esther, nor did he name a son, Edmond, but other records show that he had a daughter and a son so named.

Edmond Brannock, son of Edmond and Jane Brannock, married Rebecca Sergeant in 1703 (see Marriage Index at Hall of Records, Annapolis, Maryland - DLR 3 OLD 173 of August 7, 1679 - DLR 4 1/2 OLD 39 of July 12, 1685 - DLR 9 OLD 61 of May 2, 1733 - all three Land Records concerning the tract of land called "Canterbury"). After Edmond died his widow, Rebecca, married John Harwood (DLR 8 OLD 100).

The will of Rebecca (Sergeant - Brannock) Harwood was dated October 5, 1741, and was probated July 19, 1742 (Wills 22,504). In her will she named daughters Mary Owens, Rachel Orrells, and Rebecca Nicholls; grandson Thomas Noal; son Thomas Brannock. DLR 7 OLD 49 dated June 10, 1717, shows that Rebecca also had a daughter, Elizabeth LeCompte, wife of Peter LeCompte.

Thomas Brannock, son of Rebecca and Edmond, was referred to in the records sometimes as Thomas Brannock, Jr., again it should be remembered that it was the custom at the time these records were made to use the characterizations "Senior and Junior" to distinguish an older person from a younger person, both with the same name. The characterization did not necessarily represent a father-son relationship. The term Junior was applied to Thomas Brannock, son of Rebecca and Edmond, no doubt, to distinguish him from his uncle, the older Thomas Brannock.

BRICE (145)

On February 20, 1669, Richard Butwell, planter, sold to William Brice "Butwell's Choice" containing 100 acres of land located near the head of Little Choptank River adjoining the land of Robert Winsmore (DLR 1 OLD 8).

Dorchester Land Record 4 OLD 124 names the wife of William Brice as Elinor.

No additional information has been found in the records on William Brice.

BROOKS (14)

Michael Brooke, son of John Brooke of Yorkshire, England, immigrated to Calvert County in 1654. He represented Calvert County in the Assembly in 1658 thru 1660 and was a justice of Calvert County in 1655 thru 1661. Patent Record L5 F59 shows that he received a gift of 400 acres of land from the Governor and Council for public service.

On April 16, 1662, a 250 acre tract of land called "Brooks Landing" was surveyed for Michael Brooke of Calvert County (Pat. L5 F231). The tract was located in what became Dorchester County, between Jordan Point and Manning Point. Jordan Point later became known as Hills Point, and Manning Point later became known as Cook Point. On that same day he had a 100 acre tract surveyed on the west side of Oyster Creek, on Taylors Island, called "Hog Point Neck."

Michael and Frances Brooke were the parents of one son, John. The records show that Dr. John Brooke, the son, was still living in Calvert County in 1667. There are no records to indicate that Michael ever lived in Dorchester County.

Prior to 1665 Frances, the widow of Michael, married Henry Trippe of Dorchester County.

By 1671 Dr. John Brooke had moved to Dorchester County and in that year he became a justice of that county. He later represented the county as a burgess in the Maryland Assembly. Dr. John married Katherine Stevens, widow of Robert Stevens. John and Katherine had two daughters, Ann and Mary.

Ann married Thomas Cook and had four children: Babington, Mary, Ann and John. When Thomas Cook died, his widow, Ann, married John Stevens (see "Early Dorchester" by C. W. Mowbray, page 61).

Mary, the daughter of Dr. John and Katherine, married Joseph Ennalls and they had the following children: William, Bartholomew, Joseph, Thomas, Henry, Elizabeth and Mary.

After his first wife, Katherine, died, Dr. John Brooke married Judith, the widow of John Newman. Dr. Brooke died in 1692. His will showed that his dwelling plantation was in Transquaking. (Note: The maiden name of Judith Newman was probably Judith Winsmore.)

BROWN (100)

Patent Record L5 F203 shows that Thomas Brown was transported to Maryland in 1662.

On August 29, 1667, a 100 acre tract of land called "Brown's Rest" was surveyed for him (Pat. L11 F388). "Brown's Rest" was located at the head of Tar Bay.

On May 20, 1672, a 150 acre tract of land called "Angels Hold" was surveyed for him and it was also located on Tar Bay.

Dorchester Land Record 3 OLD 189, dated December 18, 1679, shows that Elizabeth Brown was the widow of Thomas Brown.

In Dorchester Land Record 6 OLD 64, dated May 10, 1705, Thomas Johnson and his wife, Elizabeth, of Cecil County transferred part of "Brown's Rest" and "Angels Hold."

BURTON (117)

Patent Record L12 F359 shows that William Burton of Dorchester County immigrated from Virginia in 1669.

In that same year, a 150 acre tract of land was surveyed for him. It was called "Burton's Lott" and it was located on the Northeast Branch of the Chicamacomico River.

Rent Roll Record L10 F364 shows for "Burton's Lott:" "No heirs to be found."

## BUSSEY (6)

George Bussey immigrated to Calvert County in February of 1653 with his wife and two sons, George and Henry. On August 13, 1659, he had a tract of land surveyed that was located north of what is now the town of Cambridge in Dorchester County. The tract was called, "Busby," and it consisted of 500 acres (Pat. L4 F373). It encompassed "Bussey's Marsh," now called Great or Grays Marsh, and it was the sixth tract surveyed in what eventually became Dorchester County.

Henry Sewall, merchant of North Yarmouth in the County of Norfolk, acquired "Busby" and on December 22, 1664, he sold it and "Sewall's Point" (an adjoining tract that Sewall had patented to William Dorrington, gent of Patuxent [Arch. of Md., Vol. 49, pages 338-339]).

When George Bussey made his will, he was still an inhabitant of Calvert County. In the will (Wills, 1,316), he named his wife, Ann, executrix. There is nothing in the records to indicate that George Bussey or any of his immediate family ever became inhabitants of Dorchester County.

But, "Busby" became a land-mark estate of the County. At one time or another, it was owned all or in part by such staid Dorchester families as Dorrington, Hambrook, from which the names Hambrook Point and Hambrook Bay originated; Caile, Murray, Steele, Henry and many others. Along the way the property was divided and the part nearest Jenkins Creek became known as "Algonquin", or the Sandy Hill Property.

## BUTTON (151)

On April 1, 1676, John Hudson, planter of Dorchester County, sold to John Southy, planter, and John Button, cooper, "Turkey Point," a tract of land which was located on the Blackwater River and which contained 100 acres.

On May 1, 1683, the two divided the 100 acres (DLR 4 OLD 80).

John Button in the next few years acquired several tracts in the vicinity of "Turkey Point." The area is known today as "Buttons Neck" and the neck is partially bordered by a creek called Buttons Creek.

On October 3, 1706, John Button made a will which was probated August 10, 1710 (Wills 13,347). In it he named his wife, Mary, sons, John, Peter and William, and daughters, Elizabeth, Mary and Rachel.

BUTWELL (110)

On December 31, 1668, a 100 acre tract of land was surveyed for Richard Butwell. The tract was named "Butwell's Choice" and it was located at the head of Sharp's Creek (now Lee's Creek) and adjoined the land of Robert Winsmore. On February 20, 1669, Butwell sold the tract to William Brice.

On September 14, 1697, Richard Butwell made a will which was probated September 27, 1700. In his will, he named no children nor did he name a wife.

CADGER (29)

On March 11, 1663, a tract called "Cadger's Island" consisting of 200 acres was surveyed for Robert Cadger (Pat. L7 F262).

The certificate of survey gave the location of the tract as: "by a marsh belonging to Annemessex Bay...by a line drawn south to the Streights mouth standing against Potomac River and running along the Streights mouth...along the Great Bay."

In the Archives of Maryland, Volume II, page 530, is shown that an Act of the Maryland Assembly was passed at its May-June 1676 session which confirmed the stipulations contained in the will of Robert Cadger of St. Georges Hundred in the County of St. Mary's. Robert Cadger devised all his property for the maintenance of a protestant ministry in St. George's and Poplar Hill Hundreds. His will was dated January 24, 1675, and was probated February 4, 1675 (Wills L2 F383). The will named no relatives.
      NOTE: In the records in several instances, the name Cadger was spelled Kedger. It is very possible that this is the origin of the name, Kedgers Straits.

CAILE (XX)

John Caile, Jr., son of John Caile and Margaret Hall, came to Dorchester County about 1744. He was a merchant in Cambridge and served as Clerk of Court in Dorchester County from 1745 to 1766 when he was succeeded by his son-in-law, Richard Sprigg.

John Caile, Jr., married Rebecca Ennalls, daughter of Henry Ennalls and his wife, Mary (Hooper) Ennalls. Their only child, Margaret, married August 1, 1765, to Richard Sprigg of "Cedar Park," Anne Arundel County, son of Thomas Sprigg of "Longmeadow" and his wife, Elizabeth (Calloway) Sprigg. Richard Sprigg was Clerk of Court for Dorchester County from 1766 to 1777, succeeding his father-in-law. John Caile, Jr. died April 27, 1767 at the age of 47. At the time of his death, he was living at "Hambrook." He was buried in Christ Church Cemetery.

Hall Caile, son of John Caile and Margaret (Hall) Caile, was born May 28, 1733. On June 2, 1754, he married Elizabeth Haskins, daughter of Thomas Haskins and Mary (Loockerman) Haskins. He came to Dorchester County about 1750 and on October 27, 1758, he was appointed to the office of High Sheriff, a position which he held until his death on January 30, 1761. He was buried in Christ Church Cemetery. He was 27 when he died. His wife, Elizabeth, survived him for many years, and, at her death, she was buried in White March Church Yard, Talbot County.

Hall Caile and his wife, Elizabeth, had three children:

1. Mary Caile, born September 10, 1756, died February 24, 1812; married (1) November 18, 1773, John Caile Harrison, son of Christopher Harrison and Mary Caile; (2) December 22, 1789, Thomas James Bullitt, son of Hon. Cuthbert Bullitt and Helen (Scott) Bullitt. Thomas James Bullitt was a judge of Talbot County, Maryland.

2. Margaret Hall Caile, born March 15, 1759, died July 2, 1826; married February 16, 1777, to Gustaus Scott, son of Rev. James Scott and Sarah (Brown) Scott.

3. John Hall Caile, born August 14, 1761; died February 14, 1783, and was buried in Christ Church Cemetery.

NOTE: A continuation of the Caile genealogy can be found in "Maryland Historical Magazine," Volume II, beginning on page 11.

CANE (104)

In 1668 a 100 acre tract of land was surveyed for William Cane. It was called "Cane's Rest" and it was located on the east side of Hungar River near the head of Staplefort Creek (now known as Russell Creek).

No further information has been found on William Cane.

CHAPLINE (2)

Isaac Chapline immigrated to Virginia in 1610 and his wife, Mary (Calvert) Chapline, followed in 1622[1]. William I (1625-1669), the son of Isaac and Mary Chapline, married Mary Hooper and this couple immigrated from Virginia to Calvert County, Maryland[2]. William I and Mary (Hooper) Chapline of Calvert County had three children: Elizabeth, born in 1651; William II, born in 1659; and Mary, born in 1663[3].

On July 1, 1659, William Chapline I of Calvert County had a 300 acre tract of land surveyed on what became known as Hoopers Island[4]. The tract was called "Chapline's Holme" and it was the second tract surveyed in the area that eventually became Dorchester County.

William Chapline I died in Calvert County in 1669 and he left to his wife, Mary, dower rights. His son, William II, was to receive, when he reached the age of sixteen, the home plantation in Calvert County. "Chapline's Holme," on Hoopers Island was devised to his daughter, Elizabeth. The other daughter, Mary, was devised personalty[5].

William II married Susannah Kimball[6] and while he acquired the home plantation in Calvert County by his father's will, a land record of Dorchester County (7 OLD 59) shows that he disposed of his Calvert County holdings and became an inhabitant of Dorchester County prior to his death. The same record shows that he died prior to June 5, 1718, and that Matthew Travers became guardian of his three sons: William III, Solomon and John.

Elizabeth, daughter of William Chapline I (1625-1669), married William Travers of Patuxent and thru their sons, Matthew, William and Thomas, were the progenitors of the South Dorchester County branch of the Travers family.

The last male Chapline of record in the original Dorchester Chapline Line was Solomon Chapline, son of William II (1659-1718). The will of Solomon was dated March 3, 1765, and in it he named daughters, Ann Chapline and Susannah Conway.

Summarizing, the records show that William Chapline I, the patentee of "Chaplin's Holme," while never an inhabitant of the area that became Dorchester County was, nevertheless, an ancestor, thru his daughter Elizabeth, of one of the largest and most influential families of the County, the South Dorchester County branch of the Travers family.

### Notes

(1)  Isaac Chapline was a Captain in the Royal Navy and a member of the King's Council. Mary (Calvert) Chapline was a sister of the first Lord Baltimore.
(2)  Mary Hooper was a sister of the first Henry Hooper who settled in Dorchester County - confirmation of this relationship can be found in Dorchester Land Record 4 OLD 20. Also William Chapline I referred to Richard Hooper in his will as his kinsman.
Volume XLIX, page 43, of the Archives of Maryland shows the following from the Provincial Court Session of September 8, 1663: "Richard Smith informs the court that Captain Thomas Manning did marry William Chaplin and Mary Richardson, without either license or publication made, sometime in August last." Manning was fined 5000 pounds of tobacco (page 85). No other information has been found concerning this marriage and if it was the same William Chapline who is the subject of this sketch, it would be his second marriage.
(3)  Colonial Families of U.S.A. by George N. Mackenzie, Vol. 2, pages 174-177.
(4)  Patent Records, Liber 4, Folio 156.
(5)  Probate Records, Wills, Liber 1, Folio 365.
(6)  Probate Records, Wills, Liber 13, Folio 346.

## CHOREN (12)

On August 29, 1659, a 100 acre tract of land called "Castle Haven" was surveyed for Dennie Choren (Pat. L4 F436). He received the tract for transporting himself and John Raby into the Province of Maryland.

No further information has been located in the records about Dennie Choren. Dorchester Land Record 3 OLD 207 dated September 21, 1663, shows that Andrew Skinner of Talbot County sold "Castle Haven" to Thomas Martine, who in turn, sold it to Peter Underwood of Dorchester County on November 7, 1671.

Peter Underwood sold one-half of the tract to John Whitley and he, Underwood, operated a tavern on the other portion of the tract as early as 1674 (Arch. of Md., Vol. 2, page 434). When Peter Underwood died, his daughters sold his part to John Harwood. Harwood also acquired the other one-half portion of the tract from David Jenkins who had obtained it when John Whitley had died.

John Harwood was the son of Robert Harwood and Elizabeth (Gary) Harwood, daughter of John and Judith Gary and step-daughter of Peter Sharp (see the "Strangest Courtship on Record", pages 153-156 of Early Dorchester by C. W. Mowbray).

The records show that John Harwood operated a ferry from the site across the Choptank to Cloras Point (Dorchester Court Record - File 8499). He was also an innkeeper as shown by DLR 5 OLD 3 dated August 15, 1692.

On May 29, 1717, John Harwood leased the house and land at "Castle Haven" to Margaret Noell, wife of James Noell, Sr., for the remainder of her natural life (DLR 7 OLD 46).

On September 19, 1726, Rebecca Harwood, widow of John Harwood, sold to Bazell Noell, planter, "Castle Haven" containing 100 acres more or less, also "Underwoods Chance," "Five Pines" and other properties.

The above records show that "Castle Haven" was not part of "Saint Anthony," the tract that was patented by Anthony LeCompte, as some historians have claimed.

John Harwood died in 1724 (Wills 18,325) and he named in his will Mary, wife of Stephen Owen, and Rebeca Nicholls as well as his own wife, Rebecca.

In her will (Wills 22,504) which was probated September 19, 1742, Rebecca mentioned daughters Mary Owens, Rachel Orrells, Rebecca Nicholls, and a grandson, Thomas Noell, as well as Thomas Brannock, her son by her first marriage with Edmond Brannock.

In Dorchester Land Record 2 OLD 148 dated January 15, 1722, John and Rebecca Harwood also mentioned a daughter named Ann Brannock.

The records do not indicate whether or not Dennie Choren ever lived at "Castle Haven," but the name he gave to his tract has endured until today for the land is still known as "Castle Haven

Point" and it is located in what is still called "Castle Haven Neck."

## CLARK (52)

Daniel Clark immigrated from Virginia to Maryland in 1665. In that year, he received five grants for land in what became Dorchester County. The grants totaled five hundred and fifty acres and all in the area of the Little Choptank River. He also purchased from Peter Sharp in that same year a 200 acre tract called "Sharp's Point." This tract was also located on the Little Choptank River (Arch. of Md., Vol. LVII, page 93).

Daniel Clark was elected to the Lower House of the Assembly of Maryland as a delegate from Talbot County in 1669 (Arch. of Md., Vol. II, pages 156-157). At the time of the election, the area between the Nanticoke and the Great Choptank was considered as a part of Talbot County and Daniel Clark was a resident of that area (he lived on the Little Choptank). It was that same year that Dorchester County was erected and in the next election, 1671, Daniel Clark was elected as a delegate to represent Dorchester County. He served in that capacity from 1671 until 1674 and again from 1686 until 1688. He was also a justice of Dorchester County for the period from 1671 until 1674. He served as sheriff in the years 1674 thru 1676.

Stephen Gary sued Daniel Clark in 1676 claiming that while Clark was sheriff on December 20, 1675, he came to Gary's home on Little Choptank River (Clark lived across the creek from Gary) where he assaulted, beat, wounded, evil-handed and finally imprisoned him, all illegally. Gary won the suit in Provincial Court. Clark was fined 2000 pounds of tobacco, and Gary was awarded damages of 2000 pounds of tobacco and 1500 pounds of tobacco for costs (Arch. of Md., Vol. 66, pages 427-428).

Apparently, Daniel Clark had a knack for getting into trouble. On November 20, 1688, the Upper House of the Assembly received a message which said in part:

"On the 30th of October last "Petition and Complaint" was made to their hounours by the wife of the said Clark of divers inhumane usages and beastly crimes acted and committed by her said husband (Arch. of Md., Vol. 13, page 166)."

On February 8, 1691, Clark, apparently reached a settlement with his wife. On that date he deeded his 200 acre home plantation, "Sharp's Point," to Walter Campbell. Campbell, in return, agreed to pay to Katherine, Clark's wife, 3000 pounds of tobacco, yearly, for the term of her natural life (DLR 1 OLD 155).

As a result of Clark's action, another petition ensued in June of 1692:

"To his Excellency the Governor and his Honorable Council.

The Petition of Edward Cook of Dorset County Humbly Sheweth:

That one Daniel Clark of the same County living publickly in Adultery with your Petitioners wife in Comtempt and despite both the Law of God and Man and to the great Grief and Affliction of your Petitioner doth Violence and Opposition to all Authority keep and detain your Petitioners said wife refusing to deliver her to your Petitioner but Continues to live incontinently with her notwithstanding any Warrant or Order of Court to the Contrary to your Petitioners Great Damage grief and trouble as aforesaid.
     Your Petitioner humbly prays your Excellencys special warrant for the Apprehending securing and taking into Custody both the said Daniel Clark and your Petitioners said wife so as to have them before your Excellency or such other of your Council or their Majestys Provincial or County Court to Answer the Premises and to Receive such Condign Punishment as so foul a Crime may Justly deserve and your Petitioners Wife required to return to your Petitioner and live with him as becometh a wife or be otherwise disposed of at a Greater distance from the sight and knowledge of your petitioner."

_____ And shall pray &c.

"By his Excellency the Governor and Council June the 6th, 1692.

Ordered that the Sheriff of Dorset County forthwith to Apprehend and take into Custody the Body's of Daniel Clark and Katherine Cook, the wife of Mr. Edward Cook of the same County (With whom he the said Clark doth incontinently live in Adultery and detains her from going to and Cohabiting with her, so that to have them both before this Board with all Expedition to answer the Premises and the further Complaint of the said Edward Cook whereof let there be no fail at perill.)"

To the Sheriff of Dorsett County or his Deputy, signed p Order J. Llewellin Clk.

The two communications appear on pages 339 and 340 of Volume 13 of The Archives of Maryland.

Apparently Clark lived an active, if sometimes turbulent, life. The inventory of his possessions after his death and the land records of Dorchester County indicate that he was a person of considerable means.  Oddly, all of his worldly possessions were willed to his housekeeper, Mary Bussett (Wills 11, 245).  It would seem, therefore, that he had no descendants.

CLARKE (35)

On January 20, 1664, a 400 acre tract of land was surveyed for Thomas Clarke.  The tract was located on what is now called Fowling Creek in Caroline County and the tract was called "Cabin Ridge" (Pat. L9 F107).  The grant was made to Clarke for transporting himself, Sarah his wife, Robert his son, Sarah his daughter, Mary Girdler and Hugh Jenkins.

On March 18, 1674, Thomas Clarke of Calvert County made a will which was probated July 19, 1675. His wife, Sarah, was named Executrix with instructions that his possessions were to be divided between his two children: son Robert, and daughter Mary, his wife to have use of the property for her natural life (Wills L2 F347).

On April 20, 1677, Robert Clarke, son and heir of Thomas Clarke, late of Calvert County, deceased, sold to John Edmondson of Talbot county the tract called "Cabin Ridge" (4 OLD 22). John Edmondson in turn sold it to William Edmondson (5 OLD 58) on March 2, 1694. William in turn in 1699 sold it to William Stevens of Dorchester County (5 OLD 141).

On January 3, 1702, Robert Clarke of Talbot County made a will which was probated August 23, 1703. In it he named Sarah Mason (his sister), wife Mary, son Oliver and daughter Mary (Wills L11 F375).

There is nothing in the records to indicate that either Thomas Clarke or any of his children were ever inhabitants of Dorchester.

COOKE (165)

At a Council held at St. Johns on January 9, 1661, licenses were given to John Nuttall, Vincent Atcheson, Andrew Cooke and William Boreman granting them the right to trade with any inhabitant of the Province for any beaver furs, skins or any other commodity and to that end authority was given them to pass upon or through any river or creek of the Province and authority was given them to trade with any Indian or Indians...(Archives of Md., Vol. 3, pages 445-446).

In 1662 Andrew Cooke purchased "Mauldin" from Thomas Manning. "Mauldin" a 1000 acre tract of land was characterized as "Mannings Point" and it is presently known as "Cooks Point;" it lies on the south side of the Choptank River at the confluence of that River with the Chesapeake Bay. On April 11, 1664, Andrew Cooke also purchased from Thomas Manning a 200 acre tract called "Papae Thicket," and this tract was located in Fishing Creek of the Little Choptank River (DLR 1 OLD 71).

The records indicate that Andrew Cooke I and his wife, Elizabeth, had the following children: Andrew II, Thomas, Edward, and Henry. The records further indicate that Andrew Cooke I resided for a time in Calvert County and then he returned to England. There is nothing in the records to show that he ever resided in what eventually became Dorchester County.

Andrew Cooke II left his portion of "Mauldin" to his two children: Ebenezer and Anne. This fact is shown in his will, a copy of which can be found in the Dorchester Land Records (DLR 8 OLD 46) and his will shows that he was, when it was made, a resident of the Parish of St. Giles, in the Fields, in the County of Middlesex, England. The will was dated December 31, 1711.

The records show that Andrew Cooke II was married in London, England, on August 1, 1665, to Anne Bowyer. Ebenezer Cooke, son of Andrew and Anne, in 1708, published in London a poem called the "Sot-Weed Factor." Some historians tell us that the children of Andrew Cooke II and Anne Bowyer, namely Ebenezer and Anne, were never actually inhabitants of the Province of Maryland but the Land Records of Dorchester County show otherwise.

The Land Records show that on October 11, 1717 (DLR 7 OLD 46) Anne Cooke "Of Dorchester County" sold to Captain Henry Trippe of the same county one-half of "Mauldin" at the mouth of the Great Choptank River, containing 500 acres.

The Land Records also show that on October 30, 1717 (DLR 7 OLD 47) Ebenezer Cooke "Of Dorchester County" sold to Edward Cooke, of the same County, one-half of "Mauldin" at the mouth of Great Choptank River, the one-half containing 500 acres.

Edward Cooke, son of Andrew Cooke I and Elizabeth, of the Patuxent made his will on December 10, 1702, and it was probated May 11, 1703. Edward's will was filed in the Dorchester County Records so it is very possible that he was living in Dorchester County when he died. In his will he devised 250 acres of "Mauldin" to his son, Andrew. To his daughter, Sarah, he devised personalty. To his son, Edward, he devised the residue of "Mauldin."

Henry Cooke, son of Andrew Cooke I and Elizabeth, never came to the Province of Maryland.

Thomas Cooke, son of Andrew Cooke I and Elizabeth, became sheriff of Dorchester County in 1692. He married Anne Brooke, daughter of Dr. John Brooke, their children were: Babington Cooke, Mary Cooke, Anne Cooke and John Cooke (Wills 2, 305). After her husband, Thomas Cooke, died Anne married John Stevens II.

John Cooke, son of Thomas and Ann Cooke, married Mary Peterkin, daughter of David and Mary Peterkin, and they had two children, Thomas and Anne.

Edward Cooke, son of Edward and Grandson of Andrew I, made a will on September 23, 1747 (Wills 27, 283). In the will he devised "Mauldin" to his sons Babington and John. He also named son, Thomas; daughters, Ann Polson, Mary wife of Roger Childerston, Esther wife of William Thomas, Elizabeth wife of Edward Spedden, Rachel wife of Joseph Thomas.

CORBREATH (61)

On April 6, 1665, a 1000 acre tract of land called "Billingsleys Reserve" was surveyed for John Corbreath. The tract was located on the Transquaking River and the grant was received on an assignment from Captain Brent and Captain Cornwallis.

Rent Roll Records, L10 F349 shows the tract in the possession of Thomas Billingsly.

John Corbreath made a will dated October 27, 1687, and it was probated March 6, 1688/9. The will shows that he was an inhabitant of "Ye Clifts in Calvert County." In the will he named sons John and Aaron; and daughter, Jane.

There is nothing in the records to indicate that John Corbreath or any of his family were ever inhabitants of Dorchester County.

COVINGTON (XX)

Nehemiah Covington I (1628-1681) first settled in Northampton County, Virginia. His name appears in a number of records of that County in the mid 1600's. In 1662 he moved to what became Somerset County, Maryland. Nehemiah I married (1) Mary (last name unknown) and they had the following children: Jane, who married David Williams; Katherine, who married Edward Wright; Sarah, who married Julian Messick; Margaret, who married Richard Allingsworth; Nehemiah II. Nehemiah Covington I married (2) Anne Ingram, widow of Robert Ingram, and they had the following children: Elizabeth, Thomas, Anne, Jeremiah. Nehemiah Covington I died in 1681.

John Covington, son of Nehemiah I and Mary, married Mary (last name unknown) and they had the following children: John, Abraham, Mary, Nehemiah and Philip. John Covington died in 1692.

Nehemiah Covington II, son of Nehemiah and Mary, became an Indian interpreter (Arch. of Md., Vol. XIII, page 251). He married Rebecca Denwood in 1676. He amassed a considerable estate. The children of Nehemiah II and Rebecca (Denwood) Covington were: Nehemiah III; Levin; Elizabeth who married Benjamin Wailes; Priscilla who married Robert King; Sarah who married (1) Maj. Gen. Edward Lloyd of Talbot County, Governor of Maryland (2) James Hollyday of Queen Ann's County, Council member and Judge of Provincial Court.

Descendants of Nehemiah Covington I acquired property in the Nanticoke area of Dorchester County and some of the descendants intermarried with inhabitants of Dorchester County. Thomas Hicks I of Dorchester County married Sarah Denwood, sister of Rebecca Denwood who married Nehemiah Covington II.

COWLEY (111) (Cooley)

L9 F38 of the Patent Records shows that George Cowley immigrated to the Province of Maryland in 1664.

In 1669 a 600 acre tract of land was surveyed for him; it was called "Yarford" and it was located on the southside of the Great Choptank River and one-half of a mile from a creek called Marsh Creek in what is now Caroline County. In that same year a 400 acre tract was surveyed for him on the Blackwater River, it was called "Darby."

On August 11, 1674, he disposed of "Darby" (DLR 3 OLD 75) and at that time he was shown as an inhabitant of Talbot County. No further information has been found in the records about him.

## CURTIS (136)

On April 25, 1668, Isaac Abraham of Calvert County, planter, sold to Robert Curtis 150 acres of land called "Ashburne" (TLR Li F37). The tract was located at the head of an Indian field near the head of Blackwater River.

Robert Curtis was the son of John Curtis and Jane Powell of Virginia. His children were Robert, born June 5, 1675; Edmond; Thomas; Sarah; Jane who married John Trevallion; Katherine who married John Corley; and Elizabeth who married Griffith Evans of Talbot County.

Although a daughter of Robert Curtis, Jane Trevallion, became an inhabitant of Dorchester County and some of his descendants became inhabitants of neighboring Talbot County there is nothing in the records to indicate that he (Robert) ever was an inhabitant of Maryland.

## DALE (57) (Deale)

On April 2, 1665, a 100 acre tract of land was surveyed for David Dale; the tract was called "Dale's Right: and it was located on the northwest side of Hudson Creek. On February 6, 1666, a 60 acre tract called "Deale's Desire" was surveyed for David Deale; it was located on the east side of Hudson Creek and at the head thereof.

Rent Roll Record, L10 F452, on "Deale's Desire" was noted as follows: "No heirs to be found - supposed to be taken up by Thomas Killman since the death of Deale."

## DANIELL (X)
On April 26, 1682, a 150 acre tract of land was surveyed for Thomas Daniell; the tract was called "Daniell's Helicon" and it was located on the north side of a beaver dam branch that issued out of the south side of the Chicamacomico River (Pat L SD#A F425). On August 22, 1685, Thomas Daniell made a will which was probated April 3, 1686 (Wills 4,264). In his will he named sons Thomas and William; wife, Jane; and John North.

## DAVIS (X)

On April 8, 1680, a 200 acre tract of land was surveyed for Thomas and Walter Davis on an assignment from Walter Davis, Sr. The tract was called "Barrell Green" and it was located on the west side of Davis Creek that issues out of the north side of Slaughter Creek in Taylors Island (the Creek is still known today as Davis Creek). In the months that followed, Walter and Thomas acquired individually a number of tracts in the area.

Dorchester Land Record 6 OLD 105 dated June 28, 1704, shows that Thomas Davis, son of Walter, Sr., had become an inhabitant of St. Mary's County. No further information has been found on Walter, the brother, son of Walter, Sr.

Henry Davis (no relation is shown in the records to the above) acquired "Paradise" by his marriage to the widow of Lawrence Woodnet. "Paradise" was located on the south side of Fishing Creek of the Little Choptank River. Dorchester Land Record 2 OLD 49 dated August 11, 1720, shows Elizabeth as the wife of Henry Davis. Elizabeth was the daughter of John Mackeele (Wills 7,209). No further information has been found in the records about Henry and Elizabeth.

DAWSON (94)

Patent Record L8 F89 shows that Anthony Dawson was transported to Maryland in 1665 by his father, William Dawson, Sr., along with William Dawson, Jr., Samuel Abbott, Sr., and Jane Abbott. Patent Record L WC2 F391 shows that Anthony Dawson married Rebecca Osbourne, daughter of Henry Osbourne.

On April 13, 1667, Henry Osbourne, Thomas Walker and Anthony Dawson had a 650 acre tract of land surveyed; the tract was called "Alexander's Place" and it was located on the westernmost side of the Northwest Branch of the Transquaking River (Pat. L11 F45). Walker and Dawson had married the daughters of Osbourne. Henry Osbourne died prior to 1678.

On February 16, 1673, a 300 acre tract of land called "Dawson's Chance" was surveyed for Anthony Dawson; it was located between "Malden" and "Cedar Point" on the southside of the Great Choptank River (Pat. L19 F72). Dawson sold this tract on August 4, 1678, to John Brooke (DLR 3 OLD 183).

On January 11, 1683, Thomas Walker of Kent County, Pennsylvania, and Sarah, his wife, sold their one-half interest in "Alexander's Place" to Anthony Dawson, carpenter, of Dorchester County.

Anthony Dawson pledged "Alexander's Place" as a performance bond on a contract to build a courthouse in Cambridge. He reneged on the contract and the County sold "Alexander's Place" on June 3, 1700, to Hugh Eccleston.

William Dawson, father of Anthony, made his will on December 19, 1666, and it was probated July 21, 1668 (Wills 1,327). In his will he named son, Anthony; sons William and Samuel Abbott; daughters Jane and Joice Dawson; Samuel, son of Samuel Abbott; Anthony, son of Joseph Cox.

In 1678 Captain Anthony Dawson was paid 1300 pounds of tobacco for his service in the Militia in an expedition against the Nanticoke Indians (Arch. of Md., Vol. VII, pages 92-94).

In 1683 Anthony Dawson was named as a member of the Commission to lay out ports and towns in Dorchester County.

On December 6, 1684, Anthony Dawson, carpenter, contracted to build a courthouse in Cambridge; he reneged on the contract and his dwelling house in Cambridge and his plantation, "Alexander's Place," on the Transquaking River which he had used as a performance bond were forfeited.

Rebecca, his wife, said that he had estranged himself from the county (Addendum to DLR 4 1/2 OLD 44).

No further information has been found on Anthony or Rebecca Dawson.

## DEAN (X)

On February 26, 1678, William Dean had a 100 acre tract of land surveyed on the west side of the north branch of Fox Creek that issues out of Hungar River. The tract was called "Dean's Choice" and Rent Roll L10 F398 (1706) showed the tract in the possession of William Dean, son of William Dean.

William Dean I married Elizabeth, the daughter of Michael and Margaret (Insley) Todd. He (William) made a will dated October 25, 1698, and it was probated March 13, 1699. In it he named his wife, Elizabeth; his daughters Sarah, Mary, and Elizabeth Johnson; and four sons, William, Richard, John and Henry (Wills 6,304). Elizabeth Johnson was the wife of Robert Johnson.

William Dean II made his will on February 10, 1760 (Wills 33,18). He named his wife, Sarah; his sons William and Henry; his daughters Elizabeth Cannon, Mary Graham; and his granddaughters Deliah Dean and Sarah Dean. William Dean II devised "Dean's Choice" to his son, William Dean III.

Henry Dean, blacksmith, son of William Dean I and Elizabeth his wife, made a will dated November 25, 1746 (Wills 25, 33). In his will he named his wife, Elizabeth; sons John, Henry and Thomas; daughter, Mary Farguson.

Elizabeth Dean, widow of Henry Dean, made a will dated June 1, 1751 (Wills 31,934). In it she named her sons John and Thomas; and her grand-children George Farguson, Mary Farguson and Elizabeth Farguson.

## DELENDER (71)

On July 18, 1665, a 600 acre tract of land was surveyed for Brett Delender (Pat. L8 F33); the tract was called "Brett's Hope" and it was located on the south side of Smith's Creek (now Hunting Creek).

Brett Delender transferred "Brett's Hope" to John Edmondson, his attorney, prior to 1671.

No other information has been found in the records on Brett Delender.

## DENWOOD (118)

On January 24, 1669, a 250 acre tract of land was surveyed for Thomas Denwood; it was called "Denwood's Lott" and it was located on the Chicamacomico River.

Rent Roll Record L10 F456 shows: "No Heirs to be found and no Patent taken out."

Patent Record L10 F229 shows that Thomas Denwood was transported to Maryland in 1667 with Elizabeth, Mary and Rebecca Denwood, daughters of Levin and Mary Denwood, by Roger Woolford. The Denwood and Woolford families settled in Somerset County, Maryland.

Levin Denwood and his wife Mary (Cutting) Denwood had in all the following: Arthur, Thomas, Levin II, Luke, Susanna who married Thomas Browne, Mary who married Roger Woolford, Elizabeth who married Henry Hooper II, Rebecca who married Nehemiah Covington II, and Sarah who married Thomas Hicks in 1679.

## DICKENSON (87) (Dickinson)

On March 6, 1666, a 100 acre tract of land was surveyed for Walter Dickenson; the tract was called "Dickenson's Rights" and it was located on the north side of Hunting Creek adjoining John Pitt's land (Pat. L11 F509).

Rent Roll Record L10 F449 shows the tract in the possession of William Dickenson (1706).

Walter Dickenson was born in 1620 and migrated to Virginia with his brothers Henry and John in 1654. He settled on the Rappahannock in Lancaster County, Virginia, where he married the daughter of a neighbor. He moved to Maryland in 1659 where he located at North Point on the Patapsco. Shortly thereafter he moved to Talbot County to land he had purchased on Reeds Creek.

Walter Dickenson died in 1681 and he named in his will (Wills 2,136) sons William, Charles and Walter; daughter Rachel; cousin Mary Dickenson, daughter of John Dickenson.

John Dickenson, brother of Walter, made a will dated October 7, 1714, (Wills 14,582) which was probated April 29, 1718. In his will he named wife, Rebecca; sons John and Charles, daughter Sidney and Mary Kersey.

## DICKSON (65) (Dixon)

On April 14, 1665, a 300 acre tract of land was surveyed for Robert Dickson; the tract was called "John's Garden" and it was located on the southside of the Choptank River in Todds Bay (Pat.

L8 F313).

On December 13, 1667, Robert Dickson, planter of Calvert County, sold to James Williams, planter of Calvert County, "Johns Garden" (Arch. of Md., Vol. 57, pages 268-269).

On January 6, 1673, James Williams of Calvert County, planter, and Mary, his wife, sold "John's Garden" to Richard Owen of Dorchester County (DLR 3 OLD 34).

Robert Dickson (Dixon) of the Cliffs in Calvert County made a will dated May 1, 1688 (Wills 7,51) which was probated May 21, 1695. In his will Robert named sons John, James and Robert; daughters Elizabeth, Mary, Sarah and Rosamon; and wife, Elizabeth.

There is nothing in the records to indicate that Robert Dickson or any of his family was ever an inhabitant of Dorchester County.

DORRINGTON (30)

William Dorrington immigrated from Bristol, England, to Calvert County in 1655. In that year Captain Peter Johnson, who had commanded the Militia during the Puritan uprising, died and William Dorrington was appointed manager of Johnson's extensive land-holdings. The will of Anne Johnson, widow of Captain Peter Johnson, dated May 27, 1656, contained the following provision: "William Dorrington, personalty in trust for testatrix' children until their majority. Said William Dorrington to remain on plantation until he remarries" (Wills 1,64). The will was in the form of a deed of gift made on the eve of the marriage of Anne Johnson, widow of Captain Peter Johnson, to William Dorrington. Anne Johnson and William Dorrington were married soon thereafter.

On May 18, 1663, a 100 acre tract of land called "Hogg Hole" on Jenkins Creek was surveyed for William Dorrington of Patuxent (Pat. L5, F521). On December 22, 1664, Henry Sewall, merchant of North Yarmouth in the County of Norfolk sold "Busby" containing 500 acres and "Sewalls Point" containing 50 acres to William Dorrington, Gent. of Patuxent River (Arch. of Md., Vol. 49, pages 338 and 339). The latter two tracts which Dorrington purchased adjoined "Hogg Hole" which he had patented earlier. Later Dorrington acquired "Clifton" and several other tracts in the same general area.

Dorrington's first wife, Anne Johnson, died and he married Elizabeth Winsloe, sister of William Winsloe (DLR 1 OLD 106). Elizabeth also preceded William in death. The will of William Dorrington named a son, William; and two daughters, Sarah and Anne (Wills 7,290). Anne, the daughter, married Richard Hooper. Sarah, the other daughter, first married Thomas Fisher and when he died she married Thomas Foulke (DLR 4 OLD 3). William, the son, married Mary (last name unknown) and his will (Wills 14,246) which was probated March 12, 1716, indicated that they had only one child, a son named William. Mary Dorrington, widow of

William, married John Smith, tailor, after the death of William
(Wills 18,45).

DORSEY (146)

Genealogists and Historians have written that three Dorsey
brothers brought the name of Dorsey to Dorchester County. This
contention, apparently, stems primarily from the will of James
Preston who mentioned in his will three kinsmen.

James and John Dossey were given certain reversionary interests
and the will states: "Four hundred acres of land at the head of
Little Choptank River 1/3 part I have already given to my kinsman
Ralph Dossey the other 2/3 to belong to John Dossey. Ralph
Dossey to get cattle owed by William Tick a dutchman of Little
Choptank. John Dossey goods valued at 20 pounds ..."

On November 26, 1683, John Dossey, planter of Little Choptank in
Dorchester County, leased to Daniell Willard "Old Field" being
part of "Preston" on the east side of Little Choptank for the
lifetime of said Willard (DLR 4 OLD 99).

No mention has been found in the Dorchester Records of either
Ralph or James Dorsey. On the other hand, a James Dorsey is
mentioned in the Calvert County Probate Records as a witness in
1684 and in 1685.

A John Dossey and a William Dossey are mentioned in the
Dorchester Land Records as early as February 20, 1669 (DLR 1 OLD
8), and they are mentioned many times thereafter in the next few
years. Patent Record L18 F 116 shows John Dossey "Service 1674,
of Dorchester County."

On January 4, 1679, William Dossey of Dorchester County, planter,
acquired from William Jump of Talbot County, carpenter, a 200
acre tract of land called "End of Controversie." It was located
on Little Choptank River and Fishing Creek near a tract called
"Teverton" (DLR 4 OLD 12).

William Dossey I married Mary, the daughter of John MacKeele
(Wills 7,209).

On November 29, 1703, William Dossey I made a will which was
probated December 4, 1703. In the will he devised all his lands
equally to his two sons, William and John. He also named three
daughters, Isabell, Dorothy and Mary (Wills 3,7).

Dorchester Land Record 6 OLD 208 shows the wife of William Dossey
II as Elizabeth. William II made a will dated August 25, 1714,
which was probated December 18, 1714. In his will he devised "The
End of Controversy" to his son, William. He devised "Olive
Branch" to his son John and personalty to his son, Edward (Wills
14,57).

## DOWNING (128)

On June 10, 1669, a 100 acre tract of land was surveyed for William Downing. The tract was called "Copartnership" and was located on Hungar River adjoining "Bentleys."

Rent Roll Record L10 F267 shows "No heirs to be found." No other mention of William Downing has been found in the Dorchester County Records.

## EARLY (123)

On March 4,1669, a 150 acre tract of land was surveyed for John Early; it was called "Early's Neck" and it was located on the west side of Tar Bay.

Rent Roll Record L10 F363 (1706) notes: "Let fall being taken away by "Barren Island."

However, Dorchester Land Record 6 OLD 258 dated March 28, 1715, shows the sale of "Early's Neck" by John Early and Elizabeth his wife to Matthew Travers. The Earlys were involved in several land transactions in the area in the early 1700's.

John Early made a will dated November 24, 1717, which was probated June 11, 1717. In his will he named his wife, Elizabeth; several members of the Woodland family; which would indicate that his wife was either a Woodland or had a close relationship to that family.

## EASON (121)

On February 25, 1669, a 500 acre tract of land was surveyed for William Fowler and John Eason; it was called "Darby" and it was located on the easternmost side of the Blackwater River.

On May 3, 1697, John Eason of Talbot County and Mary his wife sold "Darby" to John Edmondson. No further information has been found in the records on John and Mary Eason.

## EATON (14) (This should be 36)

On June 16, 1663, a 100 acre tract called "Eatons Point" was surveyed for James Eaton (Pat. L7 F93). It was located on Shallow Creek (now called Shoal Creek).

Rent Roll Record L10, F347 shows this tract in the Choptank Indian Reservation, consequently, its identity as a tract was lost and no further information has been found in the records on James Eaton.

## ECCLESTON (XX)

Hugh Eccleston immigrated from England to Dorchester County in the mid 1600's and settled in the Transquaking River area where he acquired large land holdings. He served as Clerk of Court from 1692 until his death in 1710. In his will dated November 25, 1710 and probated April 2, 1711, he made a number of bequests (Wills 13,357); following is an abstract of the will:

"To son Hugh, dwelling plantation and additions to same, also house and lot at Cambridge, bought of John Haselwood, and a house newly built.

To son John, plantation up the river, "Millington's Green," where David Coarson lives, also part of "Andersons Neck," bought of Benj. Palmer; son John to make over to son Thomas, at majority, certain land bequeathed said sons jointly by Morice Matthews, failing to do so, son Thomas to possess equally with son John "Millington's Green" and part of "Anderson's Neck" aforesaid.

To daughter Margaret, 94 acres, "Merchants Good Will" on Long Branch, Blackwater River.

To daughter, Elizabeth, at marriage or 25 years of age, personalty, including sum of money due by Thomas Brannock on account of his brother, John Brannock.

To daughters Mary and Rachell, 940 acres, "Retalliams."

To daughter Sarah, 400 acres, "Utopia" on north east branch of Nanticoke River, one-half of said land to be sold to Dennis Bryan, conditionally.

To daughters aforesaid, personalty, including that of their deceased Mother.

Testaor desires to be buried by his wife in Cambridge Church."

NOTE: The only church known to have existed in Cambridge in 1710/11 would have been what is now known as Christ Church and there is nothing in the Christ Church Cemetery Records to show that either Hugh Eccleston or his wife is buried there. The wife of Hugh Eccleston was Elizabeth, the daughter of Edmond and Jane Brannock (See Will 12, 224).

Hugh Eccleston II married Mary, widow of Rev. James Hinderman and daughter of Jacob Loockerman. Hugh II died prior to 1718 and left no children. His widow married Francis Allen.

John Eccleston, son of Hugh Eccleston I, married Dorothy Skinner, daughter of Andrew Skinner. John and Dorothy had the following children:
    1. Hugh Eccleston, who married Elizabeth Trippe, daughter of John Trippe.
    2. Rachel Eccleston.
    3. Thomas Firman Eccleston, who married Milcah, widow of Robert Pitt and daughter of Rev. Thomas Airey.
    4. Dorothy Eccleston, who married Joseph Richardson.

Dorothy (Skinner) Eccleston died July 11, 1759, age 45, she and her husband, John, were buried at "Yarmouth" in Bucktown District.

Not much information has been found concerning the five daughters of Hugh Eccleston I. Mary married Francis Voss; Rachel married Walter Stevens; Margaret married Bazell Nowell; Elizabeth married John White after the death of his first wife, Margaret.

Thomas Eccleston (1701-1745), son of Hugh Eccleston I, married Eleanor (last name unknown) and they had nine children.

A grandson (son of Charles and Margaret) of Thomas Eccleston was John Eccleston who was born in 1750. He married Rebecca Hodson. This John Eccleston died on March 11, 1798. John and Rebecca had a son named Nathaniel Green Eccleston who married Susan Pattison; a daughter, Elizabeth, who married Col. William Gist; a daughter, Anna Maria, who married Col. Joseph Byus; and a daughter, Mary; and another son, John.

An incongruity of our local histories is the utter lack of proper information about the Dorchester heroes of the Revolutionary War. What little information is shown in those local histories is in the main inaccurate and in most instances almost no information has been supplied. The latter is such in the case of John Eccleston (1750-1798). Following, in brief, is the service record of John Eccleston:

"2d Lieutenant of Barrett's Independent Maryland Company, 14th January, 1776; 1st Lieutenant, July, 1776; Captain 2d Maryland, 10th December, 1776; Major 5th Maryland, 10th December, 1777; taken prisoner at Charleston, 12th May, 1780; released 30th December, 1780; transferred to 1st Maryland, 1st January, 1781; Lieut. Col. 1st Md. 22nd December 1782 and served until November 3, 1783."

Bounty Land Warrant No 671 (no date) shows that Col. John Eccleston was awarded 400 acres of land for his services.

James McSherry in his History of Maryland wrote (page 308) that at the first meeting of the Maryland Society of the Cincinnati on November 21, 1783, the officers of the Maryland Line assembled at Annapolis and elected officers. Lieutenant Colonel John Eccleston was named assistant treasurer of the Society.

EDLOE (95)

On April 16, 1667, a 200 acre tract of land was surveyed for Joseph Edloe; it was called "Edloe's Purchase" and it was located near the head of St. John's Creek. On August 29, 1667, a 100 acre tract called "Punch Point" located on Drumm Cove of Slaughter Creek was surveyed for him.

Rent Roll Record L10 F356, (1706) shows "Edloe's Purchase" in the possession of James Edloe.

In Volume 66, page 132, of the Archives of Maryland there is set forth a "Provincial Court Case of 1675" which shows that Joseph Edloe of Calvert County was deceased and it also named a Joseph Edloe, Jr.

Joseph Edloe, Sr., made a will dated July 3, 1666, which was probated August 30, 1666 (Wills 1,266). In his will he devised his estate equally to his two sons Joseph and John.

There is nothing in the records to indicate that any of the Edloes ever became inhabitants of Dorchester County.

EDMONDSON (40)

John Edmondson was transported in 1658 to Calvert County as an indentured servant by John Horne, a merchant of London. After his service to Horne he moved to Talbot County where he became a very successful merchant and he also carried on a widespread land operation. The records show that he obtained in just the area that became Dorchester County alone a total of 16 patents representing 9650 acres. His operations in land transactions in other counties were also very widespread. The first tract that he obtained in the area that eventually became Dorchester County was called "Gotham;" a 150 acre tract that adjoined "Sarke" on Todds Bay. "Gotham" was surveyed for him on March 6, 1664.

Edmondson represented Talbot County in the Maryland Assembly where he became the center of a controversy for his failure to take the required oath because of his Quaker beliefs.

John Edmondson married (1) Sarah Parker, daughter of William Parker and (2) Sarah Loockerman, daughter of Jacob Loockerman II and after John Edmondson died, Sarah married Howell Powell, Jr. John had the following children:
1. John, who married Sussannah Omealy, daughter of Bryan Omealy.
2. James, who married Magdalen Stevens, daughter of John Stevens.
3. William, who married Sarah Sharpe, daughter of Wm. Sharpe.
4. Thomas, who married Mary Grason.
5. Samuel.
6. Sarah, who married William Johnson of Radecliffe, England.
7. Elizabeth, who married William Stevens Jr.
8. The records indicate that John Edmonson also had several other daughters.

John Edmondson, Jr., preceded his father, John, Sr., in death and in his will dated February 13, 1689, which was probated March 26, 1687 (Wills 4,284), John, Jr., devised his property to his father, mother, brothers and sisters so, apparently, his wife had died and they must have had no children.

John Edmondson, Sr., made a will dated October 9, 1697, which was

probated April 9, 1698 (Wills 6,95).  In his will John, Sr.,
named his wife, Sarah; sons James, William, Thomas, Samuel;
daughter, Elizabeth Stevens; deceased son, John, Jr.  He also
named a son, Abraham Morgan, and the exact relationship of
Abraham Morgan to John Edmondson has not been determined.

The wills of both John, Sr., and John, Jr., indicated that they
were both inhabitants of Talbot County when they died.

However, the will of William Edmondson, son of John Edmonson,
Sr., which was filed September 27, 1702, and probated November
11, 1702 (Wills 11,235) indicated that he was an inhabitant of
Dorchester County when he died.  He, William, had a number of
children and the records indicate that other descendants of John
Edmondson, Sr., became inhabitants of Dorchester County where
they became very prosperous and influential members of the
Community.

Thus, while John Edmondson was never an inhabitant of Dorchester
County, he was, nevertheless, very active in the land affairs of
the County in its early days, and he was the progenitor of the
Edmondson Line of the county.

EDWARDS (77)

On August 20, 1665, a 100 acre tract of land was surveyed for
John Edwards; the tract was named "Edwards Desire" and it was
located on the southside of the Choptank River and in the freshes
thereof.  The location was in what is now Caroline County.

On March 30, 1683, Ann James indentured her son and only child,
William, until he reached the age of 29, to John Edwards and
Susanna his wife (DLR 4 OLD 21).

On April 8, 1688, John Edwards made a will which was probated
July 5, 1688 (Wills 6, 18).  In it he devised all of his lands to
his wife, Susanna, with the stipulation that all of the lands
would pass to William James when he, William, reached the age of
21.

ELDRIDGE (32) (Aldridge)

On November 23, 1663, a 200 acre tract of land named "Eldridge"
was surveyed for William Eldridge (Pat. L8 F417).  The tract was
located at the second turning of the Choptank River on the south
side thereof and the location is in what is now Caroline County.

According to Rent Roll Record L10 F427, the tract was in the
possession of John Burk who married Eldridge's widow.  However,
this tract was devised by William Eldridge, of Anne Arundel, on
March 11, 1665, to Samuel Lane, Admr., and William Sisick along
with his entire estate, real and personal (Wills L1 F285).

"Eldridge" was acquired by Charles Goldsborough of Dorchester
County on October 28, 1761, as per the following abstract from

DLR 17 OLD 449:
"Samuel Lane of Ann Arundel County, Gent., son and heir of Richard Lane late of Calvert County, deceased, who was the eldest son and heir at law of Samuel Lane, deceased, who was the eldest son and heir at law of Samuel Lane of Ann Arundel County, deceased, to Charles Goldsborough of Dorchester County: "Eldridge" on Great Choptank River, formerly devised by the will of William Eldridge of Ann Arundel County to the last mentioned Samuel Lane and William Sisick deceased, the said last mentioned Samuel Lane having survived the said Wm. Sisick."

Obviously, William Eldridge was never an inhabitant of Dorchester County.

## ELLIOTT (XX)

Rent Roll Record L10 F353 shows "Fishing Point" in the possession of John Elliott. "Fishing Point" was on the east side of Fishing Bay on a Creek called Marsh Creek and on what became known as Elliott's Island. John Elliott was probably the first person of that surname to actually settle in Dorchester County.

However, the records show that a Henry Elliott and his wife, Ann, had a 50 acre tract of land surveyed May 7, 1662, named "Henry's Choice" and it was located at the head of Fishing Creek of Little Choptank River. The tract was acquired by a John Miller and Henry Elliott does not appear again in the records of Dorchester County.

John Elliott and his wife, Jean, are named in Dorchester Land Record 5 OLD 80 dated in 1696 when they sold a 50 acre tract called "Smith's Range" which was located on the western side of Fishing Bay.

In his will dated January 25, 1703, which was probated March 8, 1703 (Wills 3, 13), John Elliott names sons, John and Edward; daughters Mary, Elizabeth and Rose; wife, Jean. He left the plantation, "Fishing Point" to his son, John.

The will of Jean Elliott (Wills 18, 243), widow of John, shows that daughter Mary had married a Kirwan (this was Matthew Kirwan see Will 14, 413); that daughter Rose had married a Phillips (this was Benony Phillips - See Phillips 125 herein); and that daughter Elizabeth had married someone by the name of Cook.

"Fishing Point" remained in the Elliott family for several generations; Elliott's Island, of course, derived its name from John Elliott and his family.

## ENNALLS (141)

The will of Francis Hayward (York County, Virginia) dated January 1, 1657, and probated August 1657 names his son Francis; and an unborn child; his wife, Mary; and his brother, John Hayward.

Other documents show that the widow, Mary, married Bartholomew Ennalls and that the child was born and named John. Before her first marriage Mary (Hayward) Ennalls was Mary Warren.

On January 18, 1668, Bartholomew Ennalls purchased from John Edmondson a 2000 acre tract of land called "John's Purchase." The tract was located on the Transquaking River and the price for it was "A Sloop" and 1000 pounds of tobacco (TLR L1 F69). On March 2, 1669, he acquired a tract called "John's Point" located on Tobacco Stick Bay (DLR 1 OLD 11).

On March 10, 1669, Bartholomew proved his rights for transporting from Virginia into the Province of Maryland, to inhabit, (Pat. L12 F465) Mary, his wife; his children, Thomas, Bartholomew, Mary, Francis Hayward and John Hayward; and four servants.

Bartholomew Ennalls served as a justice of Dorchester and as a delegate to the Maryland Assembly and he became, probably, the largest land-owner of the county. He made his will on March 29, 1688, and it was probated January 20, 1688/9 (Wills 6, 56). In his will, he named:
1. Thomas, the eldest son, who married Elizabeth Woolford, the daughter of Roger and Mary (Denwood) Woolford.
2. William, second eldest son, who married Anne Warren.
3. Joseph, who married Mary Brooke, daughter of John and Judith Brooke.
4. John, who married Elinor Hodson.
5. Henry, who married in 1695 Mary Hooper.
6. Elizabeth, who married Roger Woolford II.
7. Mary, who married John Foster.

While he did not name his son, Bartholomew, in his will the records show that he transported a son by that name from Virginia to Maryland and the Land Records of Dorchester County also show that there was a son named Bartholomew as does the will of William, the brother of Bartholomew II (Wills 20, 301).

In his will Bartholomew I also named Elizabeth Hayward, eldest daughter of Francis Hayward. He also made bequests to "everyone of my grandchildren of the brothers Hayward" and he also named his wife, Mary. His will showed that he continued his interest in seafaring activities.

The sons of Bartholomew Ennalls, like their father, were active in the affairs of the county, and like their father, they acquired tremendous amounts of land acres. It is unaccountable that as influential and wealthy and as many Ennalls as there were in the many branches of the family, that there is no male member of the Ennalls line, bearing the Ennalls name remaining in Dorchester.

EVEROD (140)

On February 7, 1668, Robert Harwood sold 150 acres of "Harwoods Desire" to John Everod (TLR L1 F74).

On September 6, 1670, John Everod of Talbot County sold the 150 acres of "Harwoods Desire" which was located on Fishing Creek of Little Choptank River to John Edmondson.

No further information appears in the Dorchester records on John Everod.

## FALLIN (XX)

Redmond Fallin, the first of that surname to settle in Dorchester County, purchased "Coldchester" from John Spicer on January 2, 1695 (DLR 5 OLD 83). "Coldchester" was a tract of land located on the Hungar River and Fox Creek adjoining a tract called "Buckridge." It was on what is today known as "Fallins Cove;" so named after the Fallin family. The original grants of "Coldchester" and "Buckridge" make up a goodly portion of what is known today as Bishop Head.

Redmond Fallin married Frances Kemball, daughter of John Kemball (Wills 13, 346). Redmond's will was dated November 25, 1720, and it was probated March 29, 1722 (Wills 17, 116). The will names his wife Frances; sons Daniel, Redmond, John, and Barnaby; daughters Mary, Elinor, Margarett, Elizabeth and Roseanah.

Members of the Fallin family acquired a number of tracts in the area and intermarried with the MacNamaras, Wingates, Insleys, Willings, Foxwells, Pritchetts and other well-known families of the vicinity.

Daniel Fallin served with distinction as a Major in the Dorchester Militia in the Revolutionary War; other Fallins also served in that conflict with Dorchester units.

## FELTON (72)

John Felton of Patuxent River immigrated in 1651 to the Province of Maryland (Pat. L ABH F141); his wife, Katherine, immigrated in 1653 (Pat. L Q F28).

On August 5, 1665, a 250 acre tract of land was surveyed for Felton and it was called "Gloucestershire;" it was located on the west side of Limbo Harbor (Honga River) running down the river to Fishing Creek. In 1669 he also obtained an adjoining tract of 50 acres called "Rich Ridge."

John Felton made a will which was dated April 1, 1670 (Wills 1, 516) and in it he devised all his estate to his wife, Katherine.

Katherine, widow of John Felton, sometime prior to 1675 married John Phillips. There is no record of any children from the union of John Felton and Katherine.

## FERGUSON (X)

In 1685 George Ferguson acquired by patent 150 acres of land on

Hungar River called "Ferguson's Forrest." He sold this tract and acquired other lands in the Hungar River Area.

George Ferguson, ship carpenter, married Elizabeth Phillips, daughter of John Phillips (Wills 12, 212) and they had the following children: George Ferguson, Jr., and Alexander Ferguson (Wills 12, 212), and Mary Ferguson and James Ferguson (DLR 8 OLD 37) dated February 13, 1715. There may have been other children.

FISHER (120)

On February 12, 1669, a 200 acre tract of land was surveyed for Thomas Fisher; it was called "Fisher's Chance" and it was located on the easternmost side of the Blackwater River.

Thomas Fisher died prior to May 1, 1680 (DLR 4 OLD 3), and his widow, Sarah, the daughter of William Dorrington, married Thomas Foulks.

Thomas Fisher and Sarah (Dorrington) Fisher had two sons, Dorrington and Alexander.

Dorrington Fisher's will was probated December 12, 1713 (Wills 13, 668). In his will he named daughters Sarah and Mary and he showed that there was a third daughter. He also named his wife, Rachell. The records indicated that Rachell was the daughter of Pettygrew Saulsbury (Wills 16, 32).

Alexander Fisher, son of Thomas and Sarah, married Elizabeth Winsmore, daughter of Robert Winsmore I (Wills 5, 252). Alexander made a will on January 28, 1698, which was probated March 4, 1698 (Wills 6, 308). In it he named daughter Ann Pitt, widow of Philip Pitt; daughter Elizabeth; wife Elizabeth. The will did not name any sons but Alexander and Elizabeth Fisher had at least two, Alexander II and Mark, which is proven by the will of the son, Alexander II. The will of Alexander II also identifies a third daughter of Alexander and Elizabeth as Sarah.

After the death of Alexander Fisher I his widow, Elizabeth, married John Rawlings II.

In Dorchester Land Record 8 OLD 7 dated February 18, 1720, Elizabeth Rawlings deeds her lands to her son, Mark Fisher.

Alexander Fisher II made a will on January 19, 1716/7, which was probated March 25, 1717 (Wills 14, 249). In his will he named his mother Mrs. Elizabeth Rawlings; sons Thomas and Alexander; daughter Elizabeth; brother Mark; sister Sarah Marriott and her husband Mark; wife Mary and an unborn child. His wife, Mary, was probably Mary Vickers, daughter of Thomas Vickers (Wills 13, 272).

FISHER (X) Edward-William

On May 5, 1682, a 50 acre tract of land was surveyed for Edward

Fisher; it was called "Fishers Landing" and it was located on the northside of the Nanticoke River adjoining a tract of land called "St. Bartholomews." Ten days later another 50 acre tract located between "St. Bartholomews" and "The Manor of Nanticoke" was surveyed for him, and this tract was called "Weston." This "Weston" has been confused by many writers with "Weston", the 1000 acre tract located down the Nanticoke a few miles which was surveyed for Jerome White.

Edward Fisher, planter, and Frances Willis, widow of Richard Willis, were married January 8, 1699, at the Quaker Meeting House near Tuckaho Creek (Third Haven Meeting Records).

Dorchester Land Record 4 1/2 OLD 1 dated October 21, 1689, contains the will of Richard Willis. In it he named his sons Richard and John; daughter Frances; wife, Frances. The records of Third Haven Meeting show the following birth dates for those children: Richard 8/13/1684, John 7/7/1686, Frances 8/7/1688.

Edward Fisher made a will dated October 25, 1700, which was probated March 4, 1701 (Wills 11, 117). In his will he named his brother William; sister-in-law Thomasin; children of brother William - Thomas, James and Mary; wife, Frances.

Frances Fisher, widow of Edward, made a will dated February 29, 1723/4, which was probated May 7, 1729 (Wills 19, 679). In the will she named sons Richard and John Willis; daughter, Frances Newton; Edward Newton the husband of Frances; granddaughters Frances and Mary, children of Frances and Edward Newton; granddaughter Elizabeth Thompson.

William Fisher, brother of Edward, made a will dated October 25, 1698, which was probated March 26, 1702 (Wills 11, 183). In his will he named son Thomas and daughter Jane. He devised his estate to his four children (unnamed other than Thomas and Jane) and their mother (also unnamed).

The records show that William married Elizabeth Scott, only daughter of Thomas Scott, and when William Fisher died his widow, Elizabeth, married Philip Griffin (Wills 11, 19).

In Dorchester Land Record 6 OLD 240 dated March 5, 1714, Jane Fisher, Mary Fisher and Sarah Fisher, daughters of William Fisher, conveyed "Fishers Landing" to Frances Fisher.

Dorchester Land Record 8 OLD 1 dated November 18, 1720, shows that Sarah Fisher, daughter of Elizabeth and William, married Thomas Rowles.

FOOKS (X) (Foulks - Foulkes)

On December 25, 1681, Margaret Foulke had a 50 acre tract surveyed at the head of Cabin Creek called "Milverton" (Pat. L SD#A F344). Rent Roll Record L10 F414 notes in connection with this tract, "This land belongs to John Foulkes who went to sea several years ago and not heard of since. No other owners found."

On December 28, 1681, Nicholas Folkes had a 200 acre tract surveyed at the head of Cabin Creek called "Taunton" (Pat. L CB#3 F410). Rent Roll Record L10 F415 shows this tract in the possession of John Foulkes.

No further records has been found of the three Foulkes mentioned in the above accounts, nor has any further information been located on the two tracts of land.

On April 28, 1682, Thomas Foulkes had a 100 acre tract of land surveyed called "Foulkes Content" (Pat. L SD#A F159). This tract adjoined Dorrington's land called "Busby." Thomas had several other tracts patented in the months that followed.

Thomas Foulkes came to Dorchester County from Accomac County, Virginia, and was the son of James Foulkes. Thomas married Sarah, the widow of Thomas Fisher and the daughter of William Dorrington (DLR 4 OLD 3). He was characterized in DLR 4 OLD 4 of May 2, 1680, as Thomas Foulkes, Chirurgeon. In his will dated October 25, 1720, which was probated October 15, 1722, Thomas Foulkes named three sons: Daniel, William and James. He also had a son named Benjamin and five daughters: Namoi, Rachel, Sarah, Mary Warrington and Elizabeth Crippen.

Daniel Foulkes, son of Thomas and Sarah Foulkes, married Sarah Roach, daughter of John Roach of Accomac, and Daniel remained in Accomac where he raised his family. His will was probated June 24, 1740 (Accomac Will Book 1734-1740, page 237).

William Foulkes, son of Thomas and Sarah Foulkes, married Mary Foster in 1704. Mary Foster was the daughter of John and Mary Foster of Dorchester County (Third Haven Records). In 1722 William Foulkes was living in Dorchester County because in that year the Choptank Indians filed a complaint with the Council of Maryland (Md. Arch., Vol. 25, page 392) that William and James Foulkes and others refused to pay rent for Indian land that they lived on. William Foulkes and Mary and the following children: Elizabeth, who married John Rawling probably the son of Anthony Rawlings; Thomas, who married Elizabeth Anderson; Sarah, who married William Taylor; Mary, who married John Walker; John; Benjamin; Rebecca, who married Henry Hands; Namoi; and Margaret. William made his will in April of 1740 and it was probated October 23, 1740. His will declared him to be of Talbot County.

Benjamin Foulkes, son of Thomas and Sarah Foulkes, married Catherine Roach, daughter of John Roach of Accomac. Benjamin died in Worcester County, Maryland where he had raised a large family and where he married a second time.

James Foulkes, son of Thomas and Sarah Foulkes, married Elizabeth Kennerley, daughter of Joseph and Sarah Kennerley. Their children were: Priscilla, Joseph, Sarah, Mary, Ann, James,

Rosannah, and Elizabeth who married William Trippe.

Joseph Foulkes, son of James and Elizabeth Foulkes, married Mary Kirke Gunn and they had a daughter, Elizabeth, who married John Trevallion Stewart.

FORD (X)

The Provincial Court Records of 1670 show the marriage on January 12, 1669/70, of William Ford of Bristol, England, and Sarah Preston, daughter of Richard Preston of Calvert County (Arch. of Md., Vol. 57, page 502).

William Ford, thru his marriage with Sarah, obtained large tracts of land in Dorchester County which Sarah had inherited from her father, Richard Preston. Ford also acquired a number of tracts in his own right. William and Sarah made "Horne" their dwelling plantation. "Horne" was inherited by Sarah from her father and it was located on Horne Bay on the south side of the Choptank River. William Ford served as a delegate to the Maryland Assembly in 1674 and in 1675; he also served as a Justice for Dorchester County in 1674 thru 1676.

He made a will on November 16, 1678, which was probated March 11, 1679. In his will he named a son, Samuel, who was born February 22, 1673 (Third Haven Meeting Records) and a son, Josias; wife, Sarah; and an unborn child. Dorchester Land Record 3 OLD 202 dated March 1679 shows the third child of Sarah was a daughter who was named Rebecca.

After William Ford died, his widow, Sarah, married Edward Pinder I. They had at least two children: a daughter, Kath. (this probably should be Beth--short for Elizabeth) who married Thomas Taylor, Jr. (DLR 5 OLD 132 and 6 OLD 169), and a son, Edward Pinder II.

Edward Pinder II married Jane (last name unknown) and they had a son, Edward Pinder III.

Edward Pinder II made a will dated June 2, 1711, and it was probated November 17, 1711 (Wills 13, 352). In it he named his son, Edward; sister-in-law, Elizabeth Taylor; wife Jane.

After Edward Pinder II died his widow, Jane, married George Stapleford.

Edward Pinder III made a will dated January 26, 1729, and it was probated February 13, 1729 (Wills 19, 866). In it he named his sister Dorothy Staplefort; brothers Charles and Thomas Staplefort; aunt, Elizabeth Taylor.

Apparently, the will of Edward Pinder III was not legal because he died before he was of age, the following is taken from Dorchester Land Record 8 OLD 398 dated January 27, 1730.

"Samuel Preston and Margaret his wife of Philadelphia to David Peterkin of Dorchester County, Gent: Whereas Edward Pinder the son of Edward Pinder who was the son of Sarah Pinder, became in his lifetime entitled to 600 acres of land and died in his minority without heirs, said land is sold and conveyed to said Peterkin..."

Samuel Preston was the son of Richard Preston, Jr., and he, Samuel, had moved from Calvert County to Philadelphia where he was, at one time, Mayor of that City.

FOSTER (XX)

Patent Liber 11, Folio 457, shows that Henry Trippe transported John Foster to Maryland. The will of Bartholomew Ennalls (Wills 6, 56) made in 1688 shows that Mary, daughter of Bartholomew, married John Foster.

On March 2, 1685, John Foster purchased a 200 acre tract of land called "Exchange" which was located at the head of the Transquaking River.

On November 5, 1690, John Foster sold 1 acre of "Exchange" to the Quakers (DLR 1 OLD 126). The record shows that a Quaker Meeting House stood on the 1 acre tract at the time of the transaction. Other records show that the meeting house became known as "The Transquaking Meeting House."

The Third Haven Meeting Records show the birth of the following children to John and Mary Foster:
1. Susanna, born April 24, 1680, married Richard Dawson at Transquaking Meeting House on March 8, 1698.
2. Mary, born October 5, 1681, married William Foulks of Accomac, Virginia, February 2, 1704.
3. Elizabeth, born July 15, 1685.
4. Sarah, born August 14, 1688.
5. Rebecca, born August 19, 1692.
6. Ann, born April 12, 1696 (Married Deane).
7. John, born July 29, 1698.

Other records show that John and Mary Foster also had the following additional children:
8. Thomas, died 1756, married Elizabeth Smart, daughter of Captain Richard Smart and Elizabeth (Hayward) Smart (DLR 11 OLD 80 and 16 OLD 132). Thomas Foster made a will dated December 24, 1755 (Wills 30, 94). In his will he named his wife, Elizabeth; and sons Joseph and William.
9. Phoebe.
10. Joseph.
11. William.

On November 9, 1725, John Foster I made a will which was probated March 22, 1726 (Wills 19, 93). He devised part of "Exchange" at the head of the Transquaking River to his daughter, Rebecca; to daughter, Susannah Dawson, land where she now dwells; to daughter, Mary Fooks, land adjoining land of Susannah's; to daughter, Phoebe, land adjoining land of Mary Fooks'; also mentioned were daughters, Sarah and Ann Deane; as well as wife, Mary; and son, Thomas.

In his will he made a request that he be buried in Friends Graveyard, Transquaking.

FOWLER (122)

On February 25, 1669, a 500 acre tract of land was surveyed for William Fowler and John Eason; the tract was named "Darby" and it was located on the easternmost side of the Blackwater River.

No further information has been found in the records on William Fowler.

GARY (20)

Stephen Gary immigrated from Cornwall, England, to Calvert County in 1650 and his wife, Clare, followed in 1653 (Pat. LQ F204). On February 4, 1654, he was authorized by Jerome White, Surveyor General of Maryland, to lay out and survey 1500 acres of land in any part of the Eastern Shore. In 1662 surveys were made for three tracts: "Grass Reeden" (Pat. L5 F142), "Spokott," and "Spring Garden," later "Refused Neck," "Cedar Point" and "Musketta Quarter" were taken up; the surveys were actually made in some cases by Stephen Gary. All six tracts were located on the Little Choptank River. On March 4, 1667, Stephen Gary sold "Spring Garden" consisting of 100 acres to Jacob Waymaks and William Thomas (TCL L1 F33).

Gary was one of the first commissioners of Dorchester County. He served in 1669 and in 1675 thru 1677. He was high sheriff of the county beginning in 1678.

The will of Stephen Gary was dated October 27, 1675, and probated April 6, 1686. In the will (Wills 4, 202) he mentioned wife, Clare, and he devised to her "Spokott" during her life and land in the town of West Rue (alias Purpeham) in Cornwall, England. He mentioned a son, Stephen, and three daughters: oldest daughter Magdalen, youngest daughter Clare, and Susannah. He also mentioned grandchildren, Stephen Warner and Mary Warner. Magdalen Gary married William Warner and their children were the grandchildren mentioned in the will. Susannah, daughter of Stephen and Clare Warner married Henry Willmot (DLR 5 OLD 97).

Clare, daughter of Stephen and Clare Gary, married Charles Powell (DLR 5 OLD 97) and their children were: Gary, Charles, Sarah and Blanche.

After the death of Charles Powell his widow, Clare, married Thomas MacKeele.

Blanch Powell married John LeCompte (Wills 19, 701).

Sarah Powell married --- (first name unknown) Cullen.

Gary Powell made a will dated April 11, 1729, which was probated
June 11, 1729. In his will he named brother, Charles. He also
mentioned John and Blanche (Powell) LeCompte and their sons
Charles and Anthony.

John Gary immigrated to Calvert County, Maryland, in 1651 with
his wife, Judith, and four children: John, Jr., Judith, Jane and
Elizabeth. Elizabeth Gary was the lady in what was probably the
strangest courtship on record (see details under Harwood).

On December 30, 1662, a 200 acre tract named "Cedar Point" was
surveyed for John Gary (Pat. L7 F199). The tract was located on
the east side of Fishing Creek. John Gary also acquired "Timber
Point," "Head Range," and several other tracts in the Little
Choptank area.

After John Gary died his widow, Judith, married Dr. Peter Sharp
(for further details see under Sharp).

John Gary, Jr., of the Cliffs in Calvert County made a will dated
September 14, 1674, which was probated October 19, 1681, and no
male descendants were named. So, this Gary line, apparently,
ended with John, Jr.

Nothing in the records indicate that John Gary, Sr., or any
members of his immediate family were ever inhabitants of
Dorchester County.

The will of John Gary, Jr., referred to Stephen Gary as cousin.

GATHER (21)

A 160 acre tract of land named "Gatherly" was surveyed on
December 20, 1662, for John Gather (Pat. L5 F579). It was
located on Fishing Creek and Gathers Creek (now Church Creek).

John Gather, the believed son of John and Mary Gather, was born
in Virginia and was brought to Maryland by his parents around
1652. He was granted "Abington" in 1663 in joint ownership with
Robert Proctor. John Gather married Ruth Morley and Robert
Proctor married her sister. John Gather became one of the
largest and wealthiest planters in the South River Hundred of
Anne Arundel County. The children of John and Ruth Gather were:
    1. John Gaither, born January 15, 1677/8 married Jane Buck
and Elizabeth Duval.
    2. Ruth Gaither, born September 8, 1679, married John, son
of Richard and Eleanor (Brown) Warfield, February 16, 1696.
    3. Benjamin Gaither, born February 20, 1681/2, married
Sarah Burgess.
    4. Rachel Gaither, born April 19, 1687, married Samuel
White, April 18, 1706.
    5. Edward Gaither, born September 28, 1689, married three
times.

6. Mary Gaither, born April 13, 1692.
7. Rebecca Gaither, born May 24, 1695.
8. Susan Gaither, born 1697, died 1717.

On June 18, 1668, John Gather of Anne Arundel County sold "Gatherly" to Robert Harwood (TLR L1 F50) who in turn on January 16, 1668/9 sold it to Robert Long, shoemaker of York County, Virginia (TLR L1 F78). There is nothing in the records to indicate that John Gather, or any of his immediate family, were ever inhabitants of Dorchester County.

## GEOGHEGAN (XX)

William Geoghegan, progenitor of the family in Dorchester County, is said to have been born in Dublin and to have come to Dorchester County as a teacher for the LeCompte family. The records show that he was born about 1704. He married Levina LeCompte, daughter of Moses LeCompte II and his wife Levina Pattison who was the daughter of Thomas Pattison, Sr. and Levina Pattison, the widow of Matthew Driver. William Geoghegan and his wife, Levina, had seven children:

1. Philemon Geoghegan (1735-1774); married Penelope Pattison, daughter of St. Leger Pattison and Mary Pattison.
2. Levina; born September 10, 1739, married --- Smith.
3. William; born April 14, 1742, married Rebecca ---.
4. Sarah.
5. Moses; born May 19, 1747, married (1) Rose Pattison (2) Rebecca Ferguson.
6. Elizabeth; married --- Jones.
7. John.

## GOLDSBOROUGH (XX)

Nicholas Goldsborough (1640-1670) and his wife Margaret (Howes) Goldsborough came from the County of Dorset in England and settled on Kent Island in the Province of Maryland in 1670. They had the following children: Robert (1660-1746); Nicholas (--- - 1705); Judith (--- - ---).

Soon after they settled on Kent Island Nicholas died and his widow married George Robins of Talbot County.

Robert, the son of Nicholas, came into the Province of Maryland in 1678; he married Elizabeth Greenberry, daughter of Col. Nicholas and Ann Greenberry of Greenberry's Point, Anne Arundel County, Maryland. They made their home in Talbot County, Maryland where they had a family of 12 children as follows:

1. Ann, born July 13, 1698, died February 24, 1708.
2. Elizabeth, born February 13, 1700, died January 17, 1708.
3. Mary, born December 14, 1702, died January 15, 1742.
4. Robert, born February 17, 1704, died April 30, 1777.
5. Nicholas, born February 17, 1704, died November 14,

1756.
6. Charles, born June 26, 1707, died July 14, 1767.
7. William, born July 6, 1709, died September 21, 1760.
8. John, born October 12, 1711, died January 18, 1778.
9. Greenberry, born November 16, 1713, died February 2,
1716.
10. Howes, born November 14, 1715, died March 30, 1746.
11. Greenberry (2d), born November 15, 1717, died November
20, 1717.
12. Greenberry (3d), born November 19, 1718, died same day.

Nicholas Goldsborough II, son of Nicholas and Margaret (Howes)
Goldsborough, married Elizabeth (last name unknown). Elizabeth
made a will dated December 6, 1708, which was probated January 1,
1708/9. In her will she named two daughters, Mary and Elizabeth.
The will also specified that brother-in-law, Robert Goldsborough,
was to take care of husband's two children, Rachel and Nicholas
during their minority. Also mentioned was brother-in-law, Thomas
Emerson. Sister Priscilla Bruen was named executrix. Priscilla
was the wife of Dr. John Bruen.

Charles Goldsborough (1707-1767), son of Robert and Elizabeth
Goldsborough of "Ashbey" Talbot County, Maryland, became a
politically active inhabitant of Dorchester County. He was Clerk
of Court from 1727 to 1738; he was also a member of the
Provincial Council and he represented Dorchester County in the
Maryland Assembly for some time.

Charles Goldsborough, lawyer and planter, married Elizabeth
Ennalls, daughter of Joseph and Mary (Brooke) Ennalls, and they
made their home at "Horns Point" on the Great Choptank in
Dorchester County.

Charles and Elizabeth Goldsborough had two children: Elizabeth
Greenberry who was born July 4, 1731, and who married William
Ennalls; and Robert who was born December 3, 1733.

After Elizabeth, the wife of Charles Goldsborough, died, he
married on August 2, 1739, Elizabeth Dickinson and by that second
union he had a son named Charles born April 2, 1740.

Charles Goldsborough (1707-1767) died at "Horns Point" July 14,
1767.

Robert Goldsborough (1733-1788), son of Charles and Elizabeth
Goldsborough, was born at "Horns Point." He served as Attorney
General of the Province of Maryland, Member of the Council,
Member of the Committee of Defence, Member of the Council of
Safety, Deputy to Continental Convention at Philadelphia and
Member of the Constitutional Convention.

Robert Goldsborough, like his father before him, was a lawyer and
planter. The 1783 Tax Lists of Dorchester County show him as the
largest land-owner in Dorchester County with 3365 acres in the
Lower District and 5266 acres in the Middle District. He was a

large slave owner having a total of 123 slaves according to the 1783 list.

Robert Goldsborough (1733-1786) married Sarah Yerbury in England March 27, 1755, where he was finishing his education. She was the daughter of Richard Yerbury of London. They came to Dorchester County and lived at "Horns Point." Later they moved to "The Point" in Cambridge.

Like his grandfather, Robert Goldsborough and Sarah had a family of 12 children.

Descendants of Nicholas and Margaret (Howes) Goldsborough have, throughout Dorchester County history, been noted for their professional excellence. They have made their mark as physicians, lawyers, jurists and politicians. As a family they have contributed much to Dorchester County, to Maryland and to the Country.

GOODMAN (56)

Patent Record, Liber 6, Folio 90, shows that Edmund Goodman was transported in 1656 and was in service until 1662.

On March 17, 1665, a 100 acre tract of land was surveyed for him and it was called "Goodmans Purchase." The tract was located on the south side of Little Creek which was above the second turning of the Choptank River and in what is now Caroline County.

On October 1, 1709, Edmund Goodman of Queen Ann's County made a will which was probated May 2, 1710. In his will he named two sons, John and Richard; a daughter Rebecca; and wife Katherine.

There is nothing in the records to indicate that Edmund Goodman or any of his family were ever inhabitants of Dorchester County.

GOODRIDGE (31)

A 1000 acre tract of land named "Goodridge Choice" was surveyed for Timothy Goodridge on August 7, 1663 (Pat. L7 F565). It was located on the north side of Cabin Creek. Very little has been found in the records about Timothy Goodridge. No wife co-signed any of the many deeds that he made transferring parts of "Goodridge Choice" to others so apparently he never married. He was an inhabitant of Talbot County and still resided there when he made his will on November 25, 1682. It was probated May 27, 1685, and in it he named no relatives (Wills 4, 134).

Rent Roll Record, L 10 F348 shows that the tract "Goodridge Choice" was divided into many smaller tracts and owned by numerous people.

GOOTEE (X)

Patent Liber WC2, Folio 84, shows Margaret Gootee "Service 1666, wife of John and John granted warrant for wife's service."

Chapter I of the 1671 Act of the Maryland Assembly naturalized John Gootee and Margaret his wife who were born in France. Chapter Ten of the 1695 Acts naturalized John and Joseph Gootee and John and Joseph Gootee sons of the said Joseph.

On March 16, 1677, a 100 acre tract of land was laid out for John Gootee. The tract was named "Canta" and it was located on the west side of Fishing Bay adjoining Roasting Ear Point. On February 12, 1680, a 450 acre tract called "Callis" was surveyed for him; it was located on the western side of the Blackwater River.

On May 30, 1690, John Gootee, Sr., and Margaret his wife deeded to John Gootee, Jr., several tracts of land including "Insley's Point," "Bowbunck," and "Callis."

On May 4, 1699, John Gootee, Jr., made his will and it was probated August 7, 1699. He devised all of his real estate to his father and mother, John and Margaret Gootee. His father, John Gootee, was named as executor.

Joseph Gootee, Sr., planter, made a will dated January 4, 1716, and it was probated March 13, 1716 (Wills 14, 319). The abstract of his will shows that he devised "Callis" his dwelling plantation to his wife, Ann. It also named John, his eldest son, and sons Jacob, Andrew, Joseph and youngest son John. The abstract also named daughters Elizabeth Shorter, Mary Robinson, Ruth, Rosannah, Triphena, Lucy and Elinor.

In 1691 John Gootee, Sr., and his wife Margaret had deeded "Graveling" to their son-in-law and daughter, John and Judith Cole.

GOULDEN (43)

On April 13, 1664, a 300 acre tract of land was surveyed for Gabriel Goulden. The tract was located on the east side of the Transquaking River and it was called "Glansford" (Pat. L9 F171).

Rent Roll Record, Liber 10, Folio 352, shows the tract in the possession of Thomas Bowdell.

Patent Record Liber 4, Folio 55, shows by a petition dated April 25, 1661, that Francis Armstrong transported Gabriel Goulden and Mary Goulden to the Province of Maryland. No other information has been found in the records about Gabriel Goulden.

GRAY (XX)

On February 29, 1691/2, Andrew Gray purchased 100 acres of "Charleton" (DLR 1 OLD 158). The tract was located near Cabin Creek. On June 8, 1674 he bought 600 acres of "Goodridges Choice" which was also located on Cabin Creek. The Land Records of Dorchester County indicate that the activities of the Gray family were centered in this area for a number of years.

On September 6, 1692, Andrew Gray, Sr., sold to his son, Andrew Gray, Jr., 150 acres of "Goodridges Choice" (DLR 5 OLD 4).

Andrew Gray, Jr., married Philadelphia Rawlings, widow of John Rawlings I. Andrew, Jr., died in 1693 (Wills 2, 293). In his will he named son, Jacob; brother, John Rawlings; wife, Philadelphia. Jacob Gray, son of Andrew Gray, Jr., married Isabelle (last name unknown).

Andrew Gray, Sr., made a will dated January 29, 1705, which was probated March 21, 1717 (Wills 14,512). In his will he named sons Thomas and John; wife, Elizabeth. Dorchester Land Records show that Thomas married Mary, and John married Sarah (last names unknown).

Thomas Gray, son of Andrew I and Elizabeth, made a will dated August 17, 1724, which was probated September 21, 1724. In his will he names sons Andrew (DLR 12 OLD 137 shows Andrew to be 43 years old in 1743), Thomas and William; daughters Rachel, Mary, Elizabeth, Rebeckah and Elinor.

Joseph Cox Gray served as a justice of Dorchester County from 1754 to 1764 and he served several terms during the same period of time as a delegate to the Maryland Assembly. The exact parentage of Joseph Cox Gray has not been determined; his mother was probably Elizabeth Lemee. He married (1) Sarah, daughter of Govert Lookerman, and (2) Rosannah Woolford, widow of Jacob Lookerman and daughter of James Woolford. His children were James, Joseph and John; stepchildren Jacob Lookerman and Elizabeth Lookerman; daughter Sarah. Joseph Cox Gray died May 24, 1764 (Md. Gaz.)

James Woolford Gray, son of Joseph Cox Gray and Rosannah (Woolford) Gray, married Elizabeth Grifith on April 28, 1787.

James Woolford Gray was commissioned 3rd Lieutenant under Captain Thomas Bourke of Flying Camp Company August 8, 1776; 1st Lieutenant 5th Maryland, 10th December, 1776; Captain, 25th December, 1777; taken prisoner at Savannah, 9th October, 1779; exchanged 10 February, 1781; transferred to 3rd Maryland, 1st January, 1781. Brevet Major, 30th September, 1783; served to 15th November, 1783. Major Gray was an original member of the Society of the Cincinnati of Maryland. The records show that 300 acres of land was issued to Elizabeth Gray, administrator, on Bounty Land Warrant No. 856 on May 29, 1794.

GREEN (X)

On December 11, 1679, William Green of Somerset County had a 250 acre tract of land called "Bluff Island" surveyed (Pat. L21 F15). The location of this tract was shown as on an island in the marshes near the mouth of the Nanticoke River. Insofar as can be determined this was the first tract of land that was surveyed and patented on what eventually became known as Elliotts Island.

William Green patented several other tracts in the Nanticoke area: "Cow Quarter" in 1682; "Beaver Dam Neck" in 1686; "Adventure," "Green Privilege," "Moon Shine" and "Pokate" were some of the other tracts he acquired.

William Green married Elizabeth, the widow of Mark Manlove, on February 2, 1666, both were of Pocomoke (Somerset County Court Register, Liber IKL). Luke Manlove, son of Mark and stepson of William Green, patented "Pen Pipe Point" which was located a short distance up the Nanticoke from "Bluff Island." Luke sold "Pen Pipe Point" to John Rider (DLR 6 OLD 104 - 1707).

The will of William Green I was dated April 12, 1720, and was probated March 13, 1721; it named a son, William, and mentioned two daughters. A grandson, William Robertson, was named; so one of the daughters married a Robertson. Another grandson was mentioned in an unusual manner: "To supposed grandson, William (son of Elizabeth Gileard)..." William Green I was an inhabitant of Dorchester County when he made his will.

The will of William Green II was dated January 21, 1737, and probated February 13, 1737; in it were named wife, Elizabeth; sons, William and James; and daughters Mary and Rosannah.

One hundred and seventy acres of "Bluff Island" was assigned by William Green to William Hickman of Somerset County who transferred the 170 acres to James Langrell (DLR 7 OLD 57 dated 6/12/1718). The other 80 acres was transferred by Green to Thomas Wright who transferred it to John Larmore (DLR 8 OLD 149 dated 2/21/1726).

The records indicate that William Green I was the first land owner with that surname to became an inhabitant of Dorchester County.

GRIFFIN (124)

On March 9, 1669, a 200 acre tract of land was surveyed for Lewis Griffin and John Phillips; it was called "Worlds End" and it was located on the North West Branch of Charles Creek in Hungar River.

Rent Roll Record (1706) Liber 10, Folio 363, shows the tract in the possession of John Griffin; John was probably the son of Lewis.

No record has been found that would positively identify all (there were many) the members of the early Griffin families of Dorchester County. However, the records do show some of those members.

Dorchester Land Record 8 OLD 372, 373 and 374 dated August 19,

1730, names four brothers: George, Lewis, Robert and Joseph and all are identified as the sons of the elder Griffin. Since the Rent Roll Records of 1706 indicate that Lewis Griffin I had died the elder Griffin referred to as father of the four brothers was most likely John Griffin who was shown in possession of "Worlds End" in 1706. It should be pointed out that the records show that there was a John Griffin, Sr., and a John Griffin, Jr., as mentioned in Dorchester Land Record 2 OLD 155 dated May 10, 1723. The records are such that it is impossible to distinguish between the two.

On October 21, 1728, John Griffin made a will which was probated June 8, 1730 (Wills 20, 26). In his will he named sons George, Lewis, Robert and Joseph; daughter Elizabeth Baker; wife, Hannah.

In Dorchester Land Record 8 OLD 375 dated August 20, 1730, John Cole and Elizabeth Cole his wife make reference to their brother Lewis Griffin.

In Dorchester Land Record 8 OLD 84 dated June 9, 1735, Lewis Griffin, Sr., deeds land to his daughter, Mary Keene wife of Ezekiel Keene; the deed was witnessed by Lewis Griffin, Jr.

Lewis Griffin, Sr., son of John Griffin, made a will on October 4, 1745 (Wills 24, 365). In his will he devised "Worlds End" to his eldest son, Lewis Griffin. He also named sons John and Edward; mother, Hannah; wife, Frances.

Lewis Griffin made a will on July 1, 1743 (Wills 24, 506) which names wife, Elizabeth; daughters Mary and Elizabeth; son Lewis.

Lewis Griffin made a will dated January 22, 1761 (Wills 34, 237). He devised to Lewis Griffin Paul, son of Rachel Paul, his dwelling plantation called "Hoopers Fortune." He devised "Griffin's Chance" on Hungar River where his father Lewis Griffin did dwell to Sliter Griffin Paul, son of Rachel Paul. He also named sister, Mary Keene.

GRIFFITH (XX)

In 1684 a 200 acre tract called "Griffiths Chance" was surveyed for Henry Griffith; it was located on the west side of Cone Creek (Nanticoke Creek). He later had several additional tracts patented.

Dorchester Land Record 5 OLD 140 dated September 1, 1699, shows that Henry Griffith married Elizabeth Tassell, the widow of Francis Tassell.

Dorchester Land Record 5 OLD 108 dated February 1, 1697/8 shows that Henry Griffith had a daughter, Elizabeth, who married Walter Cemey.

Henry Griffith, planter of Dorchester county, made a will dated February 22, 1708, which was probated August 9, 1709. In his

will he named sons Samuel, John and Abraham; daughter Sarah
Griffith (Wills Part II - 12, 223).

HACKETT (XX)

On July 21, 1668, Nicholas Hackett and William Travers purchased
a 300 acre tract of land on the Nanticoke River called "Goodridge
Adventure" (DLR 1 OLD 88) and on September 6, 1670, William
Travers transferred his interest to Nicholas Hackett.  Hackett
transferred the tract in that same year to James Jones.  In the
next few years Nicholas Hackett obtained patents on a number of
tracts of land in Dorchester County and then his name disappears
from the records; no wife was mentioned in any of the
transactions.

Thomas Hackett, Sr., blacksmith, of Dorchester county made his
will on June 9, 1716, and it was probated November 12, 1716.
Following is an abstract of that will:

"To wife Elizabeth, 103 acres, part of "Neighborly Kindness" and
personalty.

To sons Oliver and Thomas, residue of real estate equally divided
between them, and personalty.

To grandson Theophilius, son of Oliver Hackett, and to
granddaughters Litia, daughter of Thomas Hackett, and Elizabeth,
daughter of Oliver Hackett, personalty."

Thomas Hackett II, according to his own deposition, was born in
1689.  He patented "Hackett's Adventure" in 1732, which was
described as lying on the south side of Puckham Branch that
issueth out of the Northwest Fork of the Nanticoke River.  This
became the homestead and burying ground of the Hacketts for many
generations.

HAMBROOK (XX)

On August 20, 1706, William Dorrington leased for 99 years 75
acres of a tract of land called "Busby" to John Hambrook,
blacksmith (DLR 6 OLD 101).  Four years later Dorrington leased
for 96 years another 76 acres of "Busby" to Hambrook.

The 1st wife of John Hambrook was Elizabeth (last name unknown).
By 1710 his first wife had died and he had married Mary.  Mary
was the daughter of Henry (also known as John) Wheeler.  Mary
married 1st John Hayward who died in 1692.  They had the
following children:  Henry, John, Francis, Mary and Ann.  Mary's
2nd marriage was to Robert Winsmore who only lived a year after
the marriage; by Robert she had one child, Robert Winsmore.  She
married 3rd John Stewart II by whom she had two sons, John and
Thomas.  By 1710 (See DLR 6 OLD 156) Mary had taken her 4th
husband, John Hambrook.  No record of any children by fourth
marriage has been found.

John Hambrook made a will dated January 4, 1716, which was probated March 12, 1716 (Wills 14, 247), and in his will he mentions John and Thomas Stewart and his wife, Mary.

Mary Hambrook made a will dated September 14, 1727, which was probated March 10, 1730 (Wills 20, 149). In her will she names her son, Henry Hayward, and her sons John and Thomas Stewart.

Today a road north of Cambridge is known as Hambrook Boulevard and the Bay between Hambrook Point and Grey Marsh Point is known as Hambrook Bay which names were derived from John Hambrook.

## HARPER (126)

Patent Record ABH, Folio 140, dated July 15, 1651, shows that William Harper was transported to the Province of Maryland by Richard Preston.

On March 11, 1669, a 44 acre tract of land was surveyed for William Harper. The tract was called "Insleys Lot" and was located on Hungar River bordering the land of Thomas Skillington. In the next few years William Harper acquired several adjoining tracts.

He made a will dated March 7, 1719, which was probated May 15, 1720 (Wills 16, 164). In his will he named wife, Mary; daughters, Agness, Mary and Ann Houlten; sons Francis and Joseph.

While he did not name a son, William, in his will; a land record of Dorchester County 5 OLD 21 dated November 1, 1692, shows a William Harper, Jr., and his wife, Mary.

A John Harper is mentioned in the description of one of the tracts devised in the will but no relationship is indicated.

## HARRISON (XX)

ROBERT HARRISON (Brother of John Caile Harrison)

Robert Harrison, son of Christopher and Mary (Caile) Harrison was born in Appleby, England, November 5, 1740. He migrated to Maryland in 1755 where he became a merchant in the Town of Cambridge. He was appointed sheriff of Dorchester County in 1767. He was a deputy to the Maryland Convention of June 1774, and also to the Association of the Freeman of Maryland, July 1775. He was a justice of Dorchester County for six years starting in 1777. He was a Colonel in the Dorchester Militia and in 1791 he was appointed an Associate Justice of the Fourth Judicial District.

His wife was Milcah Gale, daughter of George Gale and Elizabeth Airy, whom he married October 10, 1770. They lived at "Appleby" near Cambridge.

The children of Robert and Milcah (Gale) Harrison were:

1. Mary Harrison, born May 23, 1774; died September 14, 1840; married Jacob Loockerman October 10, 1802. Jacob was the son of Jacob Loockerman, Jr.

2. Christopher Harrison, born August 29, 1775; died April 4, 1862. He was the first Lieutenant Governor of Indiana 1816-1818, and he helped to lay out the City of Indianapolis. He was buried at "Fair View" in Talbot County.

3. Elizabeth Harrison, born August 27, 177; died October 1857; married Andrew Skinner April 28, 1803.

4. John Gale Harrison, born December 21, 1779; died January 26, 1802.

Robert Harrison died May 16, 1802, and was buried in Christ Church Cemetery beside his wife, Milcah, who died January 5, 1780.

JOHN CAILE HARRISON   (Brother of Robert Harrison)

John Caile Harrison, son of Christopher and Mary (Caile) Harrison, was born in Appleby, England, September 3, 1747.

He was Clerk of the Committee of Observation of Dorchester County in 1776. He served as Register of Wills and as Clerk of Court of Dorchester County. He also served in the Dorchester Militia.

On November 18, 1773, he married his first cousin, Mary Caile, daughter of Hall and Elizabeth (Haskins) Caile. The children of John Caile Harrison and Mary Caile were:

1. Hall Harrison, born October 13, 1774; died September 3, 1803; married Elizabeth Galt March 17, 1800.

2. Hannah Harrison, born November 20, 1777; died November 4, 1799.

3. William Harrison, born July 7, 1780; died November 29, 1827.

John Caile Harrison died November 8, 1780.

HARWOOD (55)

John Gary, a prominent attorney of Calvert County and a large landholder of what eventually became Dorchester County, and his wife Judith, had two children, John, Jr., and Elizabeth. When John died his widow, Judith, married Peter Sharp, chirurgeon, of Calvert County and also a large landholder of the area around the Little Choptank River.

Peter Sharp brought Robert Harwood into court in an effort to resolve the relationship between him (Robert Harwood) and the step-daughter, Elizabeth. The case could be probably characterized as "The Strangest Courtship on Record." The details are set forth in Volume 10 of the Maryland Archives, pages 499, 500 and 531 thru 533.

Elizabeth Gary and Robert Harwood did, eventually, become married and they moved to Talbot County. They had three sons: John, Peter, and Samuel. Robert Harwood died in 1675 (Wills 2, 354). His widow, Elizabeth, married Wenlock Christison and they had one daughter, Harney.

When Wenlock died Elizabeth took as her third husband, William Dixon. Elizabeth died 1696/7 (Wills 7, 264).

Robert Harwood obtained patents for three tracts of land in 1665 in the area that eventually became Dorchester County. They were "Harwoods Desire," 300 acres on Fishing Creek of Little Choptank River; "Cold Springs," 200 acres on The Transquaking River; and "Harwoods Reserve," 700 acres also on the Transquaking River. He later received patents on several other tracts in the area that eventually became Dorchester County. He held most of the tracts only a short period of time before selling them to others and the records indicate that he himself never became a resident of the area of Dorchester County.

It is of interest to note that "Harwoods Desire" was the location of the early Town of "Dorchester."

John Harwood, son of Robert and Elizabeth Harwood, married Rebecca Brannock, widow of Edmond Brannock. John Harwood operated a ferry and an Inn at Castle Haven for a number of years. On May 29, 1717, he leased the house and land at Castle Haven to Margaret Noell, wife of James Noell Sr.

John Harwood died in 1724 and he named his wife Rebecca in his will (Wills 18, 323). He also named Mary Owen, wife of Stephen Owen, and Rebecca Nicholls; he didn't call them his daughters although the will of his widow, Rebecca (Wills 22, 504) identifies both as her daughters.

John Harwood did not name any sons in his will and it is probable that he had no male descendants. The records indicate that the other children of Robert and Elizabeth Harwood were never inhabitants of Dorchester County.

HASKINS (XX)

Thomas Haskins, the first with that surname in Dorchester County, married Mary Loockerman, daughter of Govert Loockerman II and his wife, Sarah Woolford. His will was dated September 21, 1735, and probated March 5, 1735/6 (Wills 21, 531). In the will he named his wife, Mary; sons, William and Joseph; and daughter, Elizabeth. After Thomas Haskins died his wife, Mary, married Joseph Ennalls, son of Henry Ennalls and Mary Hooper.

William Haskins, son of Thomas and Mary Haskins, was born May 10, 1729. He married Sarah Airey on March 11, 1759. She was the daughter of the Rev. Thomas Airey and his wife Elizabeth Pitt. William was a justice of Dorchester County for seven years starting in 1764. In 1774 he was a member of the Committee of Correspondence from Caroline County.

Joseph Haskins, son of Thomas and Mary Haskins, was born February 22, 1731.  On April 15, 1759, he married Sarah Ennalls, daughter of Thomas Ennalls and his wife Ann Skinner.  Joseph was a sea captain and he died in 1788.

Elizabeth Haskins, daughter of Thomas and Mary Haskins, was born May 25, 1733.  On June 2, 1754, she married Hall Caile.  She died November 3, 1805.

HAYWARD (XX)

The will of Francis Hayward I (York County, Virginia, Records #3, 1657-1662) dated January 1, 1657/8 and probated August 24, 1659, names his son, Francis; an unborn child; brother, John Hayward; wife, Mary.  Other documents show that his widow, Mary (Warren) Hayward, married Bartholomew Ennalls and that the child was born and named John Hayward.  Bartholomew Ennalls with his wife, Mary, and her children moved to Dorchester County, Maryland in March of 1669 and settled in the Transquaking River area.  The two Hayward children grew to manhood, prospered, and married.

John Hayward married Mary Wheeler, the daughter of Henry and Alice Wheeler (Wills 7, 333).  John Hayward entered his will in Dorchester County Land Record 4 OLD 249-136 dated December 3, 1691, as per the following abstract:

"To eldest son Henry Hayward, "Merchants Adventure" on which Testator now lives; also Testators part of "Beaver Neck," the other part belonging to Testator's brother, Francis Hayward.
    To second son, John Hayward, 64 acres called "Haywards Choice."
To son, Francis Hayward, 45 acres called "Haywards Neglect."
To Testator's three sons, personalty when they come of age.
To Testator's daughter, Mary Hayward, personalty.
Testator's wife, (not named) Executrix."

NOTE:  While she was not named in his will the records indicated that John and Mary Hayward had a second daughter who was named Ann.

After John Hayward died, his widow, Mary, married Robert Winsmore II (See Will 2, 333) by whom she had one child, Robert Winsmore III.  When her second husband died she married John Stewart II by whom she had two sons, John and Thomas Stewart.  After the death of John Stewart, Mary married John Hambrook, a blacksmith, and by him she had no children.

Francis Hayward II, son of Francis and Mary Hayward, was a party to a number of land transactions shortly before his death that manifested his wishes concerning the distribution of his lands.  Following are some abstracts of some of those transactions:

8 OLD 184 March 25, 1728
    William Ennalls of Dorchester County to his cousin, William Hayward: "Francis Cottage" formerly given by Bartholomew Ennalls,

deceased, grandfather of said William Ennalls, to Francis Hayward of the same County, uncle of said William Ennalls and father of said William Hayward, the deed of said Bartholomew Ennalls not having been perfected. Land contains 200 acres more or less, on Wills Dam which runs out of Transquaking River. Life interest to Francis Hayward, to revert at his death to said William Hayward.

8 OLD 371 August 11, 1730
Francis Hayward of Dorchester County, Gent., to his son John Hayward of the same County, mariner: "Beaver Neck." Mentions Francis Hayward second son of said Francis the elder. This deed to be void of John contests the title of Thomas Hayward, grantor's grandson, to the plantation where said Francis now lives, and which has been given to said Thomas.

8 OLD 394 December 31, 1730
Francis Hayward of Dorchester County, Gent., to John Hayward of the same County, mariner, son of said Francis: "Francis Cottage" on the south side of the head of Transquaking River and on Wills Dam, containing 200 acres more or less. Also part of "Beaver Neck" on the north side of the North Branch of Transquaking River, containing 310 acres more or less. Lands to belong to said John during his natural life; he to convey and make over to Thomas Hayward, son of William Hayward, deceased, 100 acres of "Beaver Neck" when Thomas arrives at age 21, or to pay to Thomas enough tobacco to purchase 100 acres elsewhere.

9 OLD 25 December 11, 1732
Francis Hayward Senr. of Dorchester County to his daughter, Mary Jones, of the same County: One-half of "Maidens Lott" on Dear Penn Branch located below "Francis Cottage."

Francis Hayward II, son of Francis and Mary Hayward, made a will dated April 30, 1734, and it was probated September 17, 1735 (Wills 21, 454). In his will he made bequests as follows:

To son, Thomas, "Addition to Francis Hayward's Farm."
To daughter, Elizabeth, wife of Thomas Ennalls, one moyety of "Maidens Lott"...(NOTE: Elizabeth married first Captain Richard Smart - See Dorchester Land Record 10 OLD 44 - and after the Captain's death she married Thomas Ennalls, son of Joseph Ennalls).
To daughter, Mary Jones, residue of said tract; and personalty.
To three sons: John, Francis (III) and Thomas, and grandson Thomas son of son William, deceased, residue of estate divided equally.

John Hayward, son of Francis Hayward II, made a will dated April 29, 1743, and it was probated April 13, 1744 (Wills 13, 485). In his will he made the following bequests:
To sons Francis and Thomas, dwelling plantation "Francis Cottage" and "The Addition to Francis Cottage."
To nephew, Thomas, son of William, deceased, 100 acres "Beaver's Neck" according to will of testator's father.
To son, John, residue of "Beaver's Neck." He to buy for

testator's son, William, 100 acres equalling the aforesaid tract in value.
To wife, Sarah, rest of personal estate and life interest in real estate.
Exs.: Wife, Sarah, Brother-in-law, Col. Henry Hooper.

NOTE: Sarah was the daughter of Henry Hooper II and his second wife, Mary Woolford, daughter of Roger Woolford. Col. Henry Hooper was her brother, son of Henry Hooper II and Mary Woolford.

Sarah Hayward, widow of John Hayward, made a will dated March 9, 1774, which was probated February 12, 1776 (Wills 40, 730). In her will Sarah named the following:

Sons: Francis, John, Thomas and William.
Daughters: Sarah Brannock, Mary Travers, Elizabeth Manning, Rebecca Stewart, Priscilla Plitt and Rosannah Griffin.
Grandchildren: Sarah Griffin and Elizabeth Griffin, children of Rosannah and James Griffin, William, Joseph Richard and Elizabeth, children of son Thomas, Hannah, daughter of son William.

HENRY (XX)

Rev. John Henry, a Presbyterian minister, came from Ireland about 1700 and settled near Rehoboth, on Pocomoke River in Somerset County, Maryland, where he resided until his death in 1717.

Rev. John Henry (--- - 1717) married Mary Jenkins, widow of Francis Jenkins and a daughter of Sir Robert King. After Mr. Henry's death she married as her third husband, Rev. John Hampton who was also a Presbyterian minister. She had no children except by Mr. Henry, by whom she left two sons; Robert Jenkins Henry and John Henry.

Robert Jenkins Henry (1712-1716), elder son of Rev. John Henry and Mary his wife, married in May 1746 Gertrude Rousby, daughter of John Rousby, and they had two sons: Robert and Edward; and four daughters: Mary King, Ann, Elizabeth and Gertrude.

John Henry (1714-1781), the youngest son of Rev. John Henry and Mary his wife, married Dorothy Rider, youngest daughter of Col. John Rider of Dorchester County.

Col. John Henry (1714-1781) and Dorothy had the following children: Sons; Charles Rider Henry, Francis Jenkins Henry, and John Henry (1750-1798); daughters, Charlotte who married William Winder, Jr., Niturah, Dorothy who married Isaac Henry, Nancy, and Sarah.

John Henry (1750-1798), the third son of Col. John Henry and Dorothy Rider, attended West Nottingham Academy in Cecil County, Maryland; graduated from Princeton in 1769; and studied law for several years in this Country and about two and one-half years in England. Arriving home about 1775 he was elected to the

Legislature of Maryland and served successively in the
Continental Congress, the U. S. Senate and as Governor of
Maryland until shortly before his death in 1798.  He married,
March 6, 1787, Margaret, daughter of John and Elizabeth
(Goldsborough) Campbell of Caroline County.  He was survived by
two sons, John Campbell Henry (1787-1857) and Francis Jenkins
Henry (1789-1810).  His wife died about a month after the birth
of the younger son, and he remained a widower until his death.
Gov. Henry was buried at "Weston," the place of his birth.  A
monument was erected by his descendants in his memory in Christ
Church Cemetery, Cambridge.

Insofar as can be determined, the two older brothers of John
Henry, Charles Rider Henry and Francis Jenkins Henry, died
without issue.

John Campbell Henry (1787-1857) of "Hambrooks," near Cambridge,
elder son of Gov. John Henry, married in April, 1808, Mary N.
Steele, daughter of James Steele and Mary his wife.  They had the
following children:

1. Mary Steele Henry, may have died young.
2. Margaret Campbell Henry, predeceased her father.
3. John Francis Henry (1814-1847).
4. Dr. J. Weinfeld Henry (1815-1889) married Anna Maria
Campbell (1816-1889), daughter of Levin H. Campbell (1774-1819).
5. Francis J. Henry (1816-1902), married Williamina E. E.
Goldsborough (1818-1881), youngest daughter of Robert
Goldsborough and Mary Nixon.
6. Catherine (Kitty) Henry (1818-1886) married Daniel Lloyd
(1812-1875).
7. Hampton Henry, predeceased his father.
8. Daniel Maynadier Henry (1823-1899), married (1)
Henrietta Maria Goldsborough (1828-1846) (2) Susan E.
Goldsborough (1842-1883).
9. Isabelle Elizabeth Steele Henry (1825-1912), married Dr.
Thomas B. Steele (1822-1905) on June 18, 1850.
10. Rider Henry (1828-1900) married Octavia Mary Sullivane.
11. Mary Henry (1828-1911) married April 27, 1848, Richard
Tilghman Goldsborough (1826-1896), son of  Governor Charles
Goldsborough and Sarah Y. Goldsborough.
12. Charlotte A. P. Henry (1833-1908), married Judge
Charles F. Goldsborough of Shoal Creek (1830-1892).

Francis Jenkins Henry (1789-1810), youngest son of Governor John
Henry, died unmarried shortly after becoming of age.

HICKS (XX)

Thomas Hicks I came to Dorchester County in 1671; he married
Sarah Denwood, youngest daughter of Levin Denwood and Mary
Cutting, in 1679.  Elizabeth, sister of Sarah, married Henry
Hooper II (1643-1720); a 2nd sister of Sarah, Mary, married Roger
Woolford I; and a 3rd sister, Rebecca, married Nehemiah Covington
II.

Thomas and Sarah had five sons: Thomas II, Levin, Denwood, William, Henry; and one daughter, Ann.

Between 1685 and 1714 Thomas Hicks I acquired approximately 5000 acres of land made up of various tracts in the vicinity of Vienna, near the Nanticoke or the Chicamacomico Rivers. His home plantation was made up of "Sector," "Cambre Lake," and "Luck by Chance" all adjoining at the head of the Chickamocomico River (Governor Thomas Holliday Hicks was born on this plantation).

Thomas Hicks I served as a commissioner of Dorchester county; a delegate to the Maryland Assembly; a member of the 1683 "Commission to Purchase Land and Lay out Towns in Dorchester County." He died at Vienna in 1722. His will was dated July 24, 1720, and was probated August 6, 1722. Sarah (Denwood) Hicks survived her husband and died in 1731/32.

Three of the children of Thomas and Sarah (Denwood) Hicks married:

1. Thomas Hicks II married Elizabeth Woolford, daughter of Roger Woolford II and Elizabeth Ennalls.
2. Ann married John Rider.
3. Levin Hicks I married Mary Hooper, daughter of Henry Hooper II.

Levin and Mary (Hooper) Hicks had the following children: Levin, John, Henry, Denwood, Mary, Sarah and Ann Travers.

HILL (169)

On October 28, 1669, William Hill purchased 75 acres of a tract of land called "Fishing Creek Point" (DLR 1 OLD 75). The tract was located on the Little Choptank River. On November 15, 1673, he had a 50 acre tract surveyed (Pat. L19 F112). It was called "Cherry Point" and it adjoined "Fishing Creek Point." This grant was for Hill's time of service.

On June 7, 1683, he acquired a 500 acre tract of land on the Transquaking River called "Richardson's Purchase" (DLR 1 OLD 147). Apparently, William made this acquisition his dwelling place for his will characterized him as William Hill of Transquaking.

He became a sub-sheriff of Dorchester County and was a merchant as well as a planter.

The Dorchester Land Records show that possession of "Fishing Creek Point" descended to William Hill, Jr., and the records also indicate that William, Jr., had a brother named John. The wife of William Hill, Jr., was name Elinor (DLR 6 OLD 162).

William Hill, Sr., made a will dated February 10, 1691, which was probated August 21, 1694 (Wills 2, 334). In his will he named cousin, George Watkins (perhaps Matkins); wife, Mary; and only daughter, Mary, wife of Christopher Smith of London.

HILL (XX)

Henry Hill of Anne Arundel County, mariner, acquired "Jordan's Point" a 1000 acre tract of land in Dorchester County on December 19, 1699, from Thomas Taylor and his wife, Frances (DLR 5 OLD 148). This tract is known today as Hills Point.

Henry Hill was the son of Richard Hill who died in Anne Arundel County in 1700 at the age of approximately 70. Richard had three sons: Richard, Joseph and Henry (Wills 6, 394). Confirmation of this relationship can be found in the will of Joseph, the brother of Henry (Wills 18, 289).

Richard (1673-1729), the son of Richard and brother of Henry, married Hannah the widow of John Delaval. Hannah was the daughter of Thomas Lloyd. This Richard moved to Philadelphia, Pa., and he eventually became mayor of that City.

Joseph Hill (1670-1724), the son of Richard and brother of Henry, died in Anne Arundel County in 1724. In his will dated May 21, 1724 (Wills 18, 289) he named no children nor did he name a wife.

Henry, the third son of Richard and the subject of this sketch, according to the records of Somerset County (Liber IKL of Somerset Judicials, Deeds and Wills) married Mary (1676-1735) the daughter of Levin Denwood. Henry must have married a second time after Mary died in 1735 because his will named wife, Sarah, as beneficiary.

The will of Henry Hill of Anne Arundel County was dated February 10, 1738 (Wills 22, 106) and in it he named the following: Wife, Sarah; daughters, Mary Gilliss, Milcah Gale, Priscilla Dorsey; Sons, Joseph Hill, and Levin Hill; Grandson, Henry Hill son of Richard Hill; Deborrah Hill, wife of son Richard Hill; Granddaughter, Mary Hill daughter of son Richard Hill; Granddaughters Priscilla and Mary, daughters of son Levin Hill; Grandson Henry Dorsey and Elizabeth, wife of son Levin.

Two tracts of land in Dorchester County "Jordans Point" and an adjacent tract called "Worcester" were devised by Henry Hill to his granddaughters Priscilla and Mary who were the daughters of his son, Levin, and the said Levin was designated as the overseer of the two properties until the granddaughters reached maturity.

No bequest was made to his son, Richard, so Richard the son may have preceded him in death although no record has been found to verify that.

Land Record of Dorchester County 18 OLD 235 dated November 20, 1762, and 23 OLD 223 dated May 20, 1769, show that Mary Hill the granddaughter of Henry Hill and daughter of Levin Hill married John Jackson of Dorchester County and that the two of them sold Mary's portion of the two tracts to Robert Bromwell of Talbot

County who in turn sold it to Thomas Linthicum of Dorchester
County who in turn sold it to Nicholas Maccubbin of the City of
Annapolis.

Land Record 24 OLD 47 dated July 24, 1770, and 24 OLD 70 dated
August 2, 1770, show that Priscilla Hill the granddaughter of
Henry Hill and daughter of Levin Hill married Alexander Allan of
Dorchester County and that the two of them sold Priscilla's
portion of "Jordans Point" and "Worcester" to John McDuff of
Cecil County. However, the tracts were repurchased by Alexander
Allan shortly after the sale. The Land Records of Dorchester
County show that Alexander Allan was active in Dorchester County
until 1789 (DLR 2 HD 441 dated October 14, 1789). In early 1800
a Henry Hill Allan became active in the Jordan Point-Hills Point
area and this Henry Hill Allan was the heir of Alexander Allan
because in Dorchester Land Record 5 ER 51 dated April 1, 1818,
Elizabeth Allan of Baltimore City sold to Thomas Cook of
Dorchester County: real estate of Henry H. Allan, deceased,
called "Hills or Jordans Point," sold by Elizabeth as trustee
under appointment by the Chancellor of Maryland. The relations
of Elizabeth to Henry Hill Allan was not disclosed.

Levin Hill of Dorchester County, brother of Joseph Hill of Anne
Arundel County, made a will (Wills 27, 51) dated November 13,
1748, in which he named his wife, Elizabeth, and his brother,
Joseph.

HINCHMAN (73)

On August 6, 1665, a 300 acre tract of land was surveyed for
Edmund Hinchman; the tract was called "Hinchman's Neck" and it
was located on the north side of the Nanticoke River by a Marsh
called Broad Marsh.

HOLLAND (149)

On March 1, 1669/70, Thomas Taylor, High Sheriff of Dorchester
County, sold to Daniel Holland, planter, two islands called
"Taylors Islands" (DLR 1 OLD 15) and another 80 acre island
called "James Island" (DLR 1 OLD 17). Both were located near the
"Streights of Annemesick;" they became known as Holland Islands.

Daniel Holland made a will on March 31, 1672, which was probated
April 17, 1672 (Wills 1, 564). He named in his will daughter,
Elizabeth, and wife, Joyce. The will indicated that at that time
he was an inhabitant of Northumberland County, Va.

HOOPER (105)

On May 26, 1652, Robert Clark, surveyor, laid out 1000 acres of
land on the west side of the Chesapeake Bay beginning at the
southernmost bounds of Mr. Richard Preston's land and running
down the Bay 300 perches; the tract was called "Hooper's Clifts"
and it was surveyed for Henry Hooper (Pat. L Q F239).

Hooper had transported: himself; wife, Sarah (Rycroft); daughters Elizabeth and Mary; sons Richard and Henry; and a number of other persons. He was also granted "Hooper's Neck" a tract on the Patuxent below St. Leonard's Creek.

Mary Hooper, sister of Henry Hooper, married William Chapline and this couple immigrated to Calvert County from Virginia in 1651. Since Henry Hooper came to Calvert County at about the same time it seems likely that he also came from Virginia (See DLR 4 OLD 20).

In 1658 Henry Hooper was appointed a justice of Calvert County and in that same year he was commissioned a captain of the Calvert County Militia.

On January 1, 1668, a 400 acre tract of land on an island in which was destined to become Dorchester County was surveyed for him. This tract was named "Hooper's Island." While the name of the tract was eventually adopted as the name of the island, they were, of course, entirely different entities. Hooper also obtained several other grants for land in the same general area in that year and in 1669.

On May 6, 1669, Henry Hooper was commissioned one of the eight members who made up the original group of commissioners of Dorchester County.

Richard Hooper, son of Henry, died in Calvert County in the year 1673. He had two daughters: Elinor who married Hugh Chinton an Innholder of Calvert County and Sarah who married Elisha Hall of Calvert county, there may have been other children. Henry Hooper I died in 1676 in Dorchester County.

Henry Hooper II (1643-1720) migrated to Calvert County with his father in 1652; the records do not show whether or not Henry II migrated to Dorchester County with his father in 1668 but we do know that he was an inhabitant of Dorchester by 1684.

Like his father he served as a justice of Dorchester County and served as a delegate to the Maryland Assembly. He and Elizabeth Denwood, daughter of Levin Denwood of Somerset County, were married by Captain William Thorne on July 4, 1669 (Somerset County Land Records), and from that union issued: Richard Hooper, who married Anne Dorrington; Mary Hooper, who married Henry Ennalls; Elizabeth Hooper, who married Matthew Travers.

After Elizabeth died Henry Hooper II took as his second wife, Mary, daughter of Roger Woolford I, and from that union issued: Henry, Thomas, John, Robert, James, Anne Broome, Mary Hicks, Rosanna Hodson, Sarah Hayward, Rebecca Hodson, and Priscilla Stevens (See Wills 22, 248).

Most of the Hoopers had large families and their descendants are legion; it is almost a truism that most Dorchester families can prove some connection to a Hooper ancestor.

Henry Hooper II added thousands of acres to the land holdings of his father. This fact points up a remarkable characteristic of the land ownership of some of the early settlers of Maryland. Records show that, at first, travel was limited almost exclusively to the various types of watercraft; and yet, many of the early settlers sometimes owned tracts of land in several counties and sometimes from one end of a county to another. Such was the case of the land holdings of Henry Hooper II. The scope and locations of the acreage to which he held title are indicated by his will which was dated March 27, 1720, and which was probated August 30, 1720 (Wills 16, 159).

The five hundred acre tract on the east side of Preston Creek in Calvert County that was the home of his father was left to his son Henry; as was "Hooper's Chance," "Hooper's Fortune" and "Hooper's Lot" on the Chicamacomico. "Hooper's Forrest" formerly known as "Martin's Hundred" located on the Nanticoke River (later the site of the town of Seaford, Delaware) was willed to his sons, Thomas and John, as was part of the tract called "Hooper's Island" which was located on the island of the same name. The other part of "Hooper's Island" was left to his son, Roger. A lot in the town of Plymouth which was located on the north side of Fishing Creek was willed jointly to his sons Henry, Thomas and John. A three hundred acre tract called "Parpeigham" and a one hundred acre tract called "Crowes Nest" both located on the west side of the Transquaking River were left to his son, James. To Henry (son of Richard, deceased) he willed land located at the head of Worlds End Creek; this was where Richard formerly lived. To his wife, Mary, he left the home plantation which was located on the east side of Worlds End Creek.

Henry Hooper III like his father and grandfather before him served as a justice for Dorchester County and as a delegate to the Maryland Assembly. He also served as a colonel in the Maryland Militia. In 1720 he acquired "Warwick" and by 1739 had increased it to a 2550 acre estate which he named "Warwick Fort Manor." Upon the death of Henry Hooper III the following obituary appeared in the May 14, 1767, issue of the "Maryland Gazette."

"The Hon. Henry Hooper died on Monday evening (April 20), aged over 80 years of age; Chief Justice of the Provincial Court and one of His Lordship's Council of State. He was formerly a Representative for Dorchester County, and for many years Speaker of the Lower House of the Assembly. April 23, 1767, while his body lay in the house of his daughter, Mrs. Hicks, near Cambridge, the house, a brick dwelling, was destroyed by fire, and his corpse was rescued from the flames with much difficulty."

The will of Henry Hooper III was dated April 16, 1767 (Wills 35, 382), and following are some of the excerpts:

"To son, Henry Hooper, dwelling "Warwick Fort Manor.
To daughter, Ann Hicks, the wife of Denwood Hicks....
I give to the Church in Great Choptank Parish one silver

communion cup.
I give to the Church in Dorchester Parish one silver communion
cup and it is to be engraved 'For the church in Dorchester
Parish.' (NOTE: Isn't it odd that the cup that tradition
credits with being a gift of Queen Anne of England contained
exactly the same engraved words and isn't it a further oddity
that no credit has been given by historians to the gift of Mr.
Henry Hooper III?)
To grandson William Ennalls Hooper....
To daughter, Mary Hicks...."

Henry Hooper IV like his namesake served as a delegate to the
Maryland Assembly and he, too, served in the Maryland Militia.
He was commissioned a Captain, then made Colonel and during the
Revolutionary War he served as a Brigadier General of the Fifth
District with headquarters at Cambridge, Maryland.

HOOPER (X)

It should be pointed out that the Hooper family, like other large
families of early Dorchester, had many branches and it would be
practically impossible to record in a volume such as this all of
the branches of the many families listed herein. We are,
however, outlining below some genealogical information on another
member of the Hooper family. There are still other branches
which are not covered herein.

In the will of Henry Hooper II land was devised to Henry Hooper,
son of Richard Hooper, deceased, at the head of Worlds End Creek.
The Richard Hooper mentioned in this will of Henry Hooper II was
his son who married Ann Dorrington, daughter of William
Dorrington and Elizabeth Winslow, his wife.

Richard Hooper died in 1719 one year before his father. He and
Ann had two sons, Henry and William.

Henry Hooper, son of Richard and Ann Hooper, married Rebecca
Foster, daughter of John Foster and Mary Ennalls. Rebecca was
born August 19, 1692 (Third Haven Meeting Records). The children
of Henry and Rebecca were: John Hooper, Rebecca Hooper,
Elizabeth Hooper, Mary Hooper, Priscilla Hooper, and Henry
Hooper, Jr. Henry Hooper, son of Richard and Ann, died in 1749.

Henry Hooper, son of Henry and Rebecca, served as a lieutenant
during the Revolutionary War, in the Dorchester Militia. He
lived on the Transquaking River near Vienna. He married Sarah
Travers and their children were: Henry Hooper (3rd in this
branch).
    Thomas Hooper who married Hooper (Will 21, 345 shows that he
married Mary Nutter, daughter of Charles Nutter.) Issue: Mary
Hooper who married John Thomas.
    William Hooper who married Rebecca Arnett.
    Richard Hooper who married (1) Nancy Robson and (2) Margaret
Hutchison.
    Priscilla Hooper who married (1) William Hayward and (2)

Thomas Bassett.
    Rebecca Hooper who married Josiah Shenton.   Issue: Richard
Shenton.
    Elizabeth Hooper who married Mason Shehan.
    Mary Hooper who married John Hubbert.

NOTE:  Dorchester Land Record 10 OLD 100 dated August 20, 1741
shows that a Henry Hooper married Mary, the daughter of Pettigrew
Salisbury.  This may have been the second marriage of Henry, son
of Henry and Rebecca.

HOOPER (X)  (George)

On December 27, 1679, a 64 acre tract of land was surveyed for
George Hooper; it was called "Bansbury" and it was located on the
southside of the northeast branch of Charles Creek that issues
out of Hungar River.

Patent Record Liber CB#2 Folio 298 shows that George Hooper
transported himself and his son, William, to Maryland.

George Hooper made a will dated August 3, 1695, which was
probated November 25, 1695.  In the will he devised all of his
estate to his son, William.

George Hooper must have had a son named George because Dorchester
Land Record 2 OLD 163 dated July 13, 1722, shows that Mary
Insley, daughter of Andrew Insley, became the mother of George
Hooper.  This land record also shows that Silvia was the name of
the wife of George Hooper and other land records show that George
was a cooper.

HOOTEN (96)  (Horton)

Patent Liber 10, Folio 299, shows that Thomas Hooten of Calvert
County immigrated to Maryland in 1665 with his wife, Mary, and
Daughter, Sarah.  On April 17, 1667, a 50 acre tract of land was
surveyed for him; it was named "Hooten's Neck" and was located on
the Hungar River.  In the next two years six additional tracts
were surveyed for him.  The Dorchester Land Records identified
Thomas Hooten as a planter of Dorchester County and they show his
wife as Mary (DLR 3 OLD 212 dated November 6, 1671).

The Rent Roll Records (1706) on several of the tracts carried the
notation "No Heir to be Found."


No record has been found which would show what happened to either
Thomas, or his wife, Mary, or his daughter, Sarah.

HOPEWELL (98)

Patent Record Liber ABH, Folio 35, shows that Hugh Hopewell
immigrated to Maryland in 1641.  Patent Record Liber 2, Folio
580, shows that his wife, Ann, was in service, 1649.

On June 25, 1667, a 50 acre tract of land near Slaughter Creek was surveyed for him; it was called the "Shambles;" and was specifically located on what was then called Hopewell's Creek and which is today known as Boggs Gut.

Twenty years after acquiring the "Shambles" Hugh Hopewell, Sr., of Calvert County made a will which was dated May 23, 1687, and which was probated February 20, 1688. In his will he named daughters Agnes, Ann, Susanna, and Mary wife of John Keene; sons Hugh and Richard; wife Ann. Other records indicate that he also had sons named Francis and Joseph. His daughter, Ann, married (1) Adam Bell and (2) Thomas Aisquith.

His son, Richard, married Elizabeth (last name unknown) and they had the following children: Richard, Joseph, Hugh, John, Thomas, Francis, William, Ann, Mary, Susannah and Elizabeth.

After the death of Hugh Hopewell, Sr., his widow, Ann, married John Duckworth. On July 25, 1698, Ann Duckworth of St. Marys County sold to George Ferguson of Dorchester County the tract called "Shambles."

Hugh Hopewell, Jr., planter, of Calvert County married Elizabeth Hill, daughter of Francis Hill of St. Marys County (Wills 7, 295). Hugh, Jr., made a will dated March 3, 1694, which was probated September 11, 1694 (Wills 2, 325). In the will he named wife, Elizabeth; son Hugh; daughters Elizabeth and Susannah.

Hugh Hopewell, son of Hugh Hopewell, Jr., married Elizabeth Edmondson, daughter of John and Margaret Edmondson of Talbot County.

There is nothing in the records to indicate that any of the Hopewell family ever became inhabitants of Dorchester County.

HOPKINS (115)

On January 20, 1669, a 150 acre tract of land was surveyed for William Hopkins; it was called "Hopkins Lott" and it was located on the east side of the Chicamacomico River. Rent Roll Record, Liber 10, Folio 364 notes "No heirs to be found."

HORNE (8)

The records show that John Horne, merchant of London, acquired land in Patuxent on March 19, 1657 (Pat. L4 F178-180) and that he also obtained a grant named "Hornisham" on the north side of Patuxent and south side of Lyons Creek adjacent to the land of George Bussey.

In 1658 John Horne demanded land for transporting himself and his servant, Richard Marsham, and also John Edmondson and John Squire (Pat. L4 F4).

On August 13, 1659, a 600 acre tract named "Horne" was surveyed for John Horne, London merchant (Pat. L4 F377). The tract was located on the south side of the Choptank River and today it is known as Horns Point.

On July 13, 1664, John Horne and Elizabeth, his wife, sold "Horne" to Walter Dunch, mariner, of London (Arch. of Md., Vol. 49, pages 355-356). On April 3, 1668, Dunch sold it to Richard Preston, planter, of Patuxent (Arch. of Md., Vol. 57, pages 286-287).

"Horne" was devised by Richard Preston to Sarah and Rebecca, two of his daughters. Sarah married William Ford and they occupied the premises. When Ford died Sarah married Edward Pinder and they continued to live there.

Over the years "Horne" has been the home of many notable families and it became somewhat of a "showplace" estate. Today it is used as the University of Maryland Center for Environmental and Estuarine Studies. It is still known generally as "Horns Point." So, even though the records indicate that John Horne never was a resident of Dorchester County, his name is still carried on the tract which he patented in 1659.

HUBBARD (130)

On June 12, 1669, a 50 acre tract of land was surveyed for Humphrey Hubbard; it was called "Indian Quarter" and it was located at the head of Hudson Creek.

Dorchester Land Record 5 OLD 182 dated January 3, 1700, characterizes Humphrey Hubbard as a cooper and names his wife as Elizabeth.

Dorchester Land Record 6 OLD 124 dated November 16, 1706, covers the sale of the dwelling place of Humphrey Hubbard consisting of "Taylors Happ" 50 acres, "Brooks Outhold" 100 acres, and "Indian Quarter" 50 acres, to Joseph Thomas.

No further information has been found on Humphrey Hubbard but the land records show that a Charles Hubbard acquired a tract of land that adjoined the land of Humphrey Hubbard and it is believed that Charles was the son of Humphrey. The records show that Charles also had a brother named Daniel.

Charles Hubbard made a will dated December 31, 1727, which was probated March 13, 1727 (Wills 19, 334). In his will he named a sister, Mary, and a brother, Daniel.

HUDLESTONE (114)

Liber 5, Folio 416, of the Patent Records shows that Valentine Hudlestone was transported in 1663 and Liber 10, Folio 249 shows that he was in service in 1666.

On January 19, 1669, a 300 acre tract of land was surveyed for

him; it was called "The Forge" and it was located on the
Chicamacomico River. Rent Roll Record, Liber 10, Folio 364,
notes "No land or owner can be found."

## HUDSON (69)

John Hudson immigrated to Dorchester County from Virginia prior
to 1659. On June 24, 1665, a 200 acre tract of land was surveyed
for him; it was called "John's Point" and it was located on the
east side of Tobacco Stick Creek (now Woolford Creek). This
tract is said to be the site of the first courthouse and jail in
Dorchester County.

On March 2, 1669, John Hudson sold "John's Point" to Bartholomew
Ennalls. Elizabeth Ennalls, daughter of Bartholomew, inherited
it. She married Roger Woolford. "John's Point" remained in the
Woolford family for generations.

John Hudson acquired a number of tracts of land in the next few
years. He represented Dorchester County at the Maryland Assembly
for one session and he also served as a justice of Dorchester
County. His will (Wills 5, 257) was dated February 20, 1676, and
it was probated July 14, 1677. In it he named a son, John
Hudson, by a previous marriage and 3 children by his second wife
Hester: Thomas, John and Joseph. Although not named in his will,
he had a daughter, Elinor, who married John Ennalls.

The son by his second wife Hester, named John, was characterized
"Secundus" to avoid confusion between the two John Hudsons of the
same father.

John Hudson (1653-1730) immigrated to Dorchester County from
Virginia with his father and his stepmother, Hester. Like his
father he represented Dorchester County at the Maryland Assembly
and like his father he also served as a justice of Dorchester
County; he was also a Captain in the Militia. His children were
John Jr. who married Elizabeth Trippe, John Quartus, who married
Rosannah daughter of Henry Hooper (1643-1720); and James.

John Hudson, Secundus, immigrated from Virginia with his father
and mother, John and Hester. Like his father and half-brother he
also represented Dorchester County at the Maryland Assembly and
he too was a justice of the County; he was a Captain in the
Militia.

He married Anne, daughter of John and Sarah Worth of Kent County,
and their children were John, Hester Anne, Sophia, and Vienna who
married Thomas Loockerman.

## HUGHES (11)

On August 28, 1659, Richard Hughes of Talbot County had a
300-acre tract of land surveyed called "Ricarton" (Pat. L4 F434).
It was located on Hughes Creek, now called Cambridge Creek, and
eventually became the site of the Town of Cambridge.

On September 5, 1668, Philemon Lloyd (through a power of Attorney granted by Richard Hughes to Edward Lloyd, both deceased) sold "Ricarton" containing 300 acres to Daniel Jones (TLR L1 F50).

On November 3, 1671, John Kirk purchased from Daniel Jones 200 acres of "Ricarton" and almost immediately after the purchase the 200 acres along with the remainder of "Ricarton" was incorporated into the Choptank Indian Reservation. On March 7, 1672, both Kirk and Jones were compensated for their loss by the Maryland Assembly.

In 1684 the Town of Cambridge was laid out. Obviously, the land for the original survey was taken from the Choptank Indian Reservation. The records of the 1684 erection of the Town of Cambridge were lost or as the Maryland Assembly puts it, "The records being either embezzled or casually lost." While the 1684 survey records were lost there are sufficient records to determine that the Town was actually laid out and named Cambridge (see Archives of Md., Vol. 38, pages 267-268). The records disclose that following the first survey several houses were erected in the Town, and a building that was used as a courthouse was also built.

According to the existing law of Maryland any lots that had been laid out and not taken up by 1690 would have reverted to the original owners, in this case, the Indians.

On March 2, 1702, John Kirk, repurchased all that tract of land which he had originally purchased from Daniel Jones except those lots which had been taken up by others; this time his purchase was from the Indians and the price was 42 match coats.

A second commission to Lay out Ports and Towns in Dorchester County was appointed in 1706 to lay out the Town of Cambridge again, along with three other towns in Dorchester County. On July 15th the Commission proceeded to lay out the Town of Cambridge for the second time. At that time there already existed a church of "The Great Choptank Parish;" a County Court, and several dwellings. The Town which was laid out covered 100 acres and 15000 pounds of tobacco was paid to John Kirk for the acreage.

As for Richard Hughes, the only other information that has been uncovered concerning him appears in an escheat patent issued to James Phillips for part of what was originally "Ricarton." The patent, dated November 11, 1741 (Pat. L LG#B F309-311), covered a tract of land that was called "Phillips Discovery." In the preamble of the patent it states that Richard Hughes died leaving only one son as heir and that the son died intestate.

HUMPHREY (46)

Patent Liber 5, Folio 257, shows that Robert Humphrey was a soldier who assisted Governor Calvert in regaining the Province living in 1663 when he demanded land for transporting himself and others into Maryland.

On August 4, 1664, a 200 acre tract of land called "Humphries Fortune" was surveyed for him (Pat. L7 F297). It was located on the north side of Little Choptank River at the head of Fishing Creek near the land of Captain Thomas Manning.

Thomas Oliver of Dorchester County acquired the 200 acre tract and on June 10, 1672 (DLR 3 OLD 251) he and Susan his wife sold it to Samuel Pritchett.

## HUTCHINS (X)

Charles Hutchins immigrated from England to Dorchester County in 1672. He left a wife named Dorothy and a son in England. He married Ann (Burgis) Coppin, widow, (Wills 4, 56) without benefit of a divorce from his first wife. Later his first wife sued for part of his estate. He had one daughter, named Ann, by his second wife.

Nicholas Painter of Anne Arundel County in his will (Wills 4, 56) of April 17, 1684, devised to Anne Burgis, daughter of Col. William Burgis: 1000 acres, 400 acres, and 300 acres of land in Dorchester County, patented in the name of Charles Hutchins.

Hutchins was a carpenter by trade (DLR 3 OLD 62); Edward Randolph in 1692 characterized him as "broken London carpenter." He served as: Justice of Dorchester County, a delegate to the Assembly, member of the Provincial Court and as a member of the Council. He also served as a Colonel in the Dorchester Militia.

He accumulated considerable wealth before he died in 1700. Among his holdings was "Weston," a 1000 acre plantation on the Nanticoke River. He left his estate to his wife, Anne, for her lifetime after which it was to go to his grandson, John Rider. An unusual aspect of the will made by Col. Charles Hutchins on June 29, 1699, and probated October 23, 1700 (Wills 11, 127), was a bequest that he made to Ann, daughter of Thomas Hicks, a 500-acre tract of land called "Appin Forrest." Six years after Col. Charles Hutchins died his grandson, Col. John Rider, married Ann Hicks, daughter of Thomas Hicks. They were married January 23, 1706.

Col. John Rider (1686-1740) was born October 30, 1686, the only son of John Rider of England and Anne Hutchins, the only child of Col. Charles Hutchins of "Weston" in Dorchester County. Both of the parents died on a voyage from England to America and the son was received by his grandfather, Col. Hutchins, and at his death in 1699, as stated above, inherited all his property. After his wife Ann died in 1733 he married in 1734, Mary Hicks, daughter of Henry Hooper. At his death in 1740 he left one son, Charles, and three daughters, Sarah, Anne and Dorothy, surviving. Another son, John Rider, Jr. (1708-1733), had died earlier, and Charles (1716-1741) died unmarried about two years later.

Sarah Rider (1710-1790) married first, Thomas Nevett (1684-1749), father of John Rider Nevett (1747-1772); second, William Fishwick; and third, Robert Darnall.

Anne Rider (1713-1756) married James Billings of Oxford, Maryland, and after he died she married Govert Loockerman in 1751.

Dorothy Rider (1725- ---) married Col. John Henry.

Several of the tombs of the Rider and Billings were moved from "Weston" to Christ Church Cemetery. The tomb of William Fishwick is also at Christ Church Cemetery.

INGRAM (48)

Patent Liber 17, Folio 108, shows that John Ingram was transported to the Province of Maryland by George Robotham. A tract of land containing 850 acres was acquired by George Robotham and it was located on Robothams Creek. Later this Creek was called Ingrams Creek after John Ingram, it is known today as Chapel Creek.

On January 4, 1665, a 100 acre tract of land was surveyed for John Ingram; it was called "Corbaston" and Patent Liber 9, Folio 251, shows the location at the head of John Creek. Rent Roll Liber 10, Folio 353 states "No heirs to be Found."

On December 15, 1667, a 300 acre tract of land was surveyed for Thomas Thurston called "Moorefield." Patent Liber 11, Folio 209, gives the location as on Ingrams Creek in what is now Caroline County. Rent Roll Record Liber 10, Folio 447 (1706) shows "Moorefields" in the possession of the heirs of John Ingram and further states that the tract was surveyed for John Ingram.

At a meeting of the Council held at Patuxent on August 6, 1667 (Arch. of Md., Vol. 5, page 12) Thomas Ingram of Talbot County was commissioned a Major to lead an expedition against the Indians (NOTE: In 1667 the area that eventually became Dorchester County was at that time part of Talbot County.) The archival records show that Major Thomas Ingram moved to Kent County and that he became sheriff of that County. In "Old Kent" by George Hanson on page 221 the sheriff of Kent County for 1670 is shown as Major John Ingram. No verification of the correct name for the sheriff has been possible.

The St. Paul's Parish Records of Kent County show the marriage of John Ingram and Hannah Jenkins on August 10, 1669. Those records also show the marriage of John Ingram and Mary Brington on January 10, 1704. It is believed that the John Ingram who married Mary Brington was the son of the John Ingram for which Ingram's Creek was named. John Ingram and Mary Brington had the following children as shown in St. Paul's Parish Records of Kent County: William b. December 6, 1705; Robert, d. December 1, 1707; Darcus, b. December 10, 1707; Thomas, b. February 18, 1708;

Mary, b. August 11, 1712; Martha, b. January 1, 1714; John, b. September 10, 1717; Elizabeth, b. September 12, 1720; and Benjamin, b. January 25, 1723.

## INSLEY (129)

On June 11, 1669, a 50 acre tract of land on Hungar River was surveyed for Andrew Insley; it was called "Insleys Chance." Patent Record, Liber 6, Folio 27, shows that Andrew Insley was transported into the Province of Maryland in 1669 and was in service until 1667. He married Margaret Jones whom he transported in 1668 (Pat. L11 F507).

Dorchester Land Record 5 OLD 125 dated November 19, 1698, names Andrew Insley and Elizabeth, his wife. Apparently, Andrew married a second time. In deed 5 OLD 125 Andrew and Elizabeth transferred property to their son-in-law, Michael Todd, cordwayner alias shoemaker, and their daughter Margaret Todd, his wife. This same deed named Joseph Goutey (Gootee), son-in-law of Andrew and Elizabeth.

In Dorchester Land Record 2 OLD 163 dated July 13, 1722, Mary Insley, daughter of Andrew Insley, is shown as the mother of George Hooper.

Andrew Insley made a will dated April 14, 1699, which was probated August 2, 1699. In the abstract of his will he named his wife, Elizabeth; sons James and William; daughter Mary; son-in-law Michael Todd and his wife Mary (probably intended to be Margaret).

## JENIFER (60)

On April 4, 1665, a 500-acre tract of land was surveyed for Daniel Jenifer on the east side of the Transquaking River and was named "Coleman Street."

Daniel Jenifer, Chyrurgeon, of Charles County made a will dated August 22, 1728, and probated June 4, 1729 (Wills 19, 724). He named his son, Daniel, of St. Thomas Jenifer. Other records indicate that Daniel Jenifer had at least two brothers, Jacob and Michael.

Records do not indicate that Daniel Jenifer or any of his family were ever inhabitants of Dorchester.

## JENKINS (7)

On August 6, 1659, a 200-acre tract of land was surveyed for John Jenkins on the west side of what became known as Jenkins Creek (Pat. L4 F160). The tract was called "Cliff." John Jenkins transferred "Cliff" to Marke Benton on April 1, 1661;[1] it was acquired by William Stevens on June 16, 1666 (TLR L1 F38).

A Talbot County court in August of 1666 found that John Jenkins

A Talbot County court in August of 1666 found that John Jenkins and his wife Elizabeth had been massacred by the Indians.[2] The creek is still known as "Jenkins Creek."

(1) <u>Archives of Md.</u>, Vol. LIV, page 216.
(2) <u>Archives of Md.</u>, Vol. LIV, page 402.

JENKINS (X)

On November 14, 1678, a 500 acre tract of land was surveyed for Francis Jenkins; it was called "Curtisie." It was located on the north side of the Nanticoke River about 3 miles above the North West Branch up the river to Rock Creek. Col. Francis Jenkins of Somerset County and Mary his wife sold "Curtisie" on June 30, 1707, to Matthias Caustin of Dorchester County.

Col. Francis Jenkins was married three times 1st April 12, 1672, to Lucy, widow of James Weedon, 2nd Rosanna (last name unknown), 3rd to Mary King, daughter of Major Robert King. The Colonel became a wealthy and influential man in Somerset County. He held many public offices. He had one son, Francis Jenkins (died young), by his second wife, Rosanna. The Colonel died in 1710.

JOHNSON (XX)

On January 20, 1696, Thomas Johnson of Dorchester County was issued a patent (Pat. L CD, F255) for 121 acres of land. The tract was called "Johnsons Place" and it was located at the north end of Cattail Marsh between the said Marsh and Russell Swamp. Thomas Johnson married Elizabeth, daughter of William Dean (Wills 6, 304).

On July 3, 1702, a Robert Johnson was issued a patent for 54 acres of land (Pat. L DS#F, F422). The tract was called "Johnson's Chance" and it was located in Hungar River at the mouth of Fox Creek and bounded by "Ashcombs Outlett." It is believed that Robert was the son of Thomas.

Robert Johnson, carpenter, made a will dated July 24, 1720, which was probated March 14, 1720/1 (Wills 16, 360). In it he names sons Robert, William, Henry, John and Richard; daughters Elizabeth, Jane, Sarah, Mary, and Rosanna; wife Elizabeth. Elizabeth Johnson, wife of Robert, was the daughter of Richard Goostree (Wills 19, 501).

JONES (X)

The records show that several persons with the surname Jones arrived in the Province of Maryland in it formative years. One of the first to appear in the records of Dorchester County was William Jones.

William Jones had a 100 acre tract of land surveyed on June 3, 1670. The tract was called "All Three of Us" and it was located on the east side of Russell Creek. On September 30th of that same year he had a 550 acre tract surveyed on the east side of Blackwater River. He received 50 acres for his time of service and 100 acres for the time of service of James Trice and Richard Tubman. In the months that followed William Jones had patented a number of other tracts some of which were sold to Richard Tubman.

Dorchester Land Record 4 1/2 OLD 29 dated June 1, 1691, shows several of the tracts that were patented by William Jones as being transferred by John Jones and William Jones and Jennett the wife of William. The records show that the original William was deceased and the records also show Jone Kimball as the mother of John and William II. Jone was the wife of William Jones I as shown by Land Record 1 OLD 187 dated April 16, 1676. She married John Kimball after William Jones died as shown by 1 OLD 187. The will of William Jones II showed that he settled in the Cabin Creek area of Dorchester County. He and Jennett had three children: William, Sarah and Elizabeth.

Another person who appeared in the early records of Dorchester County with the surname Jones was Daniel Jones. Daniel Jones purchased "Ricarton" from Richard Hughes on September 5, 1668. "Ricarton" was the site where the Town of Cambridge was eventually erected. Daniel Jones acquired several other tracts of land in Dorchester County among them part of "Harwood's Desire" on Fishing Creek of the Little Choptank River. The records indicate that Daniel was originally an inhabitant of Talbot County but by January 25, 1687, he was living in Kent County.

James Jones, another person to appear in the early records of Dorchester County with the surname Jones. He acquired a 300 acre tract of land called "Goodridge Adventure" located on the Nanticoke River; he acquired it on June 1, 1670 (DLR 1 OLD 185). He sold the tract to Charles Hutchins on August 29, 1674 (DLR 3 OLD 62). James Jones was a planter of Somerset County. James died in 1677 in Somerset County ; he had no children.

Still another Jones appearing in the early records of Dorchester County is John Jones who married Sarah Woolford, the daughter of Roger Woolford II and Elizabeth (Ennalls) Woolford.

John Jones who married Sarah Woolford was the son of Captain Thomas Jones and Martha Davis of Somerset County. Thomas and Martha had the following children:
1. Sarah Jones, born September 20, 1691, married Levin Woolford.
2. Thomas Jones, born February 11, 1693.
3. William Jones, born 1695.
4. John Jones, born September 15, 1699.

John Jones, son of Thomas and Martha (Davis) Jones, married Sarah Woolford, daughter of Roger Woolford II and his wife Elizabeth (Ennalls) Woolford. They had the following children: Thomas Jones, Roger Jones, John Jones, Betty Jones, and Sarah Jones. After the death of Sarah, his wife, John Jones married Anne Travers.

In his will dated August 12, 1771 (Wills 40,118) John Jones showed his daughter, Betty Jones, as Betty Woolford and his daughter, Sarah Jones, as Sarah Barron. He also mentioned his granddaughter, Christian Barron, and son-in-law Joseph Barron; grandson John Jones son of Thomas was also mentioned.

Colonel Thomas Jones, son of John Jones and Sarah Woolford, was born in 1723 and he served with distinction in the Revolutionary War. He died March 24, 1808. His son, John Courts Jones, was born in 1755 and served as a Lieutenant in the Revolutionary War and as a Colonel in the War of 1812. Colonel John Courts Jones died February 7, 1818; both the father and the son are buried in "Old Trinity Church Graveyard."

JORDAN (17)

Thomas Jordan, merchant, was born in 1634 (Pat. L S, 45) and at the age of 28 on April 28, 1662 a 1000 acre tract of land called "Jordan's Point" was surveyed for him (Pat. L5, F321). He obtained the rights to the tract on assignments from Thomas Manning and Michael Brooke. The tract is known today as "Hills Point" in the Neck District of Dorchester County.

"Jordan's Point" was acquired by Thomas Taylor of Dorchester County, and Frances his wife, and on December 19, 1699 (DLR 5 OLD 148), they deeded it to Henry Hill of Anne Arundel County, mariner.

There was a Thomas Jordan of Somerset County who married Sarah, the widow of John Elzy of that county who had died in 1664. In this connection following is an excerpt from Patent Record, L4 F374, of November 15, 1671:

"Whereas there was formerly granted unto Arnold and John Elzey the asigns and sons of Sarah Jordan, the relict of John Elzey, Sr., deceased, and since married unto Thomas Jordan, late of this Province, merchant...." (Somerset County).

After Thomas Jordan of Somerset County died his widow, Sarah, married Charles Ballard who died in 1672.

JUMP (74)

On August 9, 1665, a 100 acre tract of land was surveyed for William Jump (Pat. L9, F64). The tract was called "Jump's Point" and it was located on the Little Choptank River and Hudson Creek. The tract is known today as "Butter Pot Point."

Dorchester Land Record 4 OLD 12 dated January 4, 1679, shows that William Jump was a carpenter of Talbot County and a later record, 8 OLD 172 of March 11, 1727, shows him to be an inhabitant of Queen Anne County.

KEENE (107)

Three Keene brothers: Edward, Henry and Richard immigrated from Surrey, England, to Calvert County in 1653.

Edward married Sussannah Hunt, widow of William Hunt.

Richard, who was baptized December 7, 1628, married Mary Hodgkin, widow of John Hodgkin and after Richard died she married John Griggs.

Richard acquired St. Richard's Manor in Patuxent which became his dwelling plantation and he acquired various other tracts among which was 250 acres at the head of Honga River called "Keene's Neck" that was surveyed for him in 1668 (Pat. L11, F442).

In February of 1674/5 the Maryland Assembly ordained that an ordinary be kept at Richard Keene's of Patuxent (Arch. of Md., Vol. 2, page 434). Perhaps "coincidentally" the council held some of their meetings at his palace shortly thereafter. Volume fifteen of the Maryland Archives, page 47, shows that the Governor and Council met at his place on the Patuxent on September 14, 1675, and that they planned to meet there again on the 27th of September. Page 51 of the same volume indicates that he was compensated for the expenses of the Council. Also, on page 55 of volume fifteen of the Archives we find that Richard Keene was authorized and empowered to keep ferry boats to operate from his dwelling across the Patuxent.

The will of Richard Keene indicates that he died in Calvert County where he had a brother named Henry and a brother named Edward both of whom also died in that county. In his will dated April, 1672, and probated February 7, 1675, (Wills 2 384) Richard named his father, Henry, of Wadsworth, Surrey, England, and two sons, Richard and John. Son, Richard, was devised the Calvert County property and son, John, was devised the property in Dorchester County. His wife, Mary (Hodgkin) Keene, was named executrix.

John Keene (1657-1723), son of Richard, married Mary Hopewell, daughter of Hugh Hopewell, Sr., and his wife Ann, of Calvert County (Wills 16, 7). It is of interest that Hugh Hopewell also obtained a tract of land in the South Dorchester County area. John acquired from his father three tracts of land in Dorchester County: "Clark's Outhold," 100 acres on the north side of Slaughter Creek, "Keen's Neck," 250 acres at the head of Honga River, "Keene's Neglect," 99 acres on the south side of Slaughter Creek.

The records do not show just when John Keene moved from Calvert to Dorchester County but the records show that he was in Dorchester in 1694 (DLR 5 OLD 60 dated January 12, 1694) and that by 1704 he was serving as a justice of Dorchester County; he served a number of terms in that capacity.

John Keene of Dorchester died in 1723 (Wills 18, 185). He named in his will sons Richard (born 1688, married Susanna Pollard, Henry (born 1692, married Mary Robson), Benjamin (born 1694, married Mary Stevens, daughter of John and Priscilla (Hooper) Stevens), John, Edward (see below), Ezekiel and Zebulon. He also named a daughter, Sarah (born 1688, married Matthew Travers).

John Keene devised to his son, Edward, all that tract of land that he (Edward) lived on called "Keene's Neglect." Edward married Ann Shenton, daughter of Raymond Shenton and they had the following children: Edward, Ezekiel, Phillips (see further), and Ann who married William Phillips.

Phillips Keene, son of Edward, married Mary Grantham, daughter of William Grantham and Sarah (Kennerly) Grantham and they had one son, Richard 1758-1814, who married Sarah Woodward, June 15, 1791.

Henry Keene of Wadsworth, Surrey, England, through his son, Richard, and grandson, John, was the progenitor of the Keene family of Dorchester County with its many large branches. Numbered among his Dorchester descendants were officers of the military, justices, clergymen, doctors, lawyers and other men of prominent positions.

KENNERLEY (XX)

Rent Roll Record, Liber 10, Folio 346, shows 125 acres of "Teverton" in the possession of Joseph Kennerley.

Rent Roll Record, Liber 10, Folio 401, shows 50 acres of "Teverton Addition" in the possession of Joshua Kennerley.

The will of William Tick (Wills 4, 294) shows that "Teverton Addition" was devised by him to William Kennerley.

William Kennerley and Alice, his wife, were the parents of Joseph and Joshua as shown by the will of Alice Kennerley (Wills 11, 293) dated October 24, 1702. William had predeceased Alice. One of the witnesses to the will of Alice Kennerley was Thomas Everndon, Joshua Kennerley's father-in-law. In her will, Alice, named three children of Joseph: Joseph, Elizabeth and Mary. Elizabeth Kennerley, daughter of Joseph and Sarah Kennerley, married James Fookes at Transquaking Meeting House in Dorchester on May 3, 1720. Alice also named in her will William as the son of Joshua. She left the plantation on Fishing Creek in Little Choptank River to her son, Joshua.

Joshua Kennerley, son of William and Alice Kennerley, married Martha Everndon, the daughter of Thomas Everndon. The will of Thomas Everndon named children of Joshua and Martha: Martha, Hester and William (Wills 13, 56 dated 1710). The will of Joshua (Wills 20, 532) named two additional children: daughter Sarah and son Joshua. Sarah married William Grantham. The will of Joshua also showed that his daughter, Hester, had married an Edmondson.

Solomon Edmondson, Dorchester County, carpenter, and Hester Kennerley were married at the house of Joshua Kennerley at Fishing Creek on August 3, 1723 (Third Haven Meeting Records). Solomon was the son of William Edmondson (Wills 11, 235).

Dorchester Land Record 9 OLD 110 dated March 10, 1732, shows that Martha Kennerley, daughter of Joshua and Martha Kennerley, married Edward Wright.

Joseph Kennerley, son of William and Alice Kennerley, had two children by his first wife, Sarah: Elizabeth and Mary. By his second wife, Mary Stevens whom he married on November 14, 1711, he had two sons: Samuel and Thomas. The will of Joseph Kennerley shows him as a miller and names all four of his children as well as his wife, Mary. It is noted that he did not name in his will his first child, Joseph, who was named in his mother's will; the reason for the omission is not known.

## KILLMAN (99)

On August 8, 1667, a 100 acre tract of land was surveyed for William Killman; the tract was called "Killman's Range": and it was located on James Island.

Dorchester Land Record 1 OLD 22 dated November 13, 1669, identifies the wife of William Killman as Judith.

Killman sold "Killman's Range" on May 28, 1673 (DLR 3 OLD 1).

The Dorchester Land Records show that William Killman was a party to several land transactions.

## KIRKE (X)

On April 22, 1670, John Kirke had a 200 acre tract of land surveyed called "Poplar Plaine." The tract was located near the head of the Blackwater River in Dorchester County. In the years that followed he acquired, by patent or by purchase, a number of other tracts in Dorchester. He also acquired a mill at Cabin Creek; while he was a planter and a miller, he was by profession an attorney. He served as Coroner of Dorchester County and he represented the County in the Maryland Assembly for several years. In 1706 he was appointed a member of the Commission to Lay out Ports and Towns in Dorchester County.

Most Dorchester historians refer to John Kirke as the owner of Daniel Jones' Plantation upon which the Town of Cambridge was first erected and most Dorchester historians are wrong in that reference. On November 3, 1671, John Kirke purchased from Daniel Jones 200 acres of "Ricarton" and almost immediately after the purchase the 200 acre parcel along with the remainder of "Ricarton" was incorporated into the Choptank Indian Reservation. On March 7, 1672, both Kirke and Jones were compensated for the loss by the Maryland Assembly.

In 1684 the Town of Cambridge was laid out. Apparently, the land for the original survey was taken from the Choptank Indian Reservation. The records of the 1684 erection were lost or as the Maryland Assembly put it "The records being either embezzled or casually lost." While the 1684 survey records were lost there are sufficient records to determine that the Town was actually laid out and name Cambridge (Archives of Md., Vol. 38, pages 267-268). The records disclose that following the first survey several homes were erected in the Town, and a building that was used as a Courthouse was also built.

According to the existing law of Maryland any lots that had been laid out and not taken up by 1690 would revert to the original owners, in this case the Indians.

On March 2, 1702, John Kirke repurchased all that tract of land which he had originally purchased from Daniel Jones except those lots which had been taken up by others; this time his purchase was from the Indians and the price was 42 match coats.

A second Commission to Lay Out Ports and Towns in Dorchester County was appointed in 1706 to lay out the Town of Cambridge again along with three other towns in Dorchester County. On July 15th the Commission proceeded to lay out the Town of Cambridge for the second time. The records show that at that time there already existed in Cambridge a Church of the Great Choptank Parish, a County Court, and several dwellings. The Town which was laid out covered 100 acres and 15000 pounds of tobacco was paid to John Kirke for the acreage.

John Kirke had two sisters, Alice and Maria. Maria married (?) Rogers. John Kirke also had a brother named William.

John Kirke married Sarah Mackeele, the daughter of John Mackeele, as shown in the will of John Mackeele (Wills 7, 209 dated March 13, 1695) and they had four daughters: Anne, who married James Phillips; Elinor who married John Anderson (8 OLD 121); Sarah who married Thomas Cawee (Will 21, 120); and Margaret who married (?) Gunn (Will 20, 750).

So, John Kirke, the man who was very much a part of the second survey for the Town of Cambridge, left no male members of his line.

KIRWAN (XX)

The first Kirwan to appear in the Dorchester Land Records is Matthew Kirwan. On August 4, 1701, he purchased from Walter Campbell and Susanna, his wife, three tracts of land: "Plain Dwelling" containing 50 acres, "Hoopers Indeavour" containing 150 acres, "Kendalls Chance" containing 50 acres -- all, on the east side of Charles Creek, a tributary of Hungar River (DLR 5 OLD 225).

Matthew Kirwan married Mary Elliott, daughter of John and Jean

Elliott.

He filed a will dated January 4, 1716, which was probated June 17, 1717 (Wills 14, 413); in his will he named sons John and Matthew; daughters Jane and Mary; wife, Mary.

On April 22, 1746, Mary Kirwan, widow of <u>John</u> Kirwan, devised in Dorchester Land Record 14 OLD 20 ten pounds each out of their father's estate to her children, Matthew, Elizabeth, John and Peter.

LAKE (XX)

The Somerset Court Records (Liber IKL, page 11) show that Henry Lake and Mary Cooke were married December 25, 1683, both were servants of Thomas Cottingham. The Somerset records also show that Henry and Mary had a son, Robert, who was born February 23, 1687.

About a year before he died, on June 8, 1710, John Pritchett of Dorchester County sold to Henry Leake (Lake), blacksmith, a 110 acre tract of land on Charles Creek and Hungar River called "Long Acre."

No positive proof has been found but it is believed that Robert, the son of Henry and Mary (Cooke) Lake is the Robert Lake who married Jane, the daughter of John Pritchett of Dorchester County.

When John Pritchett made his will on December 19, 1711 (Wills 17, 322), he mentioned in that will among his children Jane Leake (Lake). Jane was the wife of Robert Lake, blacksmith.

Robert Lake on May 27, 1712, purchased a 100 acre tract of land called "Bournes Landing" (DLR 6 OLD 186) located on Slaughter Creek. On September 22, 1714, he patented a 50 acre tract called "Luck" which was located on the west side of the Northwest Branch of the Blackwater River (Pat. L EE#6, F144).

Robert Lake made a will dated January 27, 1716 (Wills 14, 413) which was probated August 14, 1717. In his will he named a daughter, Mary; wife, Jane; and an unborn child.

While he did not mention any sons the probate records covering the settlement of his estate were signed by his wife, Jane and a Robert Lake (Probate Accounts, Vol. 1, Folio 114). Also the Debt Book of 1734 (Liber 20, Folio 94) shows that at that time the 100 acre tract called "Bournes Landing" was owned by Robert Lake, obviously, the son of the elder Robert.

Further the Debt Book of 1734 (Liber 20, Folio 78) also shows that the 50 acre tract called "Luck" was owned by a John Lake, and obviously too, this was another son.

On August 12, 1717, Jane Lake, widow of Robert, purchased a 50 acre tract of land on the Blackwater River called "Obscurity" (DLR 7 OLD 43). On May 18, 1733, Timothy McNamara and Jane, his wife, sold "Obscurity" (DLR 9 OLD 91). Obviously, Jane Lake, widow, had married Timothy McNamara (his second marriage).

On January 30, 1724, Henry Lake, Sr., deeded "Long Acre" to his son, Henry Lake, Jr. "Long Acre" was the dwelling plantation of Henry, Sr., and it was deeded with the proviso that the deed would not be effective until the death of Henry Sr.

Dorchester Land Record 2 OLD 145 dated November 10, 1722, shows that Henry Lake, Jr., was also a blacksmith like his father.

A will dated April 21, 1760 (Wills 31, 153) was filed by a Henry Lake and most certainly this was the will of Henry Lake, Jr., or as he will hereinafter be called Henry Lake II and not the will of Henry Lake I as some genealogists have claimed. It is believed that it was the will of Henry Lake II; first, because of the time element involved between the date of the deed of "Long Acre" from Henry I to Henry II and the will of 1760. Henry I had deeded his home plantation, "Long Acre," to his son, obviously in anticipation of his death and yet a period of 36 years had elapsed after the deed was made and before the will of April 1760. Second, the records indicate that the wife of Henry I had died prior to January 30, 1724, since no provisions were made for her in the deed and also because she was not a party to that deed; on the other hand a wife, Mary, is shown as living by the will of April 21, 1760. Finally, the debt book of 1734 (Liber 20, Folio 91) shows that "Long Acre" was in the possession of Henry Lake II as of 1734.

It may be concluded that the will of April 21, 1760, (Wills 31, 153) is, in fact, the will of Henry Lake II and not the will of Henry Lake I as some Dorchester historians have written. Incidentally, one Dorchester historian wrote that Henry Lake II was born in 1739 and died November 20, 1804; actually, those are the dates of the birth and death of Henry III. That historian, apparently, overlooked the Dorchester Land Record of 1724 in which Henry I deeded "Long Acre" to Henry II.

The will of Henry Lake II dated April 21, 1760, names the following: daughters Sarah Lake, Rachel Williams, Arinna Hooper who married James Hooper the son of Roger Hooper (both James and Arinna were buried in the Hooper graveyard on Middle Hooper Island), Elizabeth Pritchett, Mary Pritchett and Ann Grimes; granddaughter Mary Woodland; son Henry Lake; wife, Mary.

Henry Lake III was born in 1739 and died November 20, 1804 at about 65. He married Rhoda Jewett in 1762 and they had the following children:

1. Henry, drowned at sea.
2. Elizabeth, died April 4, 1799 aged 23 yrs., married Thomas Barnes.
3. Mary, married Moses Barnes.

   4.  Lavinia (Lovey), born 1766, died November 17, 1843, married John Stewart McNamara January 21, 1783.
   5.  George, born 1776, died November 21, 1831, married Mary Boyne Slacum October 23, 1802.
   6.  William, born August 1, 1767, died April 5, 1810, married Elizabeth Hart October 21, 1791.
   7.  Levin, born January 25, 1774, died February 14, 1826, married 1st Mary Keene December 24, 1800; married 2nd Ann Maria Muir December 24, 1825.
   8.  Washington, born 1784, died June 4, 1826, married Margaret Slacum February 18, 1806.  (Margaret married 2nd William Andrews.)

The Lakes have rendered conspicuous service in several wars beginning with the Revolutionary War.  They have also served in numerous political positions in the County since the first Lake arrived in the County.

LANGLEY (70)

On July 2, 1665, a 100 acre tract of land was surveyed for Thomas Langley; the tract was called "Langley's Desire" and it was located on the south side of the Choptank River at the mouth of Little Creek (now in Caroline County).  Rent Roll Record, Liber 10, Folio 353, states "No heirs to be found."

LANGRELL (XX)

The first Langrell to appear in Dorchester County records is James Langrell.  He acquired a tract of land called "Bluff Island" and other properties in the Elliott's Island area.  His will dated March 9, 1719/20 and probated May 22, 1722, names sons, George and James; daughter Sarah.  George died unmarried in 1754.  James died in 1740; he had three sons, William, James, and George.  Sarah married a Covington and had James and Isaac Covington.

LECOMPTE (10)

Anthony LeCompte immigrated to Calvert County in the mid-1650's where he acquired a 75 acre tract called "Compton" from Ishmael Wright.  He returned to his homeland in 1661 (He was born near Callis in France) and on July 11 of that year, in London, he married Hester Dottando (Dotlando) a native of Dieppe, in Normany, France (Volume 12, Maryland Historical Magazine, page 48).

In the meantime he had an 800 acre tract of land surveyed.  It was located on the south side of the Great Choptank and on Horne Bay which he named "Saint Anthony."  (NOTE:  The tract called "Castle Haven" was not part of "Saint Anthony" as some historians have written but was an entirely separate tract and the records show that "Castle Haven" was not the property of a LeCompte in, at least, the first 75 years of its existence.)

On May 6, 1669, Anthony Lecompte was appointed along with several others as one of the original justices of Dorchester County. He served until 1671.

The children and some of the grandchildren of Anthony and Hester were:

1. John married Ann Winsmore, daughter of Robert Winsmore. Issue: John, William who married Mary, daughter of Captain Richard Smart, Philemon, James, Robert Winsmore, Ann and Anthony.
2. Moses, who married Mary Skinner, daughter of Thomas Skinner. Issue: Philip, Moses, Thomas, Peter who married Elizabeth Brannock, daughter of Rebecca Brannock (DLR 7 OLD 49), Samuel, Joseph who married Mrs. Shawhawn, Anthony who married 1st Mrs. Bennett 2nd Blanch LeCompte, William who married Mrs. Martin of Talbot County, Esther, Mary who married Arthur Rigby, and Elizabeth who married James Sewers of Philadelphia.
3. Anthony, who married Margaret Beckwith. Issue: Nehemiah, Anthony, and Margaret.
4. Philip. No record of marriage.
5. Esther, married Henry Fox of Talbot County. Issue: Esther, and Mary. NOTE: After Henry Fox died Esther married William Skinner. Issue: William, Philemon, and Thomas.
6. Katharine, who married James Cullins of Annapolis, Maryland. Issue: John, William, and James. NOTE: After the death of James Cullins, Katherine married Thomas Bruff. Issue: Margaret.

Anthony LeCompte died in 1673 and his widow, Hester, in 1674, married Mark Cordea; a wealthy merchant, innkeeper, and shipowner of St. Mary's County who had been naturalized in 1671. The bay which was named after Anthony LeCompte is still called LeCompte Bay as is LeCompte Creek.

## LEE (X)

On March 31, 1673, a 2350 acre tract of land was surveyed for John Lee of Virginia; it was called "Rehoboth" and it was located on the Northwest Fork of the Nanticoke River.

Rent Roll Record, Liber 10, Folio 374, shows the tract in the possession of Col. Richard Lee of Virginia. Richard Lee was a brother of John Lee and he, Richard, inherited "Rehoboth" when John died in 1673.

Col. Richard Lee died on March 12, 1714, in the 68th year of his age. He devised "Rehoboth" to his sons Philip and Thomas.

John Smoot acquired "Rehoboth" from the descendants of Col. Richard Lee and Major Frank Turpin became the owner shortly thereafter.

There is no evidence that any of the Lees actually occupied "Rehoboth" until about a hundred years after it was patented by John Lee of Virginia and shortly before it was acquired by John

Smoot.

## LEWIS (49)

On March 19, 1665/6, William Lewis purchased a 450 acre tract of land from Thomas Boylston. The tract was called "Boylston's Neck" and it was located on the west side of the Northwest Branch of the Nanticoke River about 10 miles up the Branch (TLR L1 F12).

William Lewis made a will dated September 23, 1668; he died September 5, 1669, and his will was probated March 12, 1669/70. In his will he named his wife, Sarah, and his daughter, Sarah. He left the 450 acres on the Nanticoke to his daughter, Mary (Wills 1, 374). Apparently, William Lewis had no sons.

Sarah Lewis, widow of William, took as her second husband, Henry Wilcocks, of Talbot County; they were married at Bettys Cove Meeting House September 11, 1669 (Third Haven Marriage Records).

Sarah Lewis, daughter of William and Sarah, married Ralph Fishborn at Bettys Cove Meeting House September 9, 1673 (Third Haven Marriage Records).

Mary Lewis, daughter of William and Sarah, married Bryan Ornelia in 1676.

## LINTHICUM (XX)

The first Linthicum to come to Maryland was Thomas Linthicum, born in 1640, and transported to Maryland shortly before 1658 by Edward Selby. He settled in Anne Arundel County and married Jane (last name unknown). The oldest of the four children of Thomas and Jane Linthicum was Hezekiah who was born about 1670 and who married on October 5, 1697, Milcah, the daughter of Thomas and Ruth Francis.

The third child of Hezekiah and Milcah Linthicum was a son named Francis, born September 29, 1709. He married on October 15, 1732, Eleanor, daughter of Richard and Eleanor (Stockett) Williams. Among the eight children of Francis and Eleanor (Williams) Linthicum were Thomas Linthicum born August 29, 1743, and Richard Linthicum born April 12, 1752.

Thomas Linthicum, son of Francis and Eleanor, married Cassandra Gaither, 13th child of Benjamin and Sarah (Burgess) Gaither. Cassandra was born March 23, 1734/5 at South River in Anne Arundel County, Maryland; she and Thomas were married in 1764. The Land Records of Dorchester county show that Thomas and Cassandra moved to Dorchester County and that they had at least two sons, Edward and Benjamin. Dorchester Land Record 14 ER 134 dated November 24, 1815, identifies the children of Benjamin Linthicum, son of Thomas and Cassandra, as: Rebecca D. who married William Barker, Jr., of Baltimore, Thomas, Harriet and Benjamin.

Richard Linthicum (1752-1817), son of Francis and Eleanor (Williams) Linthicum, married Mary Lee of Dorchester County on November 25, 1778 and they settled in that County. The children of Richard and Mary Linthicum were:

1. Richard Linthicum, born May 12, 1780, married Charlotte Seward. License January 4, 1804, Dorchester County.
2. William Linthicum, born October 1781, married Mary Bromwell. License October 26, 1801, Dorchester County. He was Captain 3rd Co. 2d Bt. 48th Regt. Dorch. Co. Militia, War of 1812.
3. Elizabeth Linthicum, born July 22, 1783, married William Pattison. License January 19, 1803, Dorchester County.
4. Rachel Linthicum, born December 14, 1785, married Joseph Stewart. License November 27, 1806, Dorchester County.
5. Frances Linthicum, born October 19, 1787, married --- Jones.
6. Thomas Linthicum, born March 29, 1790, married Nancy Harrington. License January 6, 1813, Dorchester County.
7. Samuel Linthicum, born September 12, 1792, married Alafaire, daughter of John Breerwood. License January 30, 1820, Dorchester County.
8. Mary Linthicum, born October 19, 1794, married Charles Jones. License September 20, 1815, Dorchester County.
9. Zachariah Linthicum, born 1797, married Henrietta Busick. License January 30, 1824, Dorchester County.

Still another Linthicum to move from Anne Arundel County to Dorchester was Joseph Linthicum and he was one generation later than Thomas and Richard. Joseph, son of Francis and Mary (Mayo) Linthicum was born October 19, 1759, in All Hallow's Parish. Joseph was the grandson of Francis and Eleanor (Williams) Linthicum. The licenses of Dorchester County show that Joseph married Sarah Spedden on May 9, 1787. Later records show that he married a second time, a Rachel (last name unknown). The children of Joseph Linthicum were:

1. Mary Linthicum, married John P. Meekins, July 10, 1806.
2. Ann Linthicum, married John D. Meekins, May 2, 1808.
3. John Linthicum.

Thomas Linthicum settled in the Neck District of the County while Richard and Joseph settled in the Church Creek-Woolford Area.

LLOYD (37)

On March 29, 1664, a 100 acre tract of land was surveyed for Robert Lloyd. It was named "Congunn" and it was located on the Blackwater River near the land laid out for Thomas Manning (Manning's Marsh). Robert Lloyd acquired "Congunn" by Patent (Pat. L7, F198).

"Congunn" was transferred by deed dated December 2, 1665, by Lloyd to Thomas Pratt of Anne Arundel County. Pratt in turn deeded it to James Agg and William Merchant of Dorchester County

(DLR 3 OLD 254, dated August 1, 1672).

Merchant assigned his share to Agg on November 4, 1679 (DLR 3 OLD 192) and eventually it was acquired by Dr. William Murray.

There is no record to indicate that Robert Lloyd was ever an inhabitant of Dorchester County.

## LLOYD (137)

Edward Lloyd migrated to Providence (now Annapolis) from Virginia with the Puritans in 1649. In about 1661 he moved to the area that became Talbot county in 1662. He became a justice of that County in 1663 and served in that capacity for a number of years. The records show that Edward Lloyd was a planter, Indian trader, merchant and land-speculator.

On June 18, 1666, he sold a tract of land called "Cliffe" to William Stevens (TLR L1 F38). "Cliffe" is now the site of the Cambridge Country Club in Dorchester County. That was but one of the many Dorchester land transactions in which he was involved. He amassed a considerable fortune and became the owner of thousands of acres of valuable land. Among his holdings was "Hir-Dir Lloyd" which was a 3050 acre tract that was surveyed for him on August 11, 1659, and is a major part of what is known today as Oxford Neck in Talbot County.

In 1668 Edward Lloyd returned to London where he, apparently, remained until his death sometime after his will was made in 1695.

Edward was married three times. He married 1st Frances, widow of John Watkins, 2nd Alice Crouch, widow of Hawkins, and 3rd Grace Parker, also a widow, whose maiden name was Buckerfield. Edward Lloyd had only one child, Philemon, the son of his second wife, Alice.

Philmon Lloyd (1646-1685) received full power of attorney at age 21 from his father in 1668 when his father returned to England. In 1669 Philemon Lloyd married Henrietta Maria Bennett, widow of Richard Bennett the son of Richard Bennett one time Governor of Virginia. Henrietta Maria was the daughter of Captain James Neal.

After the departure of his father, Philemon Lloyd made his home at Wye House. The Talbot County Land Records show that in 1668 he had purchased of Stephen Whetstone the "Great Island in Wye River" now commonly designated as Wye Island. Col. Philemon Lloyd died June 22, 1685, in the 39th year of his age leaving 3 sons and 7 daughters, all by his wife, Henrietta Maria. The sons were Edward Lloyd II (1670-1718), Philemon Lloyd, Jr. (1672-1732) and James Lloyd the youngest.

While none of the Lloyd family included in the preceding sketch were ever inhabitants of Dorchester County, Edward I and his son

Philemon exercised a great deal of influence in the affairs of Dorchester County through their many transactions involving people of the County.

The Lloyds of Wye have produced three governors of Maryland, councilors, burgesses, captains and colonels in Colonial and Revolutionary times; certainly it can be said that the sons of Wye have been noted for their brilliant attainments.

## LONG (139)

On January 16, 1668, Robert Harwood sold "Gatherly" consisting of 160 acres to Robert Long, shoemaker, of York County, Virginia (TLR L1 F78).

Rent Roll Record, Liber 10, Folio 345, shows "Gatherly" in the possession of William Harris of Bristol as of 1706.

The record of the transfer of this property to William Harris has not been found nor has any further information on Robert Long been found.

## LOOCKERMAN (X)

Jacob Loockerman was the only child of Govert Loockerman and his second wife Marritje Jans and he was baptized in New Amsterdam March 17, 1652. His father, Govert, was one of the wealthiest merchants in New Amsterdam. On January 29, 1677/8 Jacob married Ellinor Keiting, only daughter of Nicholas Keiting of St. Mary's County. He applied for naturalization in St. Mary's County in 1678.

On May 29, 1682, a 100 acre tract of land was surveyed for Jacob Loockerman at the head of Hungar River in Dorchester county. The tract was called "Wenmons Rest."

In 1683 Jacob was named a member of the Commission to Erect Ports and Towns in Dorchester County. In the years that followed he served Dorchester County as Justice, Sheriff, Colonel in the Militia, and represented the County as a member of the Maryland Assembly.

Jacob Loockerman retained "Wenmons Rest" only a short time but he acquired numerous tracts in other areas of the County. His will (Wills 20, 109) dated July 21, 1729, and which was probated October 27, 1730, shows that his dwelling plantation was "Regulation." This tract has been confused by some historians and genealogists with a tract called "Loockerman's Manor." "Regulation" was that tract that was originally known as "Foulkes Content" and it eventually became a great part of what is known today as the "West End" section of Cambridge. "Loockerman's Manor" was actually located on the North West Fork of the Nanticoke River and it was originally known as "Taylors Promise." Incidentally, there was another "Loockerman's Regulation" which was located on Parsons Creek.

The children of Jacob and Eleanor Loockerman were:

1. Jacob Loockerman, Jr., born 1678; died 1731; married April 26, 1711, Magdalen (Stevens) Edmondson, widow of James Edmondson and daughter of John Stevens and Dorothy Preston. Jacob Loockerman, Jr., made a will dated June 28, 1731, which was probated July 27, 1731 (Wills 20, 210). In his will he named his wife, Magdalen; and a number of relatives; brothers John and Govert; sister, Mary Allen and her husband Francis Allen; Jacob Hinderman, son of sister Mary Allen (Mary had married Rev. James Hinderman before she married Francis Allen); sister, Mary Haskins, wife of Thomas Haskins; several nephews and nieces; son-in-law John Edmondson; son-in-law Howell Powell; Sarah.

2. Govert Loockerman, born 1681; died 1728; married Sarah Woolford.

3. John Loockerman, born 1686; died 1760; married 1st Mable Dawson, 2nd Mary ---.

4. Mary Loockerman, married 1st Rev. James Hinderman, 2nd before July 21, 1720 Francis Allen.

5. Nicholas Loockerman, born November 10, 1697; died March 1771; married 1721 Sally Emerson.

6. Thomas Loockerman, married 1st Vienna Hudson, daughter of John Hudson, Secundus, and Anne Worth, 2nd Mary ---. NOTE: Thomas Loockerman was the issue of Jacob and his second wife, Dorothy (Last name unknown).

The sons of Jacob Loockerman, Sr., were active in political affairs; Jacob, Jr., served in the Maryland Assembly and was Sheriff of Dorchester County. He was living in Talbot County when he died.

Govert, son of Jacob and Elinor, served as Clerk of Court, Sheriff, Member of the Maryland Assembly and he lived in Dorchester County all of his life. He married Sarah Woolford, daughter of Roger and Mary (Denwood) Woolford. They had at least five children: Jacob who married Rosannah Woolford; Govert who married Mrs. Ann (Rider) Billings; Sarah who married Joseph Cox Gray; Elizabeth; and Mary who married 1st Thomas Haskins and 2nd Dr. Joseph Ennalls.

John Loockerman, son of Jacob and Elinor, apparently, lived most of his adult life in Talbot County.

Nicholas Loockerman, son of Jacob and Elinor, moved to Delaware in 1723 and in 1745 he became the Coroner of Kent County of that State.

Jacob Loockerman, son of Govert and Sarah (Woolford) Loockerman, married Rosannah Woolford, daughter of Roger II and Elizabeth (Ennalls) Woolford. He made a will dated April 8, 1741, which was probated August 14, 1741 (Wills 22, 417). In his will he named his wife, Rosannah; sister, Sarah, wife of Joseph Cox Gray; brother Govert; son Jacob and daughter Elizabeth. After Jacob died his widow, Rosannah, married Joseph Cox Gray, her brother-in-law.

## MACE (152)

Nicholas Mace and Josiah Mace were brothers who settled in Dorchester County in the late 1600's. Nicholas settled in the Fishing Creek area of the Little Choptank River and he acquired several tracts of land in that area in the last quarter of the 1600's.

Josiah Mace, in the same period of time, acquired land near the head of Tar Bay. Rent Roll Record, Liber 10, Folio 370, shows that a tract named "Angels Hold" consisting of 150 acres on the northeast side of Tar Bay, which had been patented by Thomas Brown, came into the possession of Josiah Mace by reason of his marriage to Angell, the daughter of Thomas Brown.

Nicholas Mace made a will dated June 15, 1730, which was probated May 5, 1731 (Wills 20, 169). In it he named two sons, Thomas and John; and two daughters, Elizabeth and Ann. He named his wife, Ann, and his son as executor. The records show that Nicholas and Ann, also, had three sons which were not named in his will: Josiah, Edmond and Nicholas.

Thomas Mace, son of Nicholas and Ann, died about 1773 leaving the following children: John, Ann who married Edmond Brannock, Thomas, Edmond, Nicholas.

John Mace, son of Nicholas and Ann, married Mary --- and had one son names Nicholas.

Ann, daughter of Nicholas and Ann, married --- Shehawne.

Josiah Mace died in 1729, leaving a will (Wills 19, 869) in which he left his entire estate to his father.

Edmond and Nicholas, sons of Nicholas and Ann Mace, apparently died before their father since they were not mentioned in his will.

Josiah Mace who settled in the Tar Bay area and married Angell Brown had the following children: Josiah, Mary who married Joseph Shenton, Rachel who married --- Lain, Elizabeth who married --- Motten, and Susanna who married John Robson.

## MACKEELE (159)

On September 6, 1669, John Hodson sold to John Mackeele, planter, a 100 acre tract of land located on Tobacco Stick Bay called "Hodsons Desire" (DLR 1 OLD 64). In the next few years John Mackeele acquired by purchase or by patent a number of tracts in the Little Choptank River area.

John Mackeele served in the Dorchester Militia and rose to the rank of Lieutenant Colonel. He was a member of the 1683 Commission to Purchase Land and Lay out Ports and Towns in Dorchester County and he served for some years as a justice of the County. "Mackeele Point," between Madison Bay and Fishing Creek, derived its name from John Mackeele and his family.

The will of John Mackeele was dated March 13, 1695, and it was probated April 16, 1696. In it he named the following children: William, Thomas, Edmond, Charles, Elizabeth Davis, Sarah Kirk wife of John Kirk, and Mary Dorsey. He also had a daughter, Ann Hunt (Will 11, 135).

Charles Mackeele, son of John Mackeele, moved to Kent County where he died in 1709. His will (Wills Part II - 12, 101) devised his estate to his nephew, Thomas Hunt. His executor was his brother-in-law, Walter Campbell.

Thomas Mackeele, son of John, married Clare Powell, widow of Charles Powell and daughter of Stephen Gray. Thomas Mackeele made a will dated April 23, 1725, which was probated August 14, 1728 (Wills 19, 482). In his will he named sons John and Thomas; daughters Ann and Elizabeth; wife, Clare.

Clare Mackeele, widow of Thomas, made a will dated April 19, 1736 which was probated June 10, 1736. In her will she named her children: Charles Powell, Sarah Cullen, Blanche LeCompte, Clare LeCompte, Anne and Elizabeth, also sons John and Thomas; grandsons Charles and Anthony LeCompte.

Thomas, son of Thomas and Clare, married Mary Stevens, daughter of John Stevens and Priscilla (Hooper) Stevens and they had three children: John, Thomas and Mary. When Thomas died his widow, Mary (Stevens) Mackeele married Benjamin Keene.

MANNING (4)

Thomas Manning with his wife, Grace, and two sons, Thomas and John, immigrated to Calvert County, Maryland, in 1658 from Nansemond County, Virginia. He acquired a 600 acre tract of land in Calvert County called "Theobush Manning" (Pat. L Q, F317).

On January 31, 1660, he was commissioned Captain of all the militia forces between the coves of Patuxent River and Herring Creek (Arch. of Md., Vol. 3, page 401) and Francis Armstrong was commissioned his Lieutenant.

Manning was a burgess along with Richard Preston, representing Calvert County, at the Maryland Assembly during the 1661-1662 sessions.

In addition to "Theobush Manning" in Calvert County, Thomas Manning acquired: "The Goar" in Calvert County; "Manning's Resolution" in Somerset County; "Malden," "Pa Pa Thicket," "Pa Pa Thicket Point," and "Manning Marsh" in Dorchester County; a total of well over 3000 acres.

"Malden" identified in early Maryland records as "Manning's Point" was sold to Andrew Cook and is known today as Cook's

Point. "Pa Pa Thicket" and "Pa Pa Thicket Point" were also sold to Andrew.

"Manning Marsh" a 1000 acre tract near what is now known as Snows Turn, just south of Cambridge, was acquired by John Prindowell of Calvert County. It was subsequently divided and parts included in several other different named tracts.

"Manning's Resolution" in Somerset County was sold by Nathaniel Manning of Calvert County on December 16, 1684 to Cornelius Johnson of Somerset County (Somerset County Land Records M A No. 3, Folio 723).

Thomas Manning's will was dated October 9, 1666, and was probated March 8, 1670 (Andrew Cooke was one of the witnesses to the will). In his will, Manning, referred to his home plantation, "Theobush," which indicated that he had remained an inhabitant of Calvert County ever since he had migrated there in 1658. In his will he named his wife, Grace; and three sons: John, Thomas and Nathaniel (Wills 1, 420).

John and Thomas Manning remained in Calvert County and their descendants were identified with Calvert and adjoining county affairs for many generations.

Nathaniel Manning I married Priscilla (Pattison) Taylor, daughter of Thomas and Ann Pattison and widow of John Taylor. John Taylor II had acquired a 400 acre tract of land on Taylor's Island from his father who was John Taylor I. The tract was called "Taylor's Folly."

"Taylor's Folly" along with several other tracts on the Island descended to John Taylor III and when he died he willed to his brother, Richard Manning, part of "Taylor's Folly" and he made bequests to his brother, Nathaniel Manning II, and to his sisters, Grace and Sarah Manning, as well as to his uncle, James Pattison (Wills 13, 251).

Richard Manning, carpenter, cooper, joyner, son of Nathaniel I and Priscilla, married Jane Trevallion. On April 1, 1737, he made a will which was probated June 15, 1738 (Wills 21, 883). In his will he referred to his wife; sons Thomas and Trevallion.

Nathaniel Manning II married Rosannah, daughter of David and Mary Peterkin (Wills 21, 920).

Thus, Thomas Manning, thru his son, Nathaniel, was the progenitor of the Manning line in Dorchester County. In addition to the Pattisons and Taylors the descendants of Thomas Manning intermarried with the Cooks, Edmondsons, Gootees, Nortons, Phillips, Scotts, Stewarts, Trevallions, Whites, etc.

A Nathaniel Manning was a Captain in the Revolutionary War and an Anthony Manning was a Captain in the War of 1812.

Mannings were associated for many generations with the tract near Cambridge known as "Ashburne." A property in the Town of East New Market is, even today, known as the "Old Manning Property." Before 1702 Nathaniel Manning had purchased from Pattisons a mill on James Island and in 1783 a Nathaniel Manning perpetuated this Manning pursuit by building a wind-mill at his dwelling plantation located just west of Todds Point. As late as 1841 a William Manning was serving as postmaster at Hicksburg.

Thus, even though Thomas Manning never became an inhabitant of Dorchester County, thru his son, Nathaniel, his descendants became inextricably woven into the generations of people that have populated the County throughout its history.

MARINE (XX)

According to one genealogy of the Marine family, Milleson Marine was the first of that name to come to Maryland and supposedly he came with the Huguenots in 1655 and settled in the northwest fork of the Nanticoke River. The genealogy goes on to state that he married Lavena Major, daughter of Thomas Major of Accomac County, Virginia.

A historian states that "In 1663, Milleson Marine conveyed his land on Secretary Creek, North-West Fork, Somerset County, Maryland, to Thomas Bradley, and moved up into Delaware."

The statement of both the genealogist and the historian are somewhat suspect to say the least, certainly no white people would have been able to survive in 1655 in the land of the Nanticokes when the Nanticokes were at war with the white settlers; and, certainly there is no record of any white settlers existing that early in any of the area that eventually became Dorchester County. As for the statement of the historian, Secretary Creek was not on the North-West Fork and neither the Creek nor the Fork were ever in Somerset County.

Patent Record Liber 6, Folio 129, shows that Millison Marine was, indeed, transported to Maryland in 1655, but, that record is an assignment by Peter Walters dated November 14, 1663, to Thomas Bradley for the terms of service for ten individuals, including that of Milleson Marine, and the record shows that Thomas Bradley, in turn, assigned the rights to Timothy Goodridge. Certainly the records prove that Milleson Marine, who was transported into the Province in 1655, could not have settled anywhere in that year because he was serving his term of service.

Milleson Marine married Lavina Major, daughter of Thomas Major of Accomac County, Virginia, probably in the year 1662. Milleson and Lavina Marine had the following children:

1. Jonathan (1665-1736) married Kezia 1689 - surname not known.
2. William (1667-1716) unmarried.
3. Charles (1669-1717).

4. James (1671-1748).
5. Alexander (1673-infant).
6. Thomas (1675-1749).
7. John (1677-1716).
8. Major (1679-1680).

## MASON (58)

On April 4, 1665, a 150 acre tract of land called "Masons Hopyard" was surveyed for Miles Mason (Pat. L8 F56). The tract was located on the western side of the Transquaking River. On August 4, 1665, another tract consisting of 100 acres was surveyed for him and named "Mason's Vineyard;" it was located on Chaplins Bay and Mason's Creek (At the head of Tar Bay - Pat. L8 F49).

On March 6, 1675, Obadiah Judkin of Talbot County sold to Miles Mason of the Cliffs in Patuxent River, planter, 250 acres of Teverton on the Little Choptank River in Fishing Creek (DLR 3 OLD 54).

On February 29, 1674, Miles Mason and Ann his wife sold "Mason's Hopyard" to John Rawlins. Rent Roll Record, Liber 10, Folio 451, on "Mason's Vineyard" was noted "No heirs appearing, tract supposed to be taken up by name of "Hootons Lot."

On December 6, 1676, Miles Mason made a will which was probated May 2, 1679, in which he left his property to his wife, Ann, and his unborn child (Wills 10, 20).

On September 11, 1749, (DLR 14 OLD 375) two depositions were taken before Henry Hooper as follows:

"Deposition of Ann Tregoe of Dorchester County, widow, aged about 61 years, states that Sarah Mason was an orphan in the house of her father Peter Stokes and was later married to Thomas Shehawne by Wm. Mishie; and that Ann's said father Peter Stokes was reported to have married the mother of said Sarah Mason, who was the widow of Miles Mason.

Deposition of William Stokes aged about 57 years states that his father Peter Stokes married for his second wife Anne, widow of Miles Mason; and that said Miles left one young child named Sarah, who was brought up in said Peter's house and was later married to Thomas Shehawne by William Mishie, a magistrate."

From the above depositions it would appear that Miles Mason had only a daughter, Sarah, who married Thomas Shehawne.

The records indicate that Miles Mason made his home at "Teverton" at the head of Fishing Creek for the few years that he lived in Dorchester County.

Timothy McNamara I married Sarah Prout, daughter of John Prout; this fact is shown by the will of John Prout which was dated

October 31, 1699, and which was probated November 22, 1699 (Wills 6, 385). Timothy McNamara I and Sarah had a son Timothy McNamara II, a son Thomas, and a daughter Sarah.

Timothy McNamara II married 1st Jane Wheeler, the widow of William Reed and the daughter of Henry and Alice Wheeler and a sister of Mary Stewart the wife of John Stewart II, and 2nd Jane Lake, widow of Robert Lake. Timothy McNamara II died in 1757 and he had the following children:

1. Levin McNamara (1723-1800).
2. John McNamara who married Mary Stewart.
3. A daughter (Sarah) who married Edward Pritchett.

The will of Timothy McNamara dated October 20, 1756 shows his wife as Jean (Wills 30, 327). It named grandsons John and Timothy who were the sons of John McNamara and it named grandson Levin McNamara.

John McNamara and Mary Stewart had the following children: Levin, Mary, Timothy, and John Stewart McNamara.

Members of the McNamara family acquired a number of tracts in Lower Dorchester County and the McNamaras intermarried in such old-line families of the area as the Pritchetts, Stewarts, Lakes, Hoopers Travers and others.

Several McNamaras served in the Dorchester Militia during the Revolutionary War. John Stewart McNamara was a Captain in that conflict as was also Timothy McNamara.

MEARS (59)

On April 4, 1665, a 300 acre tract of land was surveyed for Thomas Mears; it was called "Mears Green" and it was located on the Eastern Branch of the Transquaking River.

Rent Roll Record, Liber 10, Folio 351, shows the tract in the possession of John Talbot who married the daughter of Mears.

Thomas Mears of Severn River, Anne Arundel County, died in 1674 (Wills 2, 3). In his will he named his wife, Sarah; son, Thomas; daughter, Sarah, wife of John Homewood.

There is nothing in the records to indicate that Thomas Mears was ever an inhabitant of Dorchester County.

MATTHEWS (158)

Patent Liber 12, Folio 379, shows that Morrice Mathews of Dorchester County immigrated to the Province of Maryland in 1669. His name appears in that year on several occasions in the Dorchester County Land Records as a witness.

He acquired several tracts of land in the Little Choptank River area and one on the Blackwater River.

His will was dated September 3, 1705,and was probated April 28, 1707.  Apparently, he had no family since he named neither a wife or children in his will (Wills 12, 298).

MAYNADIER (XX)

Rev. Daniel Maynadier is said to have come into the Province of Maryland about 1688-9 and settled in Talbot County where he became Rector of St. Peter's Episcopal Parish. He married Hannah Haskins on January 12, 1720.  Hannah Haskins was the daughter of Captain William Haskins of Hunting Creek and she was the widow of George Parrott. Rev. Daniel Maynadier died February 23, 1745. Rev. Daniel Maynadier and Hannah Haskins had three children as follows:

1.  Anne, born November 21, 1721 and died November 11, 1723.
2.  Jane, born January 22, 1722/3; married March 12, 1738, Richard Fedderman.
3.  Daniel, born August 26, 1724, in Talbot County and he became Rector of Great Choptank Parish of Dorchester County.  He married Mary Murray, daughter of Dr. William and Sarah (Ennalls) Murray on May 11, 1746.

Rev. Daniel Maynadier, son of Rev. Daniel Maynadier and Hannah (Haskins) Maynadier, and Mary (Murray) Maynadier had the following children (Wills 39, 526):  William, Daniel, Sarah Ennall, Hannah, Henry, Margaret and Mary.  He also mentioned in his will a granddaughter named Mary Nevitt.  (Mary Nevitt was the daughter of John Ryder Nevitt and Sarah (Maynadier) Nevitt.)

MCNAMARA (X)

Timothy McNamara I of Calvert County proved rights to 50 acres of land for service (Pat. L17 F675) on April 4, 1674.  On August 7, 1677 (DLR 3 OLD 138) Timothy purchased "Apes Hill" from Richard Meekins.  "Apes Hill" was located at the mouth of Hungar River in Dorchester County.  The deed covering this transaction characterized Timothy McNamara as a planter of Somerset County. (This writer has been unable to find any further reference which would support the Somerset County part of this characterization.)

Timothy McNamara I married Sarah Prout, daughter of John Prout; this fact is shown by the will of John Prout which was dated October 31, 1699, and which was probated November 22, 1699 (Wills 6, 385).  Timothy McNamara I and Sarah had a son Timothy McNamara II, a son Thomas, and a daughter Sarah.

Timothy McNamara II married 1st Jane Wheeler, the widow of William Reed and the daughter of Henry and Alice Wheeler and a sister of Mary Stewart the wife of John Stewart II, and 2nd Jane Lake, widow of Robert Lake.  Timothy McNamara II died in 1757 and he had the following children:

1. Levin McNamara (1723-1800).
2. John McNamara who married Mary Stewart.
3. A daughter (Sarah) who married Edward Pritchett.

The will of Timothy McNamara dated October 20, 1756 shows his wife as Jean (Wills 30, 327). It named grandsons John and Timothy who were the sons of John McNamara and it named grandson Levin McNamara.

John McNamara and Mary Stewart had the following children: Levin, Mary, Timothy, and John Stewart McNamara.

Members of the McNamara family acquired a number of tracts in Lower Dorchester County and the McNamaras intermarried in such old-line families of the area as the Pritchetts, Stewarts, Lakes, Hoopers, Travers and others.

Several McNamaras served in the Dorchester Militia during the Revolutionary War. John Stewart McNamara was a Captain in that conflict as was also Timothy McNamara.

## MEARS (59)

On April 4, 1665, a 300 acre tract of land was surveyed for Thomas Mears; it was called "Mears Green" and it was located on the Eastern Branch of the Transquaking River.

Rent Roll Record, Liber 10, Folio 351, shows the tract in the possession of John Talbot who married the daughter of Mears.

Thomas Mears of Severn River, Anne Arundel County, died in 1674 (Wills 2, 3). In his will he named his wife, Sarah; son, Thomas; daughter, Sarah, wife of John Homewood.

There is nothing in the records to indicate that Thomas Mears was ever an inhabitant of Dorchester County.

## MEEKINS (XX)

On June 10, 1670, a 200 acre tract of land was surveyed for Richard Meekins on the east side of Slaughter Creek (Pat. L14 F135); it was called "Poole Head." In the next few years Richard Meekins acquired a number of tracts in the lower part of Dorchester County, some by patent others by purchase.

Richard Meekins married twice, his first wife was named Joana as shown by the Dorchester Land Records and by 1699 those records show that his wife was name Mary. He named his wife as Mary in his will which was dated 1701 and probated June 3, 1710 (Wills 13, 68). In his will he also named sons Richard and John.

Richard Meekins II and his wife Sarah lived on a plantation called "Meekins Hope" in what is now known as Meekins Neck. His will was dated June 9, 1718, and probated November 11, 1718. In his will he named sons Abraham, Richard, William and John. He also named his wife, Sarah.

John Meekins, son of Richard Meekins II and his wife Sarah, made a will dated February 16, 1733, and it was probated May 3, 1734. In it he named wife, Mary; sons Isaac, John, Joseph, James; daughters Mary Barnes and Elizabeth Mace, Hagar, Ann and Betty.

## MERCHANT (88)

On June 24, 1666, a 100 acre tract of land was surveyed for William Merchant and James Mossley. The tract was named "Cedar Point" and it was located on the Little Choptank River at the mouth of Slaughter Creek.

William Merchant came to Maryland from Virginia as a servant for Thomas Skinner. He married Mary (Last name unknown). William and Mary had at least two children: William Merchant II and Elinor (See Wills 7, 55). After William I died his widow, Mary, married a man named Stoker (See Wills 7, 55).

William Merchant II made a will dated January 11, 1711, which was probated September 23, 1717 (Wills 14, 325), and in it he named his son, Joseph; daughter Mary Wall and her husband Alexander Wall and their children: Alexander Wall, William Wall, and Thomas Wall. He also named his son-in-law, John Stanford, Jr., and granddaughter, Margaret Standford.

## MEREDITH (X)

On May 29, 1682, John Meredith, the progenitor of the Dorchester County family, had a 100 acre tract of land surveyed; it was called "Merediths Chance" and it was located on the east side of Worlds End Creek. Rent Roll Record, Liber 10, Folio 424, shows the tract in the possession of his son, William. John Meredith acquired several tracts of land in that same general area.

John made a will dated September 21, 1702, which was probated August 16, 1703 (Wills 11, 346). In his will he named his wife, Sarah; son, William; and daughter, Sarah who was the wife of Edward Turner; also, granddaughter, Jane Turner.

William Meredith, only son of John Meredith and his wife Sarah, married Elizabeth Palmer, daughter of Sarah Palmer (DLR 6 OLD 181). William Meredith made his will on April 17, 1711 and it was probated July 6, 1711 (Wills 13, 262). In it he named his wife, Elizabeth; daughters Sarah and Mary; and son, William. He also named his mother, Sarah. After William died his widow, Elizabeth, married Lewis Griffith.

William Meredith, son of William and Elizabeth, married Mollie --- and they had three sons: William, John and Thomas.

John Meredith, son of William Meredith and Mollie, married 1st Rachel Pritchett and 2nd Jane Pritchett, both daughters of John Pritchett and his wife Rachel.

100

## MILLINGTON (X)

On August 20, 1679, a 100 acre tract of land was surveyed for Samuel Millington; it was called "Millington's Adventure." It was located on the west side of Blackwater River. On April 1, 1680, a 200 acre tract of land was surveyed for Timothy McNamara and Samuel Millington; it was called "West Chester" and it was located on the south side of Bohemia Creek (Pat. L CB#3, Folio 99). They sold this tract in 1694 to Richard Meekins (DLR 5 OLD 47). A deposition by Samuel Millington on September 8, 1682 (DLR 4 OLD 20) shows that he was 41 years of age at that time.

On August 10, 1696, he acquired "Cabin Quarter" a 50 acre tract from John Lunn; it too was located on the Blackwater (DLR 6 OLD 120).

On December 31, 1715, Samuel Millington made a will which was probated on December 2, 1716 (Wills 14, 177). In his will he named his wife, Ruth, as executrix. He devised "Cabin Quarter" to Bridget, wife of James Edgar, and "Moorfields" to John Lunn for his lifetime after which it was to pass to Samuel Harper.

## MISHEW (X)

On May 9, 1680, a 50 acre tract of land was surveyed for William Mishew and Lawrence Woodnet; it was called "Paradise" and it was located on the south side of Fishing Creek of the Little Choptank River.

William Mishew was a justice of Dorchester County in 1690 and served until his death in 1701.

He made a will dated December 29, 1701, which was probated January 9, 1701/2. His wife, Sarah, was devised his estate (Wills 11, 188).

On March 6, 1701, Sarah, widow of William Mishew, made a will which was probated October 28, 1702. In her will she named daughter, Sarah, wife of John Ryan; grandchildren with surname of Trego; grandchildren with surname Ryan; son Thomas Newton; and daughter, Elizabeth Winsmore who married John Winsmore.

## MITCHELL (XX)

A Henry Mitchell is shown as being transported to Maryland by Richard Bently in Patent Liber 4, Folio 121, covering the tract of land called "Michael Bentley;" the patent was dated June 30, 1659.

Henry Mitchell of Calvert County acquired a tract of land in Dorchester County on James Island called "Long Point." Part of this tract was later acquired by Daniel Phillips who married Henry Mitchell's daughter. Henry Mitchell and his wife, Grace, appear in some other land transactions of Dorchester County but he is always shown as an inhabitant of Calvert County.

In 1685 a 100 acre tract of land was surveyed for Thomas Mitchell; the tract was called "Hogg Quarter" and it was located in Dorchester County. Patent Record, Liber 11, Folio 388, shows that Thomas Mitchell transported himself to the Province of Maryland. Land Record 6 OLD 143 dated November 24, 1709, shows that Henry Hooper acquired "Hogg Quarter;" it also shows that Thomas Mitchell had died and his wife, Mary, had married William Arnott.

On October 29, 1677 (DLR 3 OLD 179), Marke Mitchell acquired a deed from William Willoughby for a 50 acre tract of land called "Raxall." This tract adjoined the land of Anthony LeCompte. The tract was resold by Willoughby on June 7, 1698 (DLR 5 OLD 135), to John LeCompte. Marke Mitchell made a will dated April 30, 1734, and it was probated June 12, 1734 (Wills 21, 129). His will indicated that he had four daughters (unnamed) and he devised a tract of land called "Paradise" to them. "Paradise" had been acquired by Abraham Mitchell in 1720 (DLR 2 OLD 85).

Abraham Mitchell made a will dated January 24, 1722, which was probated February 25, 1722/3 (Wills 18, 85). In his will he mentioned Ann Vickers, daughter of Thomas Vickers, and his brother, Marke Mitchell. Richard Mitchell was shown as a witness to the will.

Richard Owens died in 1713 and he devised two tracts of land to his grandson, Richard Mitchell; other records show that the grandson's father was also named Richard. The two tracts of land were "Johns Garden" and "Owens Adventure."

From the records we have been unable to determine any relationship between the above Mitchells; nor have we been able to connect any of them with John Mitchell who acquired "Johns Garden" and "Owens Adventure" from Richard Mitchell, Sr., and Richard Mitchell, Jr., the son-in-law and grandson of Richard Owens.

"Johns Garden" had been patented by Robert Dickson (Dixon) of Calvert County who sold it to James Williams of Calvert County who in turn sold it to Richard Owen of Dorchester County (See Archives of Md., Vol. 57, page 268 and DLR 3 OLD 34).

"Owens Adventure" had been patented by Richard Owen in 1704 and it was located on Todds Bay adjoining "Johns Garden."

A Francis Seward claimed ownership of "Johns Garden" and his claim was heard by the Provincial Court who denied his claim (Provincial Court Record, Liber E I No. 7, Folio 570).

Title to "Johns Garden" was transferred to John Mitchell on June 13, 1744, in Dorchester Land Record 10 OLD 412.

On October 15, 1750, John Mitchell had "Johns Garden" part of

"Owens Adventure" and some vacant land resurveyed into one tract called "Mitchell's Garden;" the tract totaled 284 acres (Cert. of Survey Liber BY & GS #2, Folio 426 -- Pat. Liber BY & GS #5, Folio 78).

John Mitchell died in 1815 at age 106. He was buried in the graveyard at "Mitchell's Garden." By his first wife, Clare, (last name unknown - see Testamentary Proceedings Liber 30, Folio 113 of 1735) John Mitchell had the following children: John, Jr., William, Richard, Aaron, Reuben, Henry, Cornelia, Sarah and Mary. By his second wife he had Zebulon.

John Mitchell, Jr., married Mary Whitely and they had the following children: John, b. January 30, 1758; William, b. Sept. 30, 1760; Augustus, b. May 20, 1764; Elizabeth, b. May 20, 1766; Bing, b. May 15, 1768; Arthur, b. July 10, 1770; Sarah, b. June 16, 1773; Mary, b. March 15, 1776; Catherine, b. December 6, 1778; Thomas, b. February 25, 1780, d. February 1794; Michael, b. March 29, 1782.

John Mitchell, Jr., died April 1814, in the 78th year of his age and was buried in the graveyard at "Mitchell's Garden." His wife, Mary, died February 12, 1819, at age 79 and she also was buried in the graveyard at "Mitchell's Garden."

Aaron Mitchell, son of John Mitchell, Sr., married Sarah Hubbard and they had the following children:

1. Elizabeth, married Charles Frazier.
2. Solomon, b. January 16, 1789, d. December 18, 1856, married 1st Eleanor Slacum 2nd Margaret Block.
3. Shadrick, married 1st Harried Cook 2nd Mary Frazier.
4. Aaron, married Mahala Kirby, he died Mary 23, 1863 at age 78, Mahala died June 28, 1844 at age 49, both were buried in the graveyard at "Mitchell's Garden."
5. Mary, married John Willoughby, when Mary died John Willoughby married Harriett, sister of Mary.
6. John.
7. Clarissa (1).
8. Clarissa (2), married 1st a Willoughby and 2nd a Tregoe.
9. Francis or Frances.
10. Lydia, married William Flint.

Aaron, son of John Mitchell, Sr., died September 5, 1811, at age 69 and Sarah, his wife, died April 25, 1833, at age 82, both were buried in the graveyard at "Mitchell's Garden."

The land on which St. John's Chapel at Cornersville now stands was once a part of "Mitchell's Garden." Following is an abstract from the Land Records of Dorchester County which shows the title transfer:

1 FJH 326                        December 20, 1851
     John Wesley Mitchell and Mary Mitchell his wife of Dorchester county to Rev. Theodore P. Barber, James Dixon, Brice

J. Goldsborough, James B. Lake, Joseph E. Muse, Jr., Samuel W.
LeCompte, Alexander H. Bayly, R. Tilghman Goldsborough and Daniel
M. Henry, Vestry of Great Choptank Parish: part of "Mitchells
Garden" in Neck District on Hills Point Road, adj. land of
Richard Mitchell of Levin and containing one acre more or less.

St. John's Chapel was consecrated on April 16, 1853, by the Right
Rev. Henry J. Whitehouse, acting for the Bishop of Maryland.

At this point an intriguing question might be asked, "Did St.
John's Chapel get its name from a biblical source or was it named
after the tract of land on which it was erected which originally
was called "St. Johns Garden"? (See Arch. of Md., Vol. 57, pages
268-269).

MODSLEY (89)  (Mosley - Mossley)

On June 24, 1666, a tract of land called "Cedar Point" was
surveyed for James Mossley and William Merchant. The tract was
located on Little Choptank River at the mouth of Slaughter Creek
and on the west side thereof (Pat. L11 F198).

Land Record 6 OLD 186 dated May 27, 1712, shows that the wife of
James Mossley was Elizabeth. Land Record 6 OLD 241 dated January
23, 1714, shows his wife as Mary.

James Mossley made a will dated September 25, 1715, which was
probated March 3, 1715/6. In his will he devised his entire
estate to his wife, Mary.

MORGAN (45)

Certificate of Survey, Liber 7, Folio 458, shows a 100 acre tract
of land was surveyed for Evan Morgan in August of 1664. The
tract was called "Hog Hole" and it was located on the north side
of Jenkins Creek. The tract could not be located in the Rent
Rolls.

Certificate of Survey Liber 5, Folio 521, shows a 100 acre tract
surveyed for William Dorrington. This tract was also named "Hog
Hole" and it too was located on Jenkins Creek, and it also could
not be located in the Rent Rolls.

It is believed that the two surveys were actually for the same
tract. In any event, "Hog Hole" ended up as the property of
William Dorrington and he devised it to his son, William.

Evan Morgan does not appear further in the records of Dorchester
County.

MOWBRAY (XX)

At the battle of Preston a Jacobite rebel by the name of William
Mowbray was captured. He was transported (along with 79 others,
most of them Scotsmen) to Maryland aboard the vessel

"Friendship." He arrived in Annapolis August 24, 1716, and was indentured to Henry Trippe of Dorchester County for seven years.

William married a Mary (Last name unknown) and became the father of five children: Aaron, Thomas, William, Anna and Clare.

On August 14, 1740, William Mowbray purchased from Henry Trippe, a tract of land which was part of "Trippe's Regulation." The fifty acres purchased by Mowbray was in a tract located on the south side of the Choptank River near a cove called Mitchell's Cove (DLR 10 OLD 50). The fifty acre tract was on what is known today as Todds Point.

On November 10, 1748, William Mowbray purchased part of a tract of land called "Danby;" it was on a branch of Watt's Creek adjoining lands of Robert Bishop in what is now Caroline County. The portion Mowbray purchased contained 115 acres (DLR 14 OLD 261).

William Mowbray died in 1760 (Wills 31, 159). He left "Danby" to his sons Aaron and Thomas; the tract at Todds Point was left to his son, William.

Both of William's daughters married Beckwiths. Anna married Henry Beckwith and Clare married Nehemiah Beckwith, Jr. (See "Findings on the Beckwith Family of Dorchester County, Maryland" By Ethol Louise Seward).

In his will William Mowbray mentions "Milcah Mowbray" it is believed that Milcah was his daughter-in-law, wife of his son, William. This belief is buttressed by a reference to a deposition dated February 6, 1797, in the land records of Dorchester county (12 HD 15) which shows that Milcah Mowbray had a son named William; this latter William would be the grandson of the original William.

MUIR (XX)

Adam Muir, merchant and shipowner, married Ann Ballard on September 10, 1726. He died November 11, 1747, and she died September 11, 1745. They left 3 children: James, Charles and Ann.

James Muir, son of Adam and Ann, was born October 23, 1727, and died September 30, 1789, he married Sarah Nevitt who was born March 27, 1749, and who died January 12, 1790. The couple lived at "Winsor" which was located on the Northwest Fork of the Nanticoke River. They had the following children:

1. Adam, born February 27, 1750.
2. Thomas, born march 24, 1752.
3. John, born September 1754, died 1810, married Catherine Steele.
4. James, born January 23, 1756, died October 10, 1799.
5. Jane, born November 22, 1759.

6.  Charles, born January 26, 1761, died May 18, 1771.
7.  Sarah, born November 24, 1763.
8.  Robert, born May 27, 1766.
9.  Henry, born May 17, 1769, died November 6, 1773.

John Muir, Jr., son of John Muir and Catherine Steele, was born in 1789 and died in 1860; he married Elizabeth Spedden only child of Hugh Spedden.

MULLIKIN (75)

On August 14, 1665, a 200 acre tract of land was surveyed for James Mullikin; the tract was named "Mullikin's Green" and it was located on the Transquaking River. On that same date another tract named "Mullikin's Orchard" consisting of 300 acres was also surveyed for him and it also was located on the Transquaking River.

Patent Record, Liber 7, Folio 498, shows that James Mullikin was transported to the Province of Maryland in 1660 and that he married the widow of John Damaull prior to 1658.

The will of James Mullikin was dated August 18, 1666, and in it he devised all of his estate to his children and to his wife, Mary. His will indicated that he was an inhabitant of Calvert County when it was made.

On October 28, 1667, Mary Mullikin of Patuxent River in Calvert County, relict of James Mullikin, transferred "Mullikins Orchard" to her son James Mullikin and "Mullikins Green" to her son John Damaull (Arch. of Md., Vol. 57, pages 215-216).

The Maryland Assembly at its March-April 1671 session appropriated to the orphans of James Mullikin of Calvert County 450 pounds of tobacco (Arch. of Md., Vol. 2, page 303).

On January 12, 1694, James Mullikin II and Jane his wife of Calvert County transferred to Thomas Atthow of Dorchester County "Mullikin's Green" and "Mullikin's Orchard."

Eventually "Mullikin's Green" was acquired by Hugh Eccleston while "Mullikin's Orchard" was taken up by a survey called "Trippes Forrest."

There is nothing in the records to indicated that James Mullikin or any of his family ever became inhabitants of Dorchester County.

MULLIKIN (19)

Patrick Mullikin migrated to Calvert County from Scotland in 1647 (Tercentenary History of Md., Vol. 4, page 518); later he settled permanently in Talbot County where he had obtained a grant of land for 200 acres called "Patrick's Choice."

On April 28, 1662, a 400 acre tract of land called "Patricks Well" was surveyed for him. It was located at the mouth of St. Stephens Creek (Now Parsons Creek) in Dorchester County. It was on the east side of the said Creek (Pat. L5 F309).

On June 5, 1678, Patrick Mullikin of Talbot county sold "Patricks Well" to John Pollard of Dorchester County (DLR 3 OLD 151).

The descendants of Patrick Mullikin were active in Talbot County affairs for many generations. There is, however, nothing in the records to indicate that Patrick or any of his immediate family were ever inhabitants of Dorchester County.

## MURRAY (XX)

Dr. William Murray (1692-1763) son of William Murray and Mary Vans was born in Scotland in 1692. He migrated to Maryland and settled on Hunting Creek. He lived for a time in Cambridge, Maryland, but when he died he was living at "The Plains" on Hunting Creek and in his will he devised the home place to his son, David. He practiced his profession in Dorchester County until his death in 1763. The Dorchester Land Records show that he dealt extensively in land transactions in the County and accumulated a great many acres.

Dr. Murray married Sarah Ennalls, daughter of Col. Henry and Mary (Hooper) Ennalls on September 21, 1719. After she died on November 19, 1742, he married Elinor Hill, eldest daughter of Clement Hill of Prince George's County. Dr. Murray requested in his will (31-1037 (1763)) that he be buried between his wives in Christ Church Cemetery and his wish was adhered to.

Dr. Murray had no children by his second marriage, by his first marriage he had the following:

1. William Vans Murray, b. September 12, 1720, d. September 22, 1729.
2. Sarah Murray, b. April 22, 1722, d. April 23, 1727.
3. Margaret Murray, b. February 21, 1725, d. June 4, 1795. Margaret married Edward Trippe.
4. Henry Murray, b. June 29, 1727, d. September 8, 1785. Married May 10, 1750, Rebeckah Orrick, daughter of John and Susannah Orrick of Anne Arundel County. Henry and Rebeckah had the following children.
    1. Sarah who married Dr. John Coats.
    2. Margaret.
    3. Rebecca.
    4. William Vans, diplomat, born at Cambridge, Maryland, 1763, died September 31, 1803, married Charlotte Hughins of London, England.
    5. John Murray, married Sophia Smyth.
    6. Henrietta Maria, married September 27, 1794, her cousin, William Murray Robertson, son of Dr. Thomas Robertson and his wife, Amelia Murray.
5. Mary Murray, b. July 7, 1729, married May 11, 1746, Rev.

Daniel Maynadier of Talbot County.
6. David Murray, b. December 24, 1731. See Will 32-135 (1764).
7. James Murray, b. January 28, 1733, d. September 4, 1784. Married Hannah Savage, daughter of Thomas and Esther Savage of Northampton County, Virginia. James and Hannah had the following children:
1. David Murray, b. March 18, 1765; drowned October 24, 1784.
2. Margaret Murray, b. June 21, 1766; died June 2, 1782.
3. William Lyttleton Murray, b. August 16, 1768; the only living child in 1792, when he died, unmarried, and left his vast estate to his cousin, William Murray Robertson, son of Thomas and Amelia (Murray) Robertson.
4. Lilly Vans Murray, b. October 31, 1770; d. October 1, 1771.
5. Sarah Murray, b. July 31, 1772; d. February 1, 1774.
6. James Murray, b. December 7, 1773; d. January 9, 1775.
7. Mary Murray, twin, born February 23, 1777; d. infant.
8. Sarah Murray, twin, b. February 23, 1777; d. 1787.
9. Hannah Murray, b. September 23; d. infant.
8. Lilly Murray, b. July 1, 1736, married Alexander Hamilton.
9. Amelia Murray, b. May 4, 1739, married in 1760 Dr. Thomas Robertson from Somerset County.
10. John Murray, b. August 26, 1741, died young.

Much has been written about Dr. William Murray (1692-1763) and his family and it probably would be possible to write a complete book about this Doctor and his family for there probably was never a more illustrious family to inhabit Dorchester County. However, since this work is a collection of genealogical vignettes only a few comments will be made.

Dr. Murray in addition to his profession and land transactions found time to serve as a justice for Dorchester from 1734 to 1756.

His son, Henry (1727-1785), was also a practicing physician in Cambridge. His daughter, Sarah, married Dr. John Coats who was the first Grand Master of the Grand Lodge of Masons of Maryland.

David Murray (1731-1764) was a mill operator, planter and merchant in Cambridge. He resided in Cambridge when he died.

James Murray (1733-1784) another son of Dr. William Murray resided at "Tullibardine" on Hunting Creek. He was a revolutionary patriot, a member of the Maryland Convention which threw off the proprietary government and adopted the provisional government, a member of the Convention which framed the first State Constitution, a member of the General Assembly, he was

active in securing troops and supplies for the revolutionary
army. he was a Colonel in the Maryland Militia, and he was a
judge of the Maryland Court of Appeals.

Some historians have written that William Vans Murray, the
diplomat, was the son of James Murray; others have written that
they were not sure whether he was the son of Henry or James. The
records show that all of the children of James had died by 1792
and the Dorchester Land Records show specifically that William
Vans Murray was the son of Dr. Henry Murray (21 HD 299).

After receiving a classical education he studied law in London
where he met Charlotte Hughins whom he later married. He
represented Dorchester county in the Maryland Assembly and was a
member of Congress from 1791 thru 1797. He was appointed by
President George Washington as Minister to the Batavian Republic
and was appointed by President Adams as an envoy to the French
Republic. He was mainly responsible for making the Convention at
Paris on September 30, 1800, between France and the United States
which averted a war between the two countries.

William Vans Murray, like his grandfather, traded extensively in
real estate. Among the tracts which were involved in his real
estate activities were: "Hambrook" which he acquired in 1796 and
sold in 1803; part of "Betsey's Grove" adjoining "Clifton" owned
at that time by his brother, John; many acres on the Blackwater
and tracts at the head of Fishing Creek; and other acreage.

William Vans Murray's parental home was on High Street in
Cambridge and that was his home until shortly before his death
when the home was destroyed by fire. This information is shown
in his letter of April 3, 1802, to John Quincy Adams. After the
fire he lived with his brother (His only brother was John
Murray). The information about the burning of his dwelling place
on High Street was also contained in his will (DLR 13 ER 565).

The 1802 letter indicated that Mr. Murray was in the process of
building a new home near Cambridge on a small farm. He was using
the bricks from the dwelling place in Cambridge that had been
destroyed by fire. In his letter he wrote that his new home was
to be a 1 1/2 story structure with three rooms, a kitchen and a
book room. He wrote further that to the utter wonder of his
neighbors it was to have a flat roof. Since his will of
September 9, 1802, was, apparently, destroyed in the 1852
Dorchester county Courthouse fire it cannot be positively
determined just where William Vans was erecting his new home;
but, it can be determined with a fair degree of accuracy. All of
William Vans Murray's lands were deeded by his widow, Charlotte,
to his brother John Murray. Among the lands disposed of by John
were some lands near Cambridge called "Murray's Addition,"
"Bellfield," "Addition to Murray's Friendship" and "Maple Branch"
commonly known as the "Dunkill'd" or "Summer House Farm"
consisting of 300 to 350 acres. The tract was, in the main, the
property on which the present Cambridge-South Dorchester High
School is located. The "Dunkill'd," a contraction, was no doubt,

derived from the unusual (for those times) type of house that William Vans Murray built.

The obituary of William Vans Murray which appeared in the December 22, 1803, issue of the Maryland Gazette stated that he died at his seat in Dorchester County on September 11, 1803. There are other accounts which state that he died while visiting Philadelphia and that he was buried there.

Responsive to a petition for John Murray the Maryland Assembly in 1808 (Chapter 76) passed an Act making valid the deed from Charlotte Murray, widow of William Vans Murray, to John Murray. The Act shows that Charlotte had never been naturalized as an American citizen; it prevented the deeded lands from being escheated for that reason.

Neither William Vans Murray nor his brother, John, had any children.

Some historians have stated that William Vans Murray, the diplomat, was born at the residence called "Ayreshire" or "Glasgow." This writer has been unable to locate any record which would indicate that either Dr. Henry Murray or his son, William Vans, ever lived there.

Some details about the early history of "Ayreshire" or "Glasgow" can be found herein under "Robertson XX."

MUSE (XX)

Thomas Muse the first of that name to appear in Dorchester County Records married Anne Ennalls, daughter of Joseph Ennalls II and great grand-daughter of Bartholomew Ennalls, on January 5, 1769. Thomas and Anne had five children: Mary, Anne, Thomas -- all three died as infants, and:

Margaret; married Dr. William Worthington Davis on July 20, 1790, and they had two daughters. After Dr. Davis died his widow, Margaret, married W. M. Craig and they had one son, Joseph Muse Craig.

Joseph Ennalls Muse; born August 20, 1776, died July 16, 1852, married on July 5, 1798, Sophia Kerr, daughter of David Kerr and Rachel Leeds Edmondson, widow of James Edmondson. They had five children:

1. Thomas; died as an infant.
2. Joseph E. Muse (1810-1858) married Anne E. A. Bayley.
3. Dr. James A. Muse.
4. Dr. William H. Muse, married Elizabeth Sulivane.
5. Mrs. Nicholas B. (Muse) Worthington.

Thomas Muse I died November 1776 during the Revolutionary War. He was a Lieutenant Colonel.

His great grandson, Brigadier General William Sulivane Muse, the son of Dr. William H. Muse and Elizabeth Sulivane was born April 8, 1842, at "North Yarmouth" in Dorchester County. William Sulivane Muse was commissioned by President Lincoln as a Second Lieutenant in the U. S. Marine Corps in January of 1864. On August 14, 1900, Brigadier General William Sulivane Muse took a medical retirement. Brigadier General was the highest rank in the United States Marine Corps at that time. General Muse died in Cambridge April 16, 1911, and was buried in the Christ Church Cemetery.

NEWTON (84)

On November 25, 1665, a 100-acre tract of land was surveyed for Thomas Newton; the tract was located on Gary's Creek of the Little Choptank River and it was called "Newtone Desire." In that same year he had two additional tracts surveyed: "Bloud Point" 100 acres on Slaughter Creek and "Georges Point" 100 acres on Salt Marsh Creek.

Dorchester Land Record 3 OLD 37 dated December 5, 1671, shows Sarah as the wife of Thomas Newton.

Dorchester Land Record 3 OLD 175 dated November 6, 1679, shows that Thomas Newton had died. This record shows as the children of Sarah and Thomas: Elizabeth Newton, John Newton and Thomas Newton.

The records indicate that Sarah Newton was the daughter of Samuel Pritchett (Wills 10, 16). The records further indicate that Sarah and Thomas Newton also had a daughter named Sarah who married William Trego (DLR 3 OLD 175). In addition Dorchester Land Record 4 OLD 30 dated March 14, 1680, shows Edward Newton as son and heir of Thomas Newton, deceased.

Thomas Newton, son of Thomas and Sarah Newton, made a will June 16, 1704, which was probated August 2, 1704. In the will he devised his plantation to his wife, Mary, and he named no children.

Edward Newton, son of Sarah and Thomas Newton, made a will on January 2, 1693, which was probated March 6, 1693. In his will he named son, Edward, and wife, Margaret (Wills 2, 295).

Edward, son of Edward and Margaret, married Frances, daughter of Frances Fisher (Wills 19, 679). He made a will dated February 29, 1723/4, which was probated May 7, 1729. In his will he named sons John, Richard, William Edward; daughters Frances Cannon, Mary and Sarah; wife, Frances.

NOELL (XX)

On January 2, 1676, John Edmondson and Sarah his wife sold to James Noell of Dorchester County a 50 acre tract of land called "Oyster Point" (DLR 3 OLD 124). The tract was located next to the land of Anthony LeCompte. Six years later, February 8, 1682, James Noell and his wife, Margaret, sold "Oyster Point" to John Pope (DLR 1 OLD 195).

On August 10, 1683, a 150 acre tract of land called "Noell's Pokety" was surveyed for James Noell (Pat. L SD#A F136). "Noell's Pokety" adjoined tracts called "Chance" and "St. Anthony" both patented by Anthony LeCompte. Six years later, on January 20, 1689/90, James Noell, planter, and his wife Margaret, sold "Noell's Pokety" to John Harwood of Dorchester County (DLR 4 OLD 70); this part of "Noell's Pokety" was originally called "Chance" which was patented by Anthony Lecompte. On June 6, 1699, James Noell, Sr., deeded to his son, John Noell, planter, 150 acres called "Noell's Pokety."

On May 29, 1717, John Harwood, carpenter, leased to Margaret Noell, wife of James Noell, Sr., for her natural life the house and land at "Castle Haven."

James Noell, Sr., made a will dated March 16, 1717, which was probated June 11, 1718 (Wills 14, 582). In his will he named sons James and Bazell; wife, Margaret; daughter-in-law, Elinor Noell and son James.

In Dorchester Land Record 5 OLD 3 dated August 15, 1692, Elizabeth was shown to be a daughter of James Noell, Sr., and his wife, Margaret; other records show that James and Margaret also had sons named Septimus and John and daughters named Ann Kempston and Hannah.

In a deposition dated June 9, 1703, Margaret Noell was shown to be 47 years old at that time. Dorchester Land Record 6 OLD 74 dated September 8, 1705, shows that James Noell, Jr., was 22 years old then and Record 6 OLD 215 dated February 8, 1713, identifies him as a carpenter. John Noell is also identified as a carpenter in 6 OLD 65 and 66 dated June 8, 1705.

Dorchester Land Record 6 OLD 162 dated January 12, 1710, shows the wife of Septimus Noell to be Jane. Septimus made a will dated October 23, 1716, which was probated January 28, 1716 (Wills 14, 175). In his will he named brothers Bazell and James; sisters Ann Kempston and Hannah; son-in-law Thomas Taylor.

John Noell made a will dated March 31, 1717, which was probated March 12, 1717/8 (Wills 14, 566). In his will he named daughters Elizabeth and Anne; wife, Eleanor.

The Land Records of Dorchester County disclose that the Noell family acquired a number of tracts in the general area of Castle Haven Neck: "Five Pines," part of "Castle Haven," "Noell's Pokety," "Saw Box," "Harwood's Chance," "Underwood's Chance," and others, were all owned by members of the Noell family at one time or another.

NORTON (9)

On August 13, 1659, a 200 acre tract adjoining "Busby" on Jenkins Creek was surveyed for John Norton (Pat. L4 F374). The tract was named "Nortonhaugh."

The Rent Rolls have no notation as to what disposition was made of this tract of land. No information has been located in the Dorchester Land Records or any other records as to either the disposition of the land or about John Norton. Apparently, it was resurveyed and taken up by others.

NUTTER (XX)

In 1683 Christopher Nutter had two tracts of land surveyed; they were called "Attowattocoqun" consisting of 1200 acres and "Tossewondoke" consisting of 130 acres and both tracts were located in the area of Dorchester County that was taken by the State of Delaware.

Christopher Nutter married Mary Dorman and they had the following children (Somerset County Records and "Old Somerset on the Eastern Shore of Maryland" by Torrence):

>     John, born 1667, died as an infant.
>     Sarah, born 1669, died as an infant.
>     John, born February 15, 1670, at Manokin, moved to Sussex County, Delaware, died 1702.
>     Mary, born at Manokin February 17, 1672, died 1702.
>     Sarah, born at Nanticoke February 18, 1674, married Capt. William Piper.
>     Christopher, born at Nanticoke January 7, 1675, died as an infant.
>     Charles, born at Nanticoke May 18, 1680, moved to Dorchester County, died 1735.
>     Thomas, born at Nanticoke December 27, 1681, died 1702.
>     Christopher, born December 4, 1683, married Margaret Mackmorie.
>     Matthew, born 1685, died 1720, married Ann Huet, daughter of Rev. John Huett.
>     William, born 1687.

Christopher Nutter who married Mary Dorman was an Indian interpreter (Arch. of Md., Vol. V. page 555-556). The names of his two tracts were, no doubt, Indian names.

Christopher Nutter of Somerset County made a will on December 2, 1702, which was probated March 22, 1702/3 (Wills 11, 311). In his will he named sons John, Christopher, Matthew, Charles and William; daughter Sarah Piper.

Christopher Nutter, Jr., of Somerset County made a will dated February 13, 1728, which was probated August 23, 1729 (Wills 19, 818). In his will he named sons Christopher and William, brother Matthew; wife Margaret.

Apparently, the only member of the Nutter family to become an inhabitant of Dorchester County was Charles, son of Christopher and Mary (Dorman) Nutter.

He made a will dated January 27, 1732/3 (Wills 21, 345) which was probated April 16, 1735. In his will he named eldest son Charles and son John; cousin John; daughter Mary wife of Thomas Hooper, daughter Alice wife of Thomas Winder, daughter Betty wife of John Mackmory, daughter Ann and daughter Majer; wife Sarah.

Charles Nutter, grandson of Christopher and Mary (Dorman) Nutter, made a will dated January 1, 1737/8 (Wills 21, 881) which was probated May 11, 1738, and in his will he devised his entire real estate to his brother John. He named his cousin, Thomas, son of William Nutter.

OGG - See AGG.

OLIVER (42)

On March 31, 1664, a 200 acre tract of land was surveyed for Thomas Oliver and Lawrence Simmons. The tract was located on James Island and was called "Long Point" (Pat. L7 F126).

On November 1, 1670, Oliver and Simmons sold the 200 acres to William Killman of James Island (DLR 1 OLD 44).

On January 15, 1673, Thomas Oliver had a 50 acre tract of land surveyed called "Humphreys Desire." The tract was located on Fishing Creek and Teverton Creek (Pat. L19, F458).

The records show that Thomas Oliver was a boatwright. His wife was named Susan (DLR 3 OLD 31) and he was involved in several land transactions in Dorchester County in the late 1600's. No other information has been found.

OSBORNE (92)

Patent Liber ABH, Folio 273, and Patent Liber WC2, Folio 391, shows that Henry Osborne and his wife, Catherine, with their daughter, Rebecca, immigrated to Maryland in 1651.

On April 13, 1667, a 650 acre tract of land was surveyed for Henry Osborne, Thomas Walker and Anthony Dawson. The tract was called "Alexander's Place" and it was located on the westernmost side of the Northwest Branch of the Transquaking River.

Patent Liber WC2, Folio 391, shows that Rebecca, daughter of Henry Osborne, married Captain Anthony Dawson; and that Sarah, daughter of Henry Osborne, married Thomas Walker.

Patent Liber 20, Folio 46, shows that Henry Osborne of Calvert County had died, intestate, prior to 1678.

On January 11, 1683, Thomas Walker of Kent County, Pennsylvania, and Sarah his wife transferred their one-half interest in "Alexander's Place" to Anthony Dawson (see Dawson herein).

OWENS (XX)

Richard Owens of Dorchester County had a 70 acre tract of land surveyed on November 28, 1702, and patented July 10, 1704 (Pat. CD F199). The tract was named "Owens Adventure" and the certificate of survey gave the location as follows: beginning at a bounded red oak upon the west side of a small cove and on the River Great Choptank and in the east north east line of a tract of land called "John's Garden...." The rent roll records (L10 F475) showed the tract in the possession of Richard Owens with no other notations. The rent roll records also showed the adjoining tract called "John's Garden" in the possession of Richard Owens (see Dickson 65).

Some historians have confused Richard Owens of Calvert and St. Mary's Counties with the Richard Owens of Dorchester County. An Act of the General Assembly passed October 20, 1678, shows that Richard Owens was a resident of Dorchester County at that time. The Assembly passed a town bill in 1683 and a member appointed to the Commission for Dorchester County was Richard Owen. The records further show that Richard Owen of Dorchester County was appointed a justice of that county in 1693 and he spent the remainder of his life in that county and did not return to the Western Shore as some historians have claimed. He served as a justice of Dorchester County as late as 1706.

A deposition which he gave on November 12, 1700 (DLR 5 OLD 178) showed that he was born in 1644. He died in 1713 and his will (Wills 13,616) showed that at his death he was an inhabitant of Dorchester County. "John's Garden" and "Owens Adventure" were devised by him to his grandson Richard Mitchell. His wife, Jane, was named executrix.

PAINTER (X)

On February 10, 1679, a 2000 acre tract of land was surveyed for Nicholas Painter of St. Mary's County. It was called "Painters Range" and it was located on the north side of Hunting Creek. The tract eventually became part of the site of what is known today as the town of Preston in Caroline County, Maryland. In that same year he obtained a tract consisting of 1000 acres called "Grove" located on the south side of Hunting Creek; another tract called "Wiltshire" consisting of 1000 acres located near Fowling Creek.

The Archives of Md. (Vol. 5, pages 342, 343) show that Nicholas Painter acted as clerk to a "Special High Chancery Court" held in the City of St. Mary's March 18, 1677. The Archives also show (Vol. 5, pages 465, 466) that he owned land in several counties of the Province of Maryland; that he left Maryland for London in April of 1684 where he made a will in September of that year and that he embarked for Maryland a few days after making the will.

He died shortly after arriving back in Maryland.

His will dated April 17, 1684 (Wills 4, 56) was probated December 27, 1684. Col. William Burges was named executor and his handling of the estate was the subject of a petition to the Council by William Bray. As a result part of Painter's lands were conveyed to William Bray who conveyed them to William Cornwallis whose heirs conveyed them to Richard Bennett of Queen Anne's County, Maryland.

"The Grove" was devised to Painter by Nicholas Courtney of St. Mary's County. Painter also devised to Anne Burges, daughter of Col. William Burges, rights of 1000 acres, of 400 acres, and 300 acres -- all in Dorchester County and which were patented in the name of Charles Hutchins.


## PARKER (X)

On August 6, 1673, a 100 acre tract of land was surveyed for Henry Parker; it was called "Hog Pen Neck" and was located on the south side of Monsieurs Creek (later known as LeCompte Creek). In September of that same year a tract of 500 acres was surveyed for him; it was called "Parker's Chance" and it was located on the western side of the north west branch of the Transquaking River.

In Dorchester Land Record 3 OLD 66 dated October 6, 1674, Henry Parker of Talbot County transferred "Parker's Chance" on the Transquaking River to Henry Bradly of Dorchester County. On November 1, 1681, Henry Parker of Talbot County transferred "Hog Pen Neck" to William Warner of Dorchester County.

On March 5, 1686/7 Henry Parker made a will which was probated July 12, 1687. In his will (Wills 4, 259) he named neither a wife nor children.

## PARROTT (78)

On August 26, 1665, a 1050 acre tract of land was surveyed for William Parrott; the tract was called "Edmondsons Reserve" and it was located on the southside of the Northeast Branch of the Great Choptank River two miles above the dividing. The location is now in Caroline County.

On March 14, 1668, William Parrott made a will which was probated May 11, 1669 (Wills 1, 337). In his will he named his wife, Ann, and four sons: William, Henry, George and Benjamin. He named as one of the executors, brother Isaac Abraham of Talbot County which could mean that Ann, the wife of William Parrott was Ann Abraham.

The Talbot County court Proceedings 1662-1674 show the marriage on the last day of November 1669 of William Parrott and Sarah Morgaine. It would seem that this latter William was the son of

William and Ann. The Third Haven Meeting Records show the following births:

Elizabeth Parrott December 22, 1670, of William and Sarah Parrott.
John Parrott November 23, 1672, of William and Sarah Parrott.
Sarah Parrott October 22, 1674, of William and Sarah Parrott.
William Parrott March 22, 1677, of William and Sarah Parrott.

Dorchester Land Record 6 OLD 131 dated March 2, 1708, shows Richard Webb and Rebecca his wife and John Baggs and Hannah his wife transferring part of "Edmondsons Reserve." The record also shows that Rebecca and Hannah were the daughters of William Parrott and the record further discloses that part of "Edmondsons Reserve" was transferred by William Parrott to his sons, John and William Parrott. All these facts would indicate that Rebecca and Hannah were the daughters of William Parrott and Sarah Morgaine.

William Parrott, son of William and Sarah, married Susannah Silvester of Talbot County on October 11, 1704, at Tuckaho Meeting House (Third Haven Meeting Records). On May 8, 1720, he made a will which was probated July 14, 1720. In his will he named his cousin, Ann, daughter of his brother John; wife, Susannah; cousins John, Michal, William and David Kirby; cousins Aron and Benjamin and Elinor Silvester.

There is no record to indicate that the Parrotts were ever inhabitants of Dorchester County but from the time in 1665 when William Parrott had "Edmondsons Reserve" surveyed there have been members of the Parrott family residing in Talbot County.

PATTISON (X)

On January 10, 1671, a 150 acre tract of land was surveyed for Thomas Pattison called "The Grove." The tract was located on James Island at the mouth of Little Choptank River (Pat. L19 F49).

Thomas Pattison was a surveyor and an attorney and in a short time he had acquired by patent several tracts at various locations in the County. He also acquired by purchase a number of additional tracts on James Island and on Taylors Island.

In 1689 Thomas Pattison served as Clerk of Court for Dorchester County. His will which was dated February 1699 and which was probated April 10, 1701 (Wills 11, 129) indicated that he was an inhabitant of James Island when it was made. In his will he named his wife, Ann; eldest son James, 2nd son Joseph, youngest son Thomas; eldest daughter Priscilla Manning (Priscilla married 1st John Taylor and 2nd Nathaniel Manning), 2nd daughter Elizabeth Robson (Elizabeth married John Robson), 3rd daughter Jone, 4th daughter Levina Driver (Levinia married 1st Matthew

Driver and 2nd Moses LeCompte), daughter Sarah and adopted daughter Mary Jacob.

Ann Pattison, widow of Thomas Pattison made a will dated January 21, 1701, and it was probated February 27, 1702 (Wills 11, 301). In her will she mentions a son Jacob and does not mention Joseph which could mean that a misprint was made in her husband's will and Joseph and Jacob were one and the same.

The children of Ann and Thomas Pattison married and had large families. Their descendants are many and can be located in practically all parts of the Country; some are still inhabitants of Dorchester County.

PETERKIN (XX)

On March 2, 1680, a 1000 acre tract of land called "Partnership" was patented by James Peterkin and Edward Newton. The tract was located at the head of the Transquaking River.

In 1681 Peterkin petitioned the Council of Maryland charging some irregularities to Sheriff Stephen Cary in a boundary dispute concerning his lands.

In 1683 James Peterkin was named a member of The Commission to Erect Ports and Towns in the County of Dorchester.

On June 4, 1714, James Peterkin made a deposition (DLR 2 OLD 70) and at that time he showed his age to be 77.

Very little additional information has been located in the records about James Peterkin, however, a James Peterkin, planter, who married Elizabeth, the widow of William Nitter is mentioned in Dorchester Land Record 15 OLD 234 dated June 9, 1755. This latter James is probably a son of the original James. Also the will of David Peterkin, planter, is on file in Liber 21, Folio 558.

The will of David Peterkin names sons James and David; daughters Ann Wing, Elizabeth Woolford, Rosannah Manning wife of Nathanial Manning, Sarah Peterkin and Lucretia Peterkin. The will of David Peterkin was dated February 27, 1735 and probated April 5, 1736.

On June 5, 1738, the will of Mary Peterkin was filed and it was probated September 12, 1738 (Wills 21, 920). This Mary Peterkin was the wife of David. In addition to others, Mary mentions in her will grandson Thomas Cook and granddaughter Ann Cook. (NOTE: Thomas and Ann Cook were the children of Thomas Cook I and Mary Peterkin; Mary (Peterkin) Cook had preceded her parents, David and Mary Peterkin, in death.)

Ann, daughter of David Peterkin and Mary his wife, married 1st Gary Warner 2nd Captain Robert Wing and 3rd John Stewart III.

PHILLIPS (General)

There were several persons with the surname Phillips who appear in early Dorchester County Records whose relationship to others of the same surname is uncertain.

A Thomas Phillips had a 600 acre tract of land called "Conqueriers Fields" surveyed on June 16, 1673. The tract was located on Phillips Creek (now known as Mill Creek) in what is now Caroline County. On October 29, 1674, he sold 50 acres of a tract of land called "Grovelling." This transaction appears in Dorchester Land Record 1 OLD 174 and in it he is characterized as Thomas Phillips of Talbot County. We have been unable to determine how or when he acquired it. On June 26, 1676, a 250 acre tract called "Piney Point" was surveyed for him and this tract was located at the head of Hogg Creek in what is now Caroline County. This Thomas Phillips, whose wife was named Mary, was deceased by 1682 as shown by Dorchester Land Record 4 OLD 55. The records also show that this Thomas Phillips was an inhabitant of Talbot County.

A Nicholas Phillips appears in the Rent Roll Records as owning 100 acres of "Cedar Point" on Fishing Creek of the Little Choptank River. The Rent Roll Records also show him as in possession of a 100 acre tract called "Westminster" located between the Chicamacomico and Transquaking Rivers. No other information has been found on this Nicholas Phillips.

In Baldwin's "Calendar of Wills" a Phillip Phillips of Dorchester County is shown as making a will on April 14, 1728, which was probated July 2, 1728 (Wills 19, 433). In his will he named daughter, Mary; wife, Alice who was the daughter of Richard Goostree and his wife Rebecca; sons Thomas and James.

The records do not disclose the proper place of the above members of the Phillips family in the Phillips Line.

PHILLIPS (125)

On March 9, 1669, a 200 acre tract of land was surveyed for John Phillips and Lewis Griffin; the tract was named "Worlds End" and it was located on the north west branch of Charles Creek a tributary of Honga River. On November 3, 1697, John Phillips deeded "Worlds End" to John Griffin (DLR 5 OLD 104).

In the interim John Phillips had married Katherine, the widow of John Felton. When he died John Felton had devised all his property to Katherine (Wills 1, 516). On July 26, 1673, Katherine Phillips deeded all her property to her husband, John Phillips (DLR 3 OLD 49).

John Phillips, Hungar River, Dorchester County, made a will (Wills 12, 212) dated December 29, 1707, which was probated February 23, 1707/8. His will indicated that he had married a

second time since he named as his sons Richard Goar and James
Goar. A second marriage for John is also confirmed in Dorchester
Land Records 4 OLD 63 dated October 10, 1682, in which the deed
was signed by John and Mary Phillips. John Phillips also named
in his will the following children: William, Mary who married
Charles Robson, Thomas, Elizabeth who married George Ferguson,
Benony, and Anne.

Thomas Phillips, son of John, married Cornelia Ross, daughter of
John and Elizabeth Ross (DLR 14 OLD 658 dated November 11, 1746).
On August 7, 1690 (DLR 1 OLD 118) John Ross and Mable his 2nd
wife sold 58 acres of "Rosses Range" to Thomas Phillips. This
acreage was located between Arthur Wrights Creek (Now Phillips
Creek) and Hudson Creek. Thomas Phillips made a will which was
dated March 23, 1703, and it was probated June 4, 1704 (Wills 2,
339). In his will he named sons Rubin and Thomas and he
indicated that there were other children. When his son, Thomas,
died he named in his will (Wills 13, 350) dated July 13, 1711,
brother William and sisters Ann Phillips and Mary Robson.

William Phillips, son of John, made a will (Wills 21, 182) dated
August 11, 1731 which was probated August 15, 1734. In his will
he named his wife, Katherine; sons Thomas and William; daughter,
Mary.

Benony Phillips, son of John, married Rosannah Elliott, daughter
of John and Jean Elliott (Wills 18, 243 and DLR 6 OLD 259). He
made a will dated June 25, 1742, (Wills 23, 11) which was
probated December 6, 1742. In his will he named the following
children: John, Benony, Thomas, Solomon, Jacob, Jereriah, Mary,
and Rosanna.

It is interesting to note that the land which John Phillips
obtained from his wife, Katherine, and which had been patented by
her first husband, John Felton, was still in the Phillips family
at the death of Benony, and that he devised it to his children.

PICKERING (41)

On March 23, 1664, a 1000 acre tract of land was surveyed for
William Smith (Pat. L7 F531). On April 1, 1665, William Smith,
innholder, and Mary his wife of St. Mary's County sold to John
Pickering, salter, of the City of Bristol, England (Arch. of Md.,
Vol. 49, pages 428-429) the tract which was called "Smiths
Delight" and which was located on the west side of the
Transquaking River.

A tract called "Bottolph" was surveyed for John Pickering on
April 27, 1665, and it too was located on the west side of the
Transquaking River.

Rent Roll Record, Liber 10, Folio 348, on "Smiths Delight" shows
that there were no heirs and the land was taken up by others.
The Rent Roll Record, Liber 10, Folio 348, on "Bottolph" shows
the tract in the possession of the heirs of Daniel Jenefer.

Nothing has been found in the records to indicate that John
Pickering was ever an inhabitant of Dorchester County.

PINDER (X)

On September 2, 1678, William Brice sold to Edward Pinder I a 100
acre tract of land called "Butwells Choice" which was located
near the head of Little Choptank River and adjoining the lands of
Robert Winsmore (DLR 3 OLD 169). Edward sold the land in 1681.

On May 1, 1684, he acquired 300 acres of a tract called
"Goodridges Choice" which was located on the north side of Cabin
Creek (DLR 4 OLD 160).

Edward Pinder served as a justice of Dorchester County in 1683
and again in 1685. He was sheriff of the county for the period
1686 thru 1688.

Edward Pinder I married Sarah, the widow of William Ford and the
daughter of Richard Preston of Calvert County, and they had at
least two children: a daughter, Kath. (this probably should be
Beth - short for Elizabeth) who married Thomas Taylor, Jr. (See
DLR 5 OLD 132 and 6 OLD 169), and a son Edward Pinder II.

Edward Pinder II married Jane (last name unknown) and they had a
son, Edward Pinder III. Edward II made a will dated June 2, 1711
and it was probated November 17, 1711 (Wills 13, 352). In it he
named his son, Edward; sister-in-law Elizabeth Taylor; wife,
Jane.

After Edward Pinder II died his widow, Jane, married George
Stapleford.

Edward Pinder III made a will dated January 26, 1729, and it was
probated February 13, 1729 (Wills 19, 866). In it he named his
sister Dorothy Stapleford; brothers Charles and Thomas
Stapleford; aunt Elizabeth Taylor (NOTE: Elizabeth Taylor was the
wife of William Taylor - see Will 20, 147).

Apparently, the will of Edward Pinder III was not legal because
he died before he was of age, the following is taken from
Dorchester Land Record 8 OLD 398 dated January 27, 1730:

"Samuel Preston and Margaret his wife of Philadelphia to David
Peterkin of Dorchester County, Gent: Whereas Edward Pinder the
son of Edward Pinder who was the son of Sarah Pinder, became in
his lifetime entitled to 600 acres of land and died in his
minority without heirs, said land is sold and conveyed to said
Peterkin..."

Samuel Preston was the son of Richard Preston, Jr., and he,
Samuel, had moved from Calvert County to Philadelphia where he at
one time was Mayor of that City.

PITT (160)

Liber 5, Folio 268, of the Patent Records shows that a John Pitt immigrated to the Province of Maryland in 1663.

Dorchester Land Record 1 OLD 68 dated September 7, 1669, shows that a John Pitt of Isle of Wight County, Virginia, sold to John Alford of Little Choptank River a tract of land called "Musketta Quarter" on Tobacco Stick Creek; the tract contained 200 acres.

The records do not connect either of the above with the Pitt family of Dorchester County.

However, a John Pitt did have a 600 acre tract of land surveyed on April 22, 1670, in Dorchester County; the tract was located on the easternmost side of the Blackwater River and it was named "Hackaday." On June 9th of that same year he had another tract surveyed and it was called "Hampton;" it contained 250 acres and was located on the west side of Hunting Creek. Here again the records do not disclose the exact relationship between this John Pitt and a contemporary named Philip Pitt. The records show conclusively that Philip Pitt did have a son named John; the question is was it the same one that acquired "Hackaday" and "Hampton."

In August of 1688 Phillip Pitt purchased a 150 acre tract of land called "Strawbery Garden" from Edward Pinder (DLR 4 OLD 228). The tract was located on the west side of the Transquaking River. On December 4, 1694, he acquired a 150 acre tract of land called "The Plains;" this tract was located on Hunting Creek (DLR 5 OLD 56). NOTE: Part of the town of Preston is now located on this tract.

The records show that Phillip Pitt was an attorney and his name appears in numerous land transactions in the Dorchester County Land Records. His name also appears on the list of lawyers admitted to practice in the first court of Cambridge.

In 1696 Phillip Pitt and other vestrymen petitioned the Maryland Assembly for permission to build a church in the town of Cambridge.

Phillip Pitt made a will dated August 9, 1698, which was probated October 2, 1698 (Wills 6, 237). In his will he devised "Strawberry Garden" to his son, John; "The Plains" on Hunting Creek was devised to his son, Phillip. In his will he also named a son, Charles, and his wife, Ann.

The Somerset County Records show that Mary Woolford, daughter of Roger Woolford and Elizabeth (Ennalls) Woolford, who was born February 29, 1691, married John Pitt.

Dorchester Land Record 15 OLD 25 dated November 30, 1753, shows that Phillip Pitt had a son, Captain John Pitt, deceased, who in turn had a son named Thomas Pitt.

POLLARD (90)

John Pollard immigrated to Maryland in 1662 (Pat. L5 F125). On
April 4, 1667, John Pollard, cooper, of Patuxent in Calvert
County, purchased from Stephen Gary, mariner, of Little Choptank
in Talbot County (NOTE: In 1667 the area that eventually became
Dorchester County was at that time a part of Talbot County), 750
acres of land on the south side of the Little Choptank (DLR 4 OLD
78). The tract was called "Grass Reeden" and it eventually
became known as Susquehanna Neck and Susquehanna Point.

Pollard was appointed one of the first commissioners and justices
of Dorchester County in 1669. He served again in 1678 and 1679.
He was one of the Commissioners appointed in 1683 to purchase
land and lay out towns in Dorchester; he was a delegate to the
Maryland Assembly in 1694 thru 1697.

John Pollard made a will dated January 25, 1700. It was probated
October 21, 1702 (Wills 11, 294). In it he named his eldest son,
William, and his younger son, Tobias; daughter, Jane, wife of
William Robson, Jr.; several grand-children and his wife, Sarah.

Tobias Pollard, younger son of John Pollard, married Jane Robson,
daughter of William Robson, in "The Parish of Dorchester" on the
12th day of November by Thomas Howell, Rector (DLR 7 OLD 64).

Tobias Pollard made a will dated November 10, 1747 (Wills 27,
290). In his will he named the following:

    Grandson, John Edmondson. (NOTE: Margaret, daughter of
Tobias, married by 1718 to John Edmondson).
    Granddaughter, Elizabeth Edmondson.
    Grandson, Pollard Edmondson and his, Pollard's daughter
Lucretia.
    Granddaughter, Ann Edmondson, widow of grandson, James
Edmondson, deceased.
    Wife, Jane Pollard.

POPE (XX)

On February 8, 1682, James Noell and Margaret his wife sold a
tract of land called "Oyster Point" to John Pope (DLR 1 OLD 195).
The tract adjoined Anthony LeCompte's land and the tract called
"Castle Haven." The tract was located on Pope's Creek.

John Pope, innholder, and Margaret his wife of Talbot County,
sold "Oyster Point" containing 50 acres to John, Moses and
Anthony LeCompte in August of 1696 (5 OLD 77).

The records show that John Pope, on September 6, 1685, acquired
Lot No. 13 in the newly erected Town of Oxford, Talbot County,
Maryland.

On December 19, 1702, John Pope of Williamstadt (Oxford), Talbot
County, made a will which was probated April 17, 1703 (Wills 11,

330). In his will he named his brother, Robert, if living; wife, Margaret; daughter, Frances Ungle.

On May 29 - August 3, 1685, Timothy McNamara and Sarah his wife sold to Robert Pope a 50 acre tract of land called "Buck Valley" (DLR 4 OLD 123). The tract was located near Transquaking Bay (Now Fishing Bay - The tract was on what is now called Goose Creek).

Robert Pope made a will dated May 20, 1700, which was probated March 4, 1701 (Wills 11, 133). In his will he named son, Robert; daughters Rose (Rosanna) Cannon, Katherine Willey, Ann, Judy, Dianna, Sarah and Mary; wife, Elizabeth.

Elizabeth Pope, widow of Robert, made a will on August 6, 1716, which was probated December 2, 1716 (Wills 14, 176). In her will she named the following: daughters Rosanna Cannon, Katherine Willey, Sarah Willis, Ann Rumley, Judy Wingate, Dianna Willey, and Mary Wingate; son-in-law John Willey; granddaughter Dorcas Allen.

In Dorchester Land Record 7 OLD 70 dated August 12, 1718, a division is shown between John Willey and Katherine his wife and James Cannon and Rosanna his wife of 50 acres called "Doe Park" 50 acres called "Buck Valley" and 80 acres called "Waterford" left to said Katherine and Rosanna by the will of their father, Robert Pope.

POWELL (85)

Patent Liber 4, Folio, shows that Thomas Powell and his brother, Howell Powell, immigrated into the Province of Maryland in 1659. They settled in Talbot County. They came from Brecknockshire, Wales, and were sons of Hugh Powell of Castle Madoc.

On March 6, 1666, Thomas Powell had a 300 acre tract of land surveyed. The tract was called "Hogg Island" and it was located in the freshes of the Great Choptank River (Pat. L10, F113).

On April 22, 1670, a 300 acre tract of land was surveyed for Howell Powell; the tract was called "Weston" and it was located on the easternmost side of the Blackwater River.

Howell Powell also acquired land on the north shore of the Great Choptank River about three miles below what is now the Town of Cambridge and from that acquisition derived the name "Howell's Point."

Howell Powell, apparently, was a devoted Quaker because the records show that he contributed to a number of Quaker endeavors. He and his family also are mentioned many times in the minutes of Third Haven Meetings.

Howell Powell, Sr., deeded "Weston" to Howell Powell, Jr., on November 3, 1693 (DLR 5 OLD 60). Howell Powell, Jr., mariner,

and Joanne his wife sold it on November 4, 1698 (DLR 5 OLD 122).
Howell Powell, Sr., died on July 7, 1704, at age 81 (Third Haven
Records).

Howell Powell, Jr., was married three times.  His third wife was
Sarah, the daughter of Jacob Loockerman II, who had first married
John Edmondson.

From the minutes of the Third Haven Meetings:

MARRIAGES
Howell Powell, Jr., and Joanne Pryer June 8, 1698, at a meeting
     house near Choptank River.
Howell Powell, Jr., planter, and Esther Bartlet February 2, 1704,
     at Third Haven Meeting House.
Howell Powell and Sarah Edmundson February 18, 1718, at Third
     Haven Meeting House.  NOTE:  This wedding also appears in
     the Records of St. Peters Parish.

BIRTHS
Joanna Powell January 18, 1704/5, of Howell and Esther Powell.
James Powell December 16, 1705/6, of Howell and Esther Powell.
Daniel Powell February 22, 1708, of Howell and Esther Powell.
Thomas Powell January 5, 1710/11, of Howell and Esther Powell.
Mary Powell February 26, 1713, of Howell and Esther Powell.
Joanna Powell November 9, 1715/16, of Howell and Esther Powell.
Jacob Powell December 19, 1719, of Howell and Sarah Powell.
Sarah Powell October 11, 1721, of Howell and Sarah Powell.
Elizabeth Powell November 13, 1722/3, of Howell and Sarah Powell.
Benjamin Powell July 11, 1729, of Howell and Sarah Powell.

DEATHS
Joanna Powell died February 3, 1705.
Esther Powell died July 1, 1717.

Thomas Powell, brother of Howell, made a will dated January 17,
1669, which was probated April 11, 1670.  In his will he named a
wife, Anne; daughter, Anne; son, Thomas; and Anne, daughter of
Howell Powell.  He also named Howell Powell and Winlock
Christison.  In naming his son, Thomas, he characterized him as
eldest son so it is very possible that he had at least one other
son.

There is nothing in the records to indicate that either Howell
Powell or Thomas Powell ever became inhabitants of Dorchester
County.

PRESTON (24)

Richard Preston immigrated from Virginia to Calvert County,
Maryland in 1650 with his wife, Margaret, and five children (Pat.
L ABH F140): Richard, Jr., James, Samuel, Margaret and Naomi.
His other two children: Rebecca and Sarah were born in Calvert
County.

In the same year that he arrived in Calvert County he was commissioned Commander of the north side of the Patuxent. In 1654 when the Puritans took over the Government the seat of that Government was established at the home of Richard Preston. He represented Calvert County in the Maryland Assembly from 1658 thru 1668. In 1669 he was elected to represent the newly formed Dorchester County at the Maryland Assembly. By that time he had acquired 2000 acres of land in the area that became Dorchester: a tract on Barren Island; "Preston" on Little Choptank River; and "Horne" on the Great Choptank were among his holdings.

Richard, Jr., the eldest son of Richard, Sr., married Margaret Marsh, daughter of Thomas Marsh. Richard, Jr., and Margaret had one child, a son named Samuel who was born in 1665.

James Preston, second son of Richard, Sr., married Elizabeth (last name unknown) and they had one child, a daughter named Rebecca. James died in 1673.

Naomi Preston, the eldest daughter of Richard, Sr., married William Berry and they had three children: William who married Naomi Whalley; James who married first Elizabeth Wolchurch and second Elizabeth Pitt; Rebecca who married James Ridley. Naomi died in 1663 and in 1670 William Berry married Margaret, the widow of Richard Preston, Jr.

Sarah Preston married William Ford of Bristoll, England, on January 12, 1670, and after his death she married Edward Pinder. The records show that Sarah, after her marriage, resided at "Horne" in Dorchester County.

Rebecca Preston married Lovelace Gorsuch who had come into Maryland from Virginia in 1660 with his brothers Charles, Robert and Richard. They were the sons of a Loyalist Anglican Clergyman, the Rev. John Gorsuch, Rector of Walkern, Herfordshire, who had been killed by the Puritans in England in 1647. The brothers had emigrated with their mother to Virginia about 1652, had become converts to Quakerism there, and were of that group of Quakers who had been driven out of Lancaster County by Governor Berkeley in 1660. The brothers had divided, Charles and Robert settling on the Patapsco and Richard and Lovelace on the Choptank.[1]

Margaret Preston, daughter of Richard, Sr., and Samuel Preston, son of Richard Sr., both died early. Thus, the only surviving male heir of Richard Preston, Sr., was his grandson, Samuel, the son of Richard Preston, Jr., who moved to Philadelphia and eventually, in 1711, became Mayor of that city. There is no indication in the records that Richard Preston was ever an inhabitant of Dorchester county (in his will he showed his home as in Calvert County).

---

[1] Archives of Md., Vol. LIV, page 25.

While Richard Preston was an ardent Puritan when he left Virginia he became a Quaker and in his last years was known as "The Great Quaker." He died late in 1669 at the age of 55.

PRITCHETT (X)

John Pritchett, chymist, first settled in Talbot County where he married Margery Price, daughter of John and Margery Price.

On April 1, 1679, John Pritchett acquired 50 acres called "Apes Hill" from Timothy McNamara which tract was located at the mouth of Hungar River in Dorchester County (DLR 3 OLD 156).

In the ensuing years John Pritchett acquired by patent or purchase a number of tracts in the general area of Hungar River. Margery died prior to 1700 and the records indicate that John Pritchett married a second wife named Abigal.

According to tradition Dr. John Pritchett used his professional skills to administer to the needs of the Indians as well as to the white people and as a consequence he was held in great esteem by the Indians. To honor the Indians he named one of his sons "Phunback" after one of the Indian Chiefs. The records do not show whether or not there is any credence to the tradition. However, the will of John Pritchett, chymist, does show that he had a son named "Phunback."

His will was dated March 3, 1711, (Wills 17, 322) and was probated December 19, 1711. Dr. Pritchett devised "Apes Hill," his home, to his son Zebulon who was born in 1690 and who married Rachel, the daughter of William and Mary Evans. Zebulon's will was dated July 9, 1740, (Wills 22, 441) and was probated March 17, 1741.

He devised "Apes Hill" to his brother, Edward.

The will of John Pritchett (Wills 17, 322) named the following children: Zebulon, Edward, John, Phunback, Lott who married Ann (last name unknown), Phillis, Mary who married Henry Fisher, Jane who married Robert Lake, and Margery.

Edward Pritchett, son of John and Margery Pritchett, made a will dated October 25, 1760 (Wills 31, 301). In it he named the following:

> Brothers, Phunback and Lott.
> Edward Pritchett, son of Lott Pritchett.
> Edward Pritchett, son of Phunback Pritchett.
> Thomas Pritchett, son of Phunback Pritchett.
> Levin Pritchett, son of Phunback Pritchett.
> Arthur Pritchett, son of Phunback Pritchett.
> Mary Pritchett, daughter of Phunback Pritchett.
> Evans Pritchett, son of John Pritchett, deceased.
> William Pritchett, son of Zebulon Pritchett.
> Henry Fisher, son of Henry Fisher, Sr., deceased.

Benjamin Todd, son of Benjamin Todd.
Edward Pritchett, son of Edward Pritchett.
John McNemara, Sr.

It is noted that Edward named neither a wife nor any children of his own.

RAWLINGS (X)

On June 8, 1671, a 150 acre tract of land was surveyed for John Rawlings I; the tract was called "The Friendship" and it was located on the western side of the Northwest Branch of the Transquaking River.

Rent Roll Record, Liber 10, Folio 388, shows the tract in the possession of Charles Thompson who married the daughter of Rawlings.

In the same week that "The Friendship" was surveyed two other tracts in the same Transquaking area were surveyed for Rawlings: "Rawlings' Range," 300 acres and "Strawberry Garden," 150 acres.

John Rawlings I, boatwright, married Philadelphia (last name unknown). Dorchester Land Record 3 OLD 25 dated November 3, 1673, shows Michaell Basey and his wife Joanna Bassey as the "father-in-law" and "mother" of John Rawlings.

John and Philadelphia had a daughter, Margaret (DLR 3 OLD 127 dated January 6, 1676). The records indicate that there was a second daughter since it is shown that one daughter married Charles Thompson (Rent Roll L10, F388) and another married John King, father of Obadiah King (DLR 5 OLD 191 dated August 4, 1701). There were at least two sons, John Rawlings II and Anthony Rawlings.

Sometime after John Rawlings I died his widow, Philadelphia, married Andrew Gray, Jr. (Wills 2, 293).

John Rawlings II made a will dated December 4, 1709, which was probated March 17, 1709/10 (Wills 13, 15). In his will he named his son-in-law (stepson), Mark Fisher; nephew, John, son of Anthony Rawlings; nephew, John King; wife, Elizabeth. The wife of John Rawlings II was Elizabeth Fisher, widow of Alexander Fisher I.

RICHARDS (36)

On January 25, 1664, a 300 acre tract of land was surveyed for John Richards. The tract was located at the head of Hunting Creek and on the east side of the Creek. It was called "Cardiff" (Pat. L9 F67).

Rent Roll Record Liber 10, Folio 447, shows that John Richards assigned his rights to the tract to John Parker.

The Land Records of Dorchester County show that John Richards was for a time an inhabitant of Dorchester County. In 1682 he acquired a tract of land called "Noble Quarter" which was located at the head of the Nanticoke River in what is now the State of Delaware. It is believed that John Richards became an inhabitant of that area.

## RICHARDSON (34)

On November 23, 1663, a 1150 acre tract of land was surveyed for George Richardson. The tract was named "Richardson's Cliff" and it was located above the second turning of the Choptank on Richardson's Creek (Pat. L6 F114). Another tract called "Richardson's Purchase" consisting of 500 acres and located on the Transquaking River was surveyed for him on September 24, 1666 (Pat. L10 F219).

Rent Roll Record, Liber 10, Folio 427, shows "Richardson's Cliff" in the possession of heirs of William Edmonson. Rent Roll Record, Liber 10, Folio 353, shows "Richardson's Purchase" in the possession of Hugh Eccleston.

On July 2, 1667, Charles Calvert issued a commission to George Richardson which read in part as follows:

"I do hereby Constitute Ordain and Appoint you Captain under me of all that troop of horse that shall march out of Choptank and St. Miles Rivers in Talbot County aforesaid...And further I do hereby give you full power and authority to you the said George Richardson and all persons under your Command as aforesaid to destroy, kill, burn and take all such Indians as shall be declared held and reputed enemies to the inhabitants of this Province... (Arch. of Md., Vol. 5, page 10).

George Richardson was a surveyor and he was killed by the Indians; the records do not disclose whether he was killed in his line of work or in his capacity as Captain of the "Troop of Horse."

He was survived by his widow, Rebecca. It seems unusual that there is so little in the records about Captain George Richardson. This writer has been unable to connect him with any other branch of the Richardson family.

## RICHARDSON (X)

On July 5, 1672, a 500 acre tract of land was laid out for John Richardson; it was called "Hunting Fields" and was located on Conquericous Creek in what is now Caroline County. He later had a number of tracts patented in Dorchester and other counties. Among the tracts patented was one called "Jamacia;" it was surveyed on May 18, 1666, and consisted of 250 acres, it was located on the north side of the Choptank River opposite Secretary Creek and the site of the tract is known today as Jamacia Point.

Dorchester Land Record 3 OLD 177 dated August 7, 1679, shows the wife of John Richardson to be Susanna. Dorchester Land Record 6 OLD 155 dated May 31, 1710, shows Susanna Richardson as a widow. John Richardson had a son named John and Dorchester Land Record 2 OLD 44 dated June 1, 1720, shows the name of the wife of the son to be Elizabeth.

John Richardson, the son, made a will on March 10, 1722, which was probated April 27, 1723 (Wills 18, 79). In his will he named wife, Elizabeth; sons John, Isaac and Solomon; daughters Sarah Thompson, Margaret Nicholis, Mary Gamble and Anne.

DLR 8 OLD 154 dated April 3, 1727, identifies Sarah Thompson as the wife of John Thompson.

RIDER (XX)

For information on the RIDER family see HUTCHINS (X).

ROBERTS (97)

On May 17, 1667, a 100 acre tract of land was surveyed for John Roberts; the tract was named "Robert's Rest" and it was located on Tar Bay.

The records show that John Roberts was transported to Maryland in 1665 and Patent Liber 17, Folio 271, shows that he received a warrant for 50 acres for term of service. Rent Roll Record, Liber 10, Folio 357 carries the note: No heir to be found." Nothing further could be found in the records about John Roberts.

ROBERTSON (64)

In May of 1665 a 350 acre tract of land was surveyed for William Robertson on the Choptank River at Marsh Creek. The tract was named "Robertson's Purchase" and it was located in what is now Caroline County.

Rent Roll Record, Liber 10, Folio 472, notes "No heirs to be found" and no other information has been found in the records concerning William Robertson.

ROBERTSON (XX)

William Murray Robertson was born January 9, 1762; the son of Amelia Murray and Dr. Thomas Robertson. His father, Dr. Thomas Robertson had studied medicine under Dr. William Murray and had married Amelia, Dr. Murray's daughter. Dr. Thomas Robertson was from Somerset County, Maryland. He was the son of Dr. William Robertson, a Presbyterian Minister who was born near Glasgow in Ayrshire, Scotland, and who left Scotland because of the religious troubles in the reign of James II. He married a Miss Horsey and their children were: William, Thomas and Amelia Robertson.

William Murray Robertson married his first cousin, Henrietta
Maria Murray, daughter of Dr. Henry and Rebeckah (Orrick) Murray.
When William Lyttleton Murray, the last living child of James
Murray, died unmarried in 1792, he left his entire estate to his
cousin, William Murray Robertson. Thus, William Murray Robertson
became one of the largest landowners in Dorchester County.
William and Henrietta had the following children:

1. William Henry Robertson, died as an infant.
2. Amelia Murray Robertson, b. Feb. 14, 1797; d. Feb. 11, 1814.
3. Wm. Vans Murray Robertson, b. Aug. 6, 1799; d. Aug. 27, 1836.
4. Dr. Lyttleton Murray Robertson, b. Sept. 1, 1801; moved to Ala.
5. John Murray Robertson, Rev., b. June 15, 1804; moved to Ala.
6. Dr. Henry Murray Robertson, b. May 2, 1806; moved to Ala.
7. Henrietta Rebecca Robertson, b. March 8, 1809; moved to Ala.
8. Vans Murray Robertson, b. July 23, 1811; moved to Ala.
9. Dr. George James Robertson, b. Sept. 27, 1813; moved to Ala.

William Murray Robertson died June 14, 1815. On July 20, 1822,
his children and heirs had 195 acres of "Loockerman's
Regulation," 160 acres of "Clifton" and 74 acres of "Ennalls
Outrange" surveyed and platted into a tract called "Ayre Shire."
This 429 acre tract eventually became known as "Glasgow." It
remained in the Robertson family until 1842 when it was acquired
by Robert F. Tubman.

An unusual action taken by William Vans Murray Robertson, son of
William Murray Robertson and Henrietta (Murray) Robertson, was a
change of his name to William Vans Murray. This change was
accomplished by an Act of the Maryland Legislature (1821-22
session, Chapter 1, passed December 7, 1821).

The fact that William Vans Murray Robertson changed his name to
William Vans Murray, apparently, has caused many historians to
confuse him with William Vans Murray, the noted diplomat and son
of Dr. Henry Murray. Many of those historians have written that
William Vans Murray, the diplomat, was born and lived at
"Glasgow;" this contention is simply not supported by the
records.

ROBOTHAM (X)

On June 10, 1672, an 850 acre tract of land was surveyed for
George Robotham; it was called "Robotham's Range" and it was
located at the head of Robotham's Creek (later called Ingram's
Creek and known today as Chapel Branch) in what is now Caroline
County.

Among the persons transported to the Province of Maryland by George Robotham was John Ingram who later acquired land on the Creek which was renamed Ingram Creek after him.

Dorchester Land Record 6 OLD 36 dated March 7, 1703, shows that George Robotham gave the 850 acre tract called "Robotham's Range" to Walter Quinton, Sr., of Talbot County. Walter Quinton, Sr., was transported to Maryland by Robotham.

The will of George Robotham of Talbot County dated February 28, 1697, which was probated April 26, 1698 (Wills 7, 358), shows that he devised "Robotham's Range" to Quinton. There is no mention in the will of either a wife or children.

George Robotham represented Talbot County in the Provincial Assembly in the years 1685 and 1686. When the Town of Oxford was laid out in Talbot County on July 29, 1684, he acquired Lot No. 6 in that Town.

There is nothing in the records to indicate that George Robotham was ever an inhabitant of Dorchester County.

ROBSON (27)

William Robson, Sr., was born in 1642 (Chancery P. C. F860) and at the age of 21, on March 4, 1663, a 100 acre tract of land called "Robson's Cove" was surveyed for him (Pat. L7 F49). It was located in the southwestern part of Taylors Island. In the next few years Robson acquired a number of tracts in the lower part of what became Dorchester County.

On October 10, 1698, William Robson, Sr., deeded his property to his children: William, Jr., John, Charles, Joseph, Elizabeth, Jane and Hagar (DLR 5 OLD 118). The deed which was tantamount to a will gave William, Jr., "Robson's Cove" and "Pleasant Point;" John was devised "Robson's Delight" and a part of "Robson's Range;" Charles was devised "Robson's Chance;" Joseph got "Fadeinworth" and a part of "Robson's Range." "Robson's Lott" to be equally divided among Elizabeth, Jane and Hagar.

William, Jr., married Jane Pollard. John who was born in 1670 (Chancery P. L. F975), married Elizabeth, the daughter of Thomas and Ann Pattison. Jane married Tobias Pollard. Hagar married John Meekins and Elizabeth married Walter Campbell after his first wife, Susannah, died.

Charles married Mary Phillips, daughter of John Phillips (Wills 13, 669). The will of Charles Robson dated March 2, 1748 (Wills 23, 371) named a son John and an unborn child. It named his wife, Elizabeth, so, apparently, he married a second time.

On June 6, 1723, John Robson II, son of John Robson I, deeded his dwelling plantation called "Widow's Neck" to his sons John and Roger at death of grantor.

## ROSS (X)

On June 12, 1677, a tract of land containing 84 acres and called
"Rosses Chance" was surveyed for John Ross. It was located near
the mouth of Arthur Wright's Creek (now known as Phillips Creek)
of the Little Choptank River.

In the ensuing years he acquired a number of additional tracts in
the same general area. The name Ross Neck derived from John Ross
and his family.

He married 1st Elizabeth (last name unknown) and 2nd Mabella, the
widow Harrington, and after he died she married Anthony Tall
(Wills 13, 462).

John Ross made a will dated July 13, 1691, which was probated
April 22, 1695 (Wills 7, 177). In his will he named sons Reuben,
Stephen, Edward and John; stepson, John Harrington, who is
characterized as son of second wife; wife, Mabella. No
information has been found on Elizabeth, the first wife of John
Ross. He had two other sons who were not named in his will,
Charles and Peter. He also had a daughter, Cornelia, who married
1st Thomas Phillips and 2nd David MacKeele (DLR 14 OLD 658 dated
November 11, 1746).

Stephen Ross, cordwinder, made a will on August 5, 1719, which
was probated May 30, 1720 (Wills 16, 35). He named wife,
Catherine, and son, Stephen.

Reuben Ross, carpenter, married Elizabeth (last name unknown) and
moved to Prince George's County where he died in 1722 (Wills 18,
1).

Charles Ross made a will December 20, 1722, which was probated
May 25, 1723 (Wills 18, 75). He named son, Charles, and two
youngest sons (who were not named) as well as his brother, Peter.

John Ross II made a will dated January 21, 1722, which was
probated May 25, 1723 (Wills 18, 76). He named son, John;
daughters, Priscilla and Sarah.

## SAVAGE (X)

Prior to 1669 Edward Savage resided in St. Mary's County. He had
been in the service of Charles Calvert. The records of the
Provincial Court show that between the years 1666 and 1669 he was
a witness to the signatures of parties in over twenty cases
before that court. He also did some work for the Provincial
Court as shown by the payments made by the Assembly on May 27,
1669 (Arch. of Md., Vol. 2, page 234). Obviously his service
under Charles Calvert placed him in close contact with the
Provincial Court activities.

In 1669 Charles Calvert granted Edward Savage fifty acres of land
in Dorchester County for services rendered (Pat. L12 F267).

By the "Commission of Peace for Dorchester County" that was issued by Charles Calvert May 6, 1669, Edward Savage was appointed Clerk and Keeper of the Records of the Dorchester County Court.

Apparently, he augmented his regular compensation by performing court related work for others. February 12, 1674, he sued John Clemens for nonpayment of a bill and in his complaint he stated:

"...he was often employed by several of the inhabitants of the Province as a clerk for the drawing, ingrossing, and recording of several conveyances, sales of land, and other writings...."

Edward lost his case in this instance. He was clerk to the Court until his death in 1678. No mention of any other member of his family appears in the Dorchester Records. In his will which was probated April 3, 1678 (Wills 9, 1), Edward devised all of his estate to Daniel Clarke.

SCOTT (102)

On December 2, 1667, a 50 acre tract of land was surveyed for Thomas Scott; the tract was named "Scott's Hall" and it was located on the east side of Fishing Creek of the Little Choptank River. On November 12, 1675, another tract called "Oyster Point" was surveyed for him; it was also located on Fishing Creek.

Dorchester land Record 8 OLD 2 dated June 13, 1700, shows that "Oyster Point" descended to Elizabeth Griffin, wife of Phillip Griffin and only daughter of Thomas Scott, deceased. Phillip Griffin was an inhabitant of Anne Arundel County.

The will of Phillip Griffin (Wills 11, 19) shows that Elizabeth (Scott) Griffin was his wife and he devised all land at Fishing Creek to Sarah Fisher, the daughter of Elizabeth.

Dorchester Land Record 8 OLD 1 dated November 18, 1720, shows that Sarah Fisher married Thomas Rowles of Baltimore County and that they transferred the land at Fishing Creek to John Mills of Dorchester County.

SEALE (142)

On February 28, 1669, Robert Seale purchased 50 acres of "Musketta Quarter" which was located on Hungar River (DLR 1 OLD 6).

No further information has been found in the records on Robert Seale.

SEALUS (108)

In August of 1668 a 50 acre tract of land was surveyed for Stephen Sealus; it was called "Sealus Chance" and it was located on the east side of Hungar River. Stephen Sealus obtained the

warrant for the 50 acre tract for time of service to William
Chaplin.

On January 26, 1675, Stephen Sealus and his wife, Mary, sold the
tract to William Jones, planter of Dorchester County. Sealus was
also identified in that record as a painter of Dorchester County.

No further information has been found in the records about
Stephen Sealus or his wife, Mary.

SELBY (119)

On February 8, 1669, a 100 acre tract of land was surveyed for
James Selby; it was called "Skarlesborough" and it was located on
the west side of Fishing Creek of the Little Choptank River.

James Selby made a will dated August 26, 1671, which was probated
October 13, 1671 (Wills 1, 444).  He named neither a wife nor
children.

SEWALL (38)

On March 2, 1663, a 1000 acre tract of land was surveyed for
Henry Sewall.  It was originally designated in the records as
"Hap Hazzard" but the name was corrected to "Warwick." The tract
was located on Secretary Creek and the south side of Sewalls
Creek (Pat. L17 F58).

Henry Sewall patented a number of other tracts in what became
Dorchester County.  He also patented numerous tracts in the other
counties of the Province.

He resided at "Mattapony Sewall" on the Patuxent River a 1000
acre tract which he had purchased on May 25, 1663. His family
consisted of wife, Jane; son Nicholas, and four daughters, Ann,
Mary, Elizabeth and Jane.

Henry Sewall filed a will dated April 25, 1664, which was
probated April 17, 1665.  In his will Henry mentioned that it was
his intentions to make a voyage to England and the records of the
Maryland Assembly confirm that he was absent for the September
1664 session because he was in England.

The records clearly show that Henry Sewall owned land in the area
that became Dorchester County for only approximately one year
before his death and in that year he spent some time in England.
Under those circumstances it is highly improbable that he ever
built a home in what became Dorchester County.

Much has been written about "My Lady Sewall's Manor" supposedly
built by Henry Sewall in 1662 in what is now the Town of
Secretary.  Henry Sewall never owned the land on which the
so-called "My Lady Sewall's Manor" was erected.  The land on
which that "so-called" manor was erected was on a tract called
"Bath" patented by Thomas Taylor in 1675.  "Bath" was acquired by

Henry Trippe II on April 20, 1720 (DLR 2 OLD 79) and it remained in the Trippe family for many years. Most likely the dwelling was built by a member of that family.

The records show that Nicholas Sewall, son of Henry, was an inhabitant of Calvert County having received the "Mattapony Estate" from Charles Calvert who had married his mother, Jane, the widow of Henry Sewall.

Jane Sewall (Calvert) was the daughter of Vincent Lowe and Ann Cavendish and sister of Col. Vincent Lowe of Talbot County.

Major Nicholas Sewall (1655-1737), son of Henry Sewall, married Susannah Burgess, daughter of Colonel William Burgess, Deputy Governor of the Province. Major Sewall became a member of the Council, a Deputy Governor of the Province and Secretary of the State.

Ann Sewall married Colonel Benjamin Rozier and when he died she married Colonel Edward Pye.

Elizabeth, daughter of Henry and Jane, married Dr. Jesse Wharton and when the Doctor died she married Colonel William Diggs.

Mary, daughter of Henry and Jane, married Colonel William Chandler and after his death she married George Brent, brother of Governor Giles Brent.

Jane, another daughter of Henry and Jane, married Philip Calvert.

There is no record to show that either Henry Sewall or any of his family were ever inhabitants of the area that became Dorchester County.

SEWARD (X)

On June 11, 1673, a 200 acre tract of land was surveyed for George Seward; it was called "Monseiurs Folley" and it was located on the south side of the Great Choptank River near the land of Anthony LeCompte. Seward obtained this land for transporting himself, his wife, Ann, and Mary his daughter (Pat. L15 F248). Rent Roll Record, L10 F379, shows the tract in the possession of William Warner.

SHAPLEY (103)

On December 24, 1667, a 117 acre tract of land was surveyed for Philip Shapley; the tract was called "Shapley's Chance" and it was located on Tar Bay on Hoopers Island adjoining the land of William Chaplin. Fifty acres of the tract was on a warrant that he had received for transporting himself in 1667 into Calvert County of the Province of Maryland.

In the next two years Shapley obtained several grants for land in the area that was to become Dorchester County.

In 1671 Philip Shapley was made Deputy Surveyor for Somerset County; he was 27 years old at that time. He later became Deputy Surveyor for Dorchester County and he is shown in the records as an inhabitant of Dorchester (DLR 6 OLD 203). By 1712, however, he is shown as an inhabitant of Northumberland County, Virginia.

SHARP (23)

Dr. Peter Sharp was one of the Puritans to immigrate from Virginia and he settled on the Lower Cliffs of Calvert County where he obtained a grant of land called "Sharp's Outlet" He later became a Quaker and remembered that group in his will. He married Judith Gary, widow of John Gary. Judith had four children by her first marriage, John, Judith, Jane and Elizabeth. Elizabeth Gary was the lady in what was probably the strangest courtship on record (See details under Harwood).

On December 29, 1662, a 150 acre tract of land named "Fishing Creek Point" located on the south side of the Little Choptank River and the west side of Fishing Creek was surveyed for Dr. Sharp of Calvert County (Pat. L7 F176). In the months that followed several other tracts were surveyed in the same general area for him. The branch of Little Choptank now called Lee Creek was in the early days of Dorchester County called Sharp's Creek.

On November 4, 1665, Peter Sharp sold to Daniel Clark of Little Choptank "Sharp's Point" (Arch. of Md., vol. 57, pages 93 and 94) containing 200 acres and located at the head of Little Choptank (this tract is now known as "Unity Hill").

Dr. Sharp and Judith had two children, William and Mary. Son, William, married Elizabeth (last name unknown) and settled in Talbot County; they had three children: Sarah, Peter and William.

Mary, the daughter of Dr. Sharp and Judith, married William Stevens of Talbot County who was the son of William Stevens of Dorchester County.

Dr. Peter Sharp was still an inhabitant of Calvert county when he made his will on March 23, 1671/2. It was probated March 28, 1672 (Wills 1, 494). In it he named his two children William and Mary; two stepchildren, John and Elizabeth; wife, Judith. He also made bequests to several Quakers.

SHENTON (X)

On June 2, 1682, a 100 acre tract of land was surveyed for William Shenton; it was called "Shenton's Neglect" and it was located at the head of Hungar River. He acquired other tracts later in the same general area.

William Shenton died in 1711 and his will dated August 9, 1711, was probated December 19, 1711 (Wills 13, 425). In his will he named a son, William, and wife, Elinor. He indicated in his will that there were other children.

William Shenton II made a will on August 20, 1758 (Wills 30, 616), and in it he named a son, William; brother, Joseph, and the son of Joseph also named Joseph; brother, Ignatius and his son, Francis.

Raymond Shenton, son of William Shenton I, made a will on April 2, 1761 (Wills 31, 443), and in it he named sons Raymond, Joseph, William and Charles; daughters Elizabeth Toon (?) and Mary Meekins; wife, Mary; brothers Joseph and William.

SIMMONS (28)

Patent Liber 6, Folio 218, shows Lawrence Symons entering rights for transporting himself, Seth his wife, Anthony Alexander his son-in-law, and Thomas Oliver his mate, all of whom were transported this present year - 200 acres.

On March 4, 1663, a 100 acre tract called "Huntington" was surveyed for Lawrence Simmons (Pat. L7 F128). The tract was located on Taylors Island and adjoined a tract called "Robson's Cove." Rent Roll Record, Liber 10, Folio 347, shows this tract in the possession of the heirs of Lawrence Simmons. On March 31, 1664, Lawrence Simmons and Thomas Oliver had a 200 acre tract surveyed on James Island. The tract was called "Long Point." On November 1, 1670, Oliver and Simmons of Talbot County sold this tract to William Killman of James Island. In this transaction, Dorchester Land Record 1 OLD 44, Seath Simmons is shown as the wife of Lawrence Simmons.

Rent Roll Record, Liber 10, Folio 347, shows 50 acres of "Long Point" in the possession of Daniel Phillips who married Henry Mitchell's daughter; 75 acres in the possession of David McKeele; 75 acres in the possession of the widow of William Harris.

SKILLINGTON (5)

On July 7, 1659, Thomas Skillington had a 100 acre tract of land surveyed in what is now known as the Golden Hill area of Dorchester County (Pat. L4 F162). The tract was called "Skillington." Thomas Skillington also had a 300 acre tract surveyed on Skillington Creek called "Skillington's Right." That tract was the first tract surveyed in what eventually became Caroline County. Time has corrupted the name of the Creek from Skillington's Creek to Skelton Creek.

The will of Thomas Skillington was dated December 19, 1698, and it was probated June 20, 1699 (Wills 6, 287), in it was mentioned his wife, Mary; son, Kenelm, and grandson, Thomas Skillington; granddaughter, Sarah Goddard; and the will shows that at the time it was made Thomas Skillington was an inhabitant of Talbot County.

The will of Kenelm Skillington, son of Thomas, was made November 11, 1733, and it was probated February 14, 1737 (Wills 21, 858), and it shows that Kenelm was also an inhabitant of Talbot County

when his will was made.  In the will he mentions wife, Liddia;
sons, Kenelm and Elijah; and daughters Rachell and Elizabeth.

There is nothing in the records to indicate that Thomas
Skillington or any members of his immediate family  were ever
inhabitants of Dorchester.

## SKINNER (163)

Patent Record Liber 14 Folio 88 shows that Thomas Skinner had a
250-acre tract of land surveyed on March 31, 1670; it was called
"Skinner's Choice" and it was located on a branch of the
Blackwater River.   Shortly thereafter he had an adjoining 50-acre
tract surveyed called "Skinner's Chance."  The tracts were
granted, in part, for transporting Elizabeth his wife, John his
son, and William Marchant his servant, from Virginia.

Thomas and Elizabeth had the following children:
1.   Thomas who married Mary Brannock.
2.   John.
3.   William, who married Esther (LeCompte) Fox, widow of
Henry Fox of Talbot County and daughter of Anthony and Hester
LeCompte, after she died he married Elizabeth Colston, widow of
James Colston.
4.   Mary, who married Moses LeCompte.

Thomas Skinner served several terms as justice of Dorchester
County.  After he died his widow, Elizabeth, married Henry
Beckwith sometime between 1675 and 1678.  They had a daughter,
Elizabeth, and two sons, Nehemiah and Henry Beckwith.

Thomas Skinner, Jr., married Mary Brannock, daughter of Edmond
and Jane Brannock (See Will 12, 224).  He made a will dated
January 29, 1705, which was probated November 6, 1707 (Wills 12,
224).  In his will he named son Martin; daughters Elizabeth who
married Samuel Willoughby, Anne who married Thomas Ennalls son of
Col. Henry and Mary (Hooper) Ennalls, Mary who married Amos Bunt;
brothers-in-law Thomas Brannock and Hugh Eccleston.

## SLACUM (XX)

On June 11, 1697, the Maryland Assembly passed an Act for the
naturalization of George Slacum who was born in Germany (Bacon's
Laws of Maryland, Chapter 14, of 1697 Acts.)

George Slacum was the first with that surname to appear in the
Dorchester Records.  In his will dated October 11, 1725 (Wills
18, 414) he was characterized as a sailor.

He devised to his son, George, a tract of land called "Timber
Swamp" which was located on the south side of Racoon Creek; to
his son, Job, he devised a tract called "Priviledge" which
adjoined "Timber Swamp."  In his will he also mentioned his wife,
Sarah, and an unborn child.

SMART (XX)

On December 10, 1712, Thomas and Elizabeth Ennalls sold to
Richard Smart, mariner, 176 acres of "Ennells Outlett" on the
north side of the Chicamacomico River at Smart's Branch.  On
February 18, 1716, the Ennalls sold to Richard Smart an
additional 348 acres of the same tract.

Captain Richard Smart married Elizabeth Hayward, daughter of
Francis Hayward (DLR 10 OLD 44), and after his death she married
Thomas Ennalls, son of Joseph Ennalls.

Captain Smart made a will dated August 1, 1727, which was
probated June 21, 1729 (Wills 19, 714).  In his will he named his
wife, Elizabeth; son Richard; daughters Mary LeCompte and her
husband William, Elizabeth, Jane and Smart Rebecca; granddaughter
Sarah, daughter of Mary and William LeCompte.  Two of the
administrators named were brother Thomas Hayward of Somerset
County and William Hayward of Dorchester County.

In Dorchester Land Record 8 OLD 298 dated February 26, 1729,
Elizabeth Smart, widow, deeds slaves, livestock and personal
property to her children:  Mary LeCompte, Elizabeth Foster
(Elizabeth married Thomas Foster, see DLR 11 OLD 80 and 16 OLD
132, they had a son named Joseph), Richard Smart, Jean Smart, and
Smart Rebecca Smart.

On December 30, 1737, Elizabeth Smart, who it appears was the
widow of Richard Smart II, the son of Richard I and Elizabeth,
made a will which was probated March 30, 1738 (Wills 21, 855).
In it she named brothers John and Joseph Scott; sisters Mary and
Betty Scott; daughter, Elizabeth.  Uncle Thomas Hayward of
Somerset was named executor and guardian.

It would appear that there were no male descendants of Captain
Richard Smart after his son, Richard.

SMITH (44)

On May 26, 1664, a 100 acre tract of land was surveyed for John
Smith.  The tract was called "Smith's Point" and was located on
the south side of the Choptank River at Smith's Creek (Now
Hunting Creek).

On October 1, 1698, Joseph Smith, planter, of Dorchester County,
sold to John Alford of the same County "Smith's Point" (DLR 5 OLD
119).  The records do not show how Joseph acquired the tract nor
do the records show the relationship between John Smith and
Joseph Smith.  No further record has been found on the John Smith
who patented "Smith's Point."

SMITH (62)

On April 6, 1665, a 200 acre tract of land was surveyed for
William Smith; the tract was called "Fishing Point" and it was

located on what is now called Elliotts Island. In that same year two other tracts were surveyed for him: "Pa Pa Island" and "Smith's Range" both were located in the same area.

The records do not show transfers of the tracts to John Elliott but he acquired them; it could be that John Elliott married a heir of William Smith.

Nothing further has been found in the records that identifies William Smith.

## SMITHSON (134)

On March 29, 1666/7, Robert Harwood sold a tract of land consisting of 700 acres to Nathaniel Smithson; the tract was called "Harwood's Reserve" and it was located on the Transquaking River (TLR L1 F17).

No other information has been found in the records about Nathaniel Smithson but it is believed that he had sons named William and Thomas Smithson and a grandson also named Thomas.

A William Smithson served as a clerk of court for Dorchester County in 1678 and he was followed in that position in 1681 by Thomas Smithson. Chancery Record P. C. Folio 847 shows that Thomas Smithson was born in 1651.

William Smithson also served as sheriff of Dorchester County in 1682. The records indicate that William Smithson was a cousin of Lord Baltimore.

Thomas Smithson of Dorchester County made a will dated June 16, 1686, which was probated November 8, 1695 (Wills 11, 35); in the will he named Jane Taylor and her brother John Taylor.

## SOUTHEY (151)

On April 1, 1676, John Hudson, planter, of Dorchester County, sold to John Southey, planter, and John Button, cooper, "Turkey Point" which was located on the Blackwater River and which contained 100 acres.

On May 1, 1683, the two divided the 100 acres (DLR 4 OLD 80).

On March 22, 1696, John Southey made a will which was probated July 7, 1697 (Wills 7, 331). In the will he named John Button and Elinor Hudson, daughter of John Hudson.

## SPEDDEN (XX)

On January 18, 1730, Hugh Spedden, planter, of Dorchester County made his will and it was probated May 10, 1734 (Wills 21, 118). Hugh left his dwelling plantation to his son, Robert. He also named sons John and Edward as well as daughters Alice Oram, Marie Bromwell and Catherine. The dwelling plantation that Hugh devised to his son, Robert, was "Dawson's Chance" and it was located near the easternmost bounds of a tract called "Maulden" (Now known as Cooks Point).

Hugh Spedden purchased "Dawson's Chance" from William Willoughby on March 26, 1711 (DLR 6 OLD 172), as shown in the following abstract:

"William Willoughby of Dorchester County, mason, and Anne his wife to Hugh Spedden of Talbot County, planter, "Dawson's Chance" adjoining "Maulden" on Armstrongs Bay containing 300 acres..."

Several years later, August 10, 1725 (DLR 8 OLD 88), Hugh Spedden purchased an adjoining property from Edward Willoughby known as "Cedar Point" containing 150 acres.

John Spedden, son of Hugh, made a will dated November 7, 1748 (Wills 27, 286), and he named only his wife, Jean, so, apparently, he had no children.

Robert Spedden, son of Hugh, married Anne Brannock, daughter of John and Margaret Brannock. In his will dated April 1742 and probated November 11, 172 (Wills 23, 9), he named his wife, Anne, and her father and mother, John and Margaret Brannock. He also named sons: Hugh, John and Robert.

The following abstract of Dorchester Land Record 10 OLD 376 dated March 10, 1742, shows some of the land transfers between the Brannock and Spedden families.

"Thomas Brannock of Dorchester County, planter, to Margaret Brannock of the same County, widow; Ann Spedding of the same County, widow; John Spedden, Robert Spedding and Brannock Spedding of the same County, sons of Robert Spedding, deceased: 250 acres between Jordans Point and Mannings Point. Also "Addition to Brooks" adj. said 250 acres. Also "Trippes Ridge," adj. "Addition to Brooks" and containing 150 acres. Also a tract of 130 acres on Little Choptank River between Brooks Creek, Island Bay and Jordans Creek. All four tracts were conveyed to said Thomas Brannock by John Brannock, deceased, during his lifetime, were bought from said Thomas Brannock by Margaret Brannock and Robert Spedding, deceased, and are hereby conveyed to Margaret and Ann and to the survivor of them for their lifetimes, and then to be equally divided between John, Robert and Brannock Spedding."

On June 11, 1745, Margaret Brannock petitioned to have all of her lands surveyed into one tract called "Margaret's Delight." In response to the petition Margaret Brannock obtained a patent for the land resurveyed in Certificate of Survey 2016 totaling 696 acres. The resurvey covered, basically, the tracts called "Brooks Landing" and "Trippes Ridge" and some vacant land all located at the head of Trippes Creek (now Brooks Creek). The tract "Margaret's Delight" as shown in Dorchester Land Record 10 OLD 376 was destined to descend to the Spedden children. It became the ancestral home of the Spedden family and remained in that family for generations.

John Brannock Spedden, son of Robert Spedden and Ann Brannock, married Elizabeth Taylor on June 23, 1781. They had the following children:

1. John, born June 18, 1782, died August 20, 1873, married Jane Frazier, born February 19, 1790, died January 6, 1867.

2. Robert Brannock Spedden, born March 11, 1786, died June 2, 1832, married Margaret Cook on August 9, 1806, born 1786, died April 30, 1852.

3. Vincent Price Spedden, born 1787, died July 12, 1872, married Nancy Seward in Dorchester County, January 9, 1810.

4. Impey Spedden, born 1796, died March 4, 1883, married Elizabeth Spedden, December 3, 1818.

5. Prudence, died at age 41, married Levi D. Travers, December 11, 1827.

6. Timothy Spedden, born November 20, 1801, died January 28, 1858, married Frances Ann Frazier on February 14, 1828, born October 25, 1805, died January 27, 1893.

7. Hugh Spedden, died 1843 left no heirs.

Robert Brannock Spedden, son of John Brannock Spedden and Elizabeth Taylor, married Margaret Cook on August 9, 1806. They had the following children: Thomas, Mary, Robert, Henry, Prudence, John, Levin and Captain Joseph H. Spedden who married Margaret Wheeler on January 1, 1855.

## SPICER (X)

On November 19, 1677, a 50 acre tract of land was laid out for Thomas Wingod and John Spicer; it was called "Waxford" and it was located on the western side of Goose Creek issuing out of Fishing Bay.

In the years that followed John Spicer acquired an interest in a number of tracts of land in the Lower Dorchester County area. Some of the records on those transactions show that his wife was named Norah.

In Dorchester Land Record 5 OLD 162 dated July 31, 1700, John Spicer is characterized as a carpenter and his wife, Norah is still living as of that date. No further information has been found on John Spicer and Norah his wife.

However, a John Spicer made a will dated August 11, 1724, which was probated July 14, 1730 (Wills 20, 35). This is in all probability the will of the son of John and Norah Spicer. The will names wife, Elinor; sons Thomas, William, Phillip, John and James; daughters Elizabeth Bright, Mary, and Rachel; son-in-law Bartholomew Gibbs.

It is, of course, possible that John and Norah Spicer had other children in addition to their son, John.

STANLEY (132)

On September 17, 1669, a 350 acre tract of land was surveyed for William Stanley; the tract was called "Stanley's Lott" and it was located on the east side of the Chicamacomico River.

Rent Roll Record, Liber 10, Folio 361 shows the tract in the possession of John Stanley.

No further information has been found on William or John Stanley.

STAPLEFORT (91)

Raymond Staplefort came to Maryland in 1660 and settled in Calvert County. It is interesting to note that his land in Calvert County adjoined that of Henry Hooper and that both eventually moved to what became the lower part of Dorchester County. Mary Staplefort, sister of Raymond, married George Thompson and they immigrated from Northumberland County, Virginia to Calvert County. Raymond Staplefort served as commissioner of Calvert County in 1664. In 1667 he obtained patents for two tracts of land in the Hungar River area of Dorchester County: "Stapleforts Hermitage" and "The Commencement." In the following year he obtained patents on two more tracts "Staplefort's Lott: and "Addition to Hermitage."

He was the first sheriff of Dorchester County and one of the first commissioners as well as one of the first justices. He was reappointed a commissioner in 1676 and 1679. As a result of complaints he was dismissed in 1679 by the Governor. The records show that he had married the widow of Thomas May prior to 1666 (Pat. L9 F355). Other records show that her name was Elinor (Arch. of Md., vol. 66, pages 128-132). Elinor was probably the daughter of George Goodrich (Wills 5, 91).

The will of Raymond Staplefort was dated August 11, 1684, and was probated September 3, 1687 (Wills 4, 265). In his will he named a son, Charles, and a son, George, as well as a daughter, Mary. While she was not named in his will he also had a daughter named Elinor who married Richard Tubman (see DLR 8 OLD 227 and Wills 19, 183).

On March 18, 1747, George Staplefort, son of Raymond and Elinor, filed a will (Wills 27, 381) naming sons, Raymond and Thomas and a daughter, Dorothy. Another son, Charles, was deceased (see Wills 24, 359). The will of Edward Pinder (Wills 19, 866) confirms the fact that Charles was the son of George. George Staplefort had married Jane, the widow of Edward Pinder II.

STEELE (XX)

Much has been written about Henry Steele and his origin, most of which has been pure conjecture.

Henry Steele and Ann Billings entered into a marriage contract on

October 28, 1756, and this contract contains much information about both and it shows the origin of Henry. The contract is contained in Dorchester Land Record 15 OLD 403 and reads in part as follows:

"Contract of marriage between Henry Steele, late of the town of Whitehaven in the Kingdom of England, merchant, and at present of Somerset County in the Province of Maryland, of the first part; Ann Billings of Dorchester County, spinster, of the second part; and John Henry of Dorchester County of the third part. Whereas Ann Billings is possessed of considerable wealth ...(continuing, Ann agrees to turn over her wealth to John Henry in trust and when vows are performed Henry Steele to obtain same under certain conditions, except specified jewels.)"

Henry and Ann Steele had the following children:
1. Catherine Steele, born February 28, 1758, died December 5, 1768.
2. James Steele, born March 18, 1760, died September 21, 1816; married Mary Nevett, daughter of John Rider Nevett and Sarah Maynadier, daughter of Reverend Daniel Maynadier.
3. Peter Steele, born August 16, 1762, died January 1, 1791.
4. John Steele, born September 4, 1765, died the 12th of the same month.
5. Charles Steele, born March 14, 1767, died August 28, 1776.
6. Isaac Steele, born November 9, 1769, died November 7, 1806.
7. Henry Steele, born March 14, 1722, died young.
8. Ann Steele, born April 11, 1775, died October 9, 1777.

Henry Steele I died February 5, 1782, and was buried at "Weston;" his body and tombstone were moved from "Weston" to Christ Church Cemetery. He had served as a justice of the County in 1759; burgess 1763-1770; represented Dorchester at the Convention in Annapolis in 1774; member of the General Assembly in 1777. He was 64 years old when he died.

Ann Steele, widow of Henry, died April 29, 1788. The tax records for the year 1783 show that Ann Steele was the 2nd largest land owner in the County with 23 tracts totalling 8344 acres; she also owned 86 slaves, 345 ounces of plate, 35 horses and 174 black cattle.

James Steele, son of Henry and Ann Steele, and his wife, Mary Nevett, had the following children:
1. Mary Nevett Steele, born October 16, 1789, married John C. Henry April 22, 1808.
2. Ann Billings Steele, born October 24,1791, married Arthur Uphsur of the Eastern Shore of Virginia, December 1810.
3. Sarah Maynadier Steele, born January 8, 1793, died June 21, 1793.
4. James Billings Steele, born October 14, 1794, married Milcah Gale, daughter of General John Gale; Milcah died August

28, 1836. James took as his second wife, Sarah Yerbury
Goldsborough, daughter of Robert Goldsborough and Mary Nixon of
Delaware. The marriage of James and Milcah took place at Cedar
Grove in Somerset County, April 15, 1817.
    5. John Nevett Steele, born February 22, 1796.
    6. Henry Maynadier Steele, born October 5, 1798.
    7. Catherine Sarah Maria Steel, born August 2, 1801.
    8. Isabella Elizabeth Steele, born December 30, 1803.
    9. Sarah Maynadier Steele, born November 5, 1805.

James Billings Steele, eldest son of James and Mary Nevett
Steele, and Milcah his first wife had the following children:
    1. James Billings Steele, born July 24, 1820.
    2. John Gale Steele, born February 21, 1822.
    3. Amelius Steele, born May 8, 1824.
    4. Charles Nevett Steele, born February 23, 1827.
    5. Maria Amelia Steele, born September 28, 1829.

James Billings Steele and Sarah, his second wife, had the
following children:
    1. Louise N. Steele, married Joseph Henry Hooper.
    2. Wilhelmina Goldsborough Steele, married Van Rensalaer
Dickson of Talbot County.
    3. Nellie Steele, married Joseph D. Richards of Pittsburgh.
    4. Sarah, married Mr. Buck of England.
    5. Clarance Hutchins Steele who died unmarried.

STEVENS (65)

William Stevens with his wife, Magealean, and his sons: William
Jr. and John, immigrated to Calvert County, Maryland, in 1651
(Pat. ABH F141). Magealen was the sister of John Hodgis of St.
Mary's County (Wills 1, 61) who immigrated from Virginia in 1651
with the Stevens family. On May 14, 1665, William Stevens had a
100 acre tract of land surveyed on the southside of Jenkins Creek
called "Armstrong Sale." On June 18, 1666, he purchased from
Edward Lloyd a 200 acre tract of land called "Cliffe" (TLR L1
F38); both of the tracts were located on the south side of the
Choptank River in what eventually became Dorchester County.

William Jr. settled in Talbot County on Dividing Creek almost
directly across the Choptank River from William Sr. William Jr.
married Mary Sharp, daughter of Peter Sharp on February 9, 1670.
The record of their marriage was entered in the Provincial Court
Proceedings (Arch. of Md., vol. 57, page 502).

Both William Sr. and William Jr. were ardent Quakers as evidenced
by the meeting held at their homes by George Fox in 1673 (see
Journal of George Fox). William Sr. was appointed one of the
first commissioners of Dorchester County in 1669. He died in
1684; his wife, Magealen, had died in 1678. In 1940 their graves
were the two oldest known graves in Dorchester County; in that
year the headstones were moved, from what had become the
Cambridge Country Club, to Christ church graveyard in Cambridge.

The 18th Governor of Maryland, Samuel Stevens, was a descendant of William Stevens, Sr., thru his son William Jr.

John, the other son of William Sr. became a leader in the political affairs of Dorchester and one of the largest landowners of the County. He represented Dorchester County as a delegate to the Maryland Assembly for three terms beginning 1678.

John Stevens married Dorothy Preston, daughter of Thomas Preston and a sister of Christopher Preston of Calvert County. Thomas Preston was named in the will of Richard Preston and they were probably brothers.

John and Dorothy Stevens had the following children (Wills 2, 285):
1. John Stevens, born in 1670, married Ann, widow of Thomas Cooke and daughter of Dr. John Brooke. John and Ann had at least two daughters, Dorothy who married Thomas Smith, and Sarah (DLR 7 OLD 53).
2. William, married in 1700 Mary Pryor.
3. Magdalen, married 1st James Edmonson and 2nd Jacob Loockerman.
4. Grace, married James Woolford.

Dorothy Stevens, widow of John, made a will November 7, 1709, which was probated November 10, 1710 (Wills 13, 194).

William Stevens, son of Dorothy and John Stevens died in 1709 and in his will (Wills 13, 18) he named sons Walter and William and daughters Johannah and Mary. He also named his wife, Mary.

STEVENS (Of Little Choptank)

William Stevens was appointed one of the first Commissioners and justices of Dorchester County in 1669; he was characterized as William Stevens of Little Choptank to distinguish him from the other William Stevens that was appointed a Commissioner at the same time and who lived on the Great Choptank. Very little has been found in the records concerning William Stevens "Of Little Choptank." In October 1671 Charles Calvert appointed him to be Coroner in Dorchester County (Arch. of Md., Vol. 5, page 97).

In Dorchester Land Record 3 OLD 169 appears the following: "Reference to Patent of "Dale's Right" on Little Choptank River, Hudson's Creek and Dale's Cove, granted May 10, 1671 to William Stevens."

On August 6, 1678, William Stevens of Little Choptank transferred "Dale's Right" to William Keyson.

In Dorchester Land Record 3 OLD 26 Henry Mitchell of Calvert County deeded to William Stevens "Cedar Poynt." This transaction was dated November 4, 1673, however, on May 28, 1679 (DLR 3 OLD 186) Henry Mitchell resold the same tract of land to Jefferson Meanly.

The above transactions could be an indication that William
Stevens "Of Little Choptank" was disposing of his holdings in
Dorchester County.

Appearing in the records of Dorchester County is a copy of a will
made December 5, 1680, and probated December 21, 1680 (Wills 2,
116), of William Steephens of Gloucester, New England.  The will
was witnessed by John Hazlewood and William Robson both
inhabitants of Dorchester County. Under the circumstances it
would seem that William Stevens "Of Little Choptank" had moved to
Gloucester where he had died.  William Steephens of Gloucester
named in his will son, James Stevens, and son-in-law, John Fish
and Mary his wife; grandchildren, William, James, Mary, Abenezer
and David, Hann and Samuel Steephens.

STEWART (76)

On August 18, 1665, John Stewart had a 350 acre tract surveyed.
The tract was called "Stewarts Place" and it was located at the
head of Stewart's Creek, a tributary of the Little Choptank River
(Pat. L8 F46).  Stewart's Creek is known today as Beckwith Creek
after Henry Beckwith who acquired "Stewarts Place."  Rent Roll
Record, Liber 10, Folio 35, shows 300 acres of "Stewarts Place"
in the possession of Henry Beckwith and 50 acres in the
possession of Arthur Wright.

On January 8, 1668, John Stewart acquired by patent (Pat. L12
F233) a 100 acre tract called "Pine Swamp."  This tract was
located near what is known today at Hills Point.  The records
show that "Pine Swamp" was the home plantation of John Stewart I.

The will of John Stewart I was filed March 16, 1688, and it was
probated September 4, 1688 (Wills 6, 27).  No immediate family
members were named in the will.  However, a deed (DLR 4 OLD 195)
dated June 8, 1687, indicates that John Stewart did have a
family.

While no records have been found to verify the relationship it
would seem that John Stewart II, a carpenter who appears in the
Dorchester Records as doing some carpentry work for Dr. John
Brooks in April of 1692 (Provincial Court Records AW#3, page 103)
could very well be the son of John Stewart I.  The records do, in
any event, show the continuation of the Stewart line from John
Stewart II so that he is without doubt an ancestor of the
Dorchester Stewart Line.

John Stewart II married in 1694/5 Mary Winsmore, the widow of
Robert Winsmore II.  Mary was the daughter of Henry Wheeler and
his wife Alice.  Mary first married John Hayward who died in
1692.  John Hayward and Mary had 5 children: Henry, John,
Francis, Mary and Ann.  After John Hayward died Mary, his widow,
married Robert Winsmore II by whom she had one child, Robert
Winsmore III.  After Robert II died Mary married John Stewart by
whom she had two sons: John and Thomas Stewart.  After the death
of John Stewart, his widow, Mary, married John Hambrook, a

blacksmith, who had purchased a part of "Busby" which is known today as Hambrook Point and which was named after him.

John Stewart III married Elizabeth Trevallion in 1723 and they had the following children: John, Mary, Thomas, Charles, James, Henry, Elizabeth and Jane. After Elizabeth died John Stewart III married Ann (Peterkin) Warner Wing. Ann was the daughter of David and Mary Peterkin. She had first married Gary Warner by whom she had a son, Stephen Gary Warner, and when her first husband died she married Captain Robert Wing. Ann and John Stewart III had one son whom they named John and this son, John, became known as "John Stewart of Ann" to differentiate him from his half-brother also named John and other John Stewarts.

Thomas Stewart, son of John Stewart and Mary (Wheeler) Hayward Winsmore, married 1st Mary Woolford, daughter of James Woolford, and 2nd Elizabeth Smart, daughter of Richard Smart and Elizabeth Hayward. In his will (Wills 31, 1035) Thomas Stewart names the following children: Joseph, John, Charles, William, Thomas, Ann, Rebecca, Mary and Elizabeth. He also mentioned his wife, Elizabeth, in his will. After the death of Thomas his widow, Elizabeth, married John Manning.

## STOKES (X)

On November 2, 1674, Peter Stokes purchased from Anthony Hardacre 50 acres of "Hayles Choice" (DLR 3 OLD 69) and this tract was located on a branch of Fishing Creek of the Little Choptank River.

On November 12, 1680, a 100 acre tract of land was surveyed for Peter Stokes; and it was named "Head Range" and was located southside of Long Branch that issued out of northwest side of Blackwater River. Rent Roll Record, Liber 10, Folio 406, showed this tract still in the possession of Peter Stokes as of 1706. In 1688 he had a tract of 34 acres patented and it was called "Peter's Adventure."

Dorchester Land Record 14 OLD 375 shows that Peter Stokes married for his second wife, Anne, the widow of Miles Mason and that the said Miles left one young child named Sarah who was brought up in said Peter's house and later married Thomas Shehawne.

The will of Peter Stokes, planter, (Wills 17, 324) was made February 27, 1710, and it was probated on June 1, 1712. In his will Peter Stokes devised "Hayles Choice" to his son, Peter, and "Peter's Fortune" to his sons, William and John. He devised 50 acres of "Head Range," where son James did live, to his grandson, Peter. He named daughters Rebecca and Alles.

Peter Stokes II married Ann, daughter of Thomas Vickers

(Wills 13, 272). He made a will in 1768 (Wills 36, 564) and
in it he named his son, James, and grandsons James, Peter
and William who were sons of James. He also named daughter
Ann the wife of Henry Brannock and daughter Mary Woodward.
Named also in his will were grandchildren Archibald Grimes,
Peter Grimes and Elizabeth Grimes as well as son-in-law
Benjamin Woodward.

## STONE (3)

William Stone immigrated from England to Virginia in 1633
where he became a justice in Accomac County and High Sheriff
of Northumberland County. In 1648 he and his family left
Virginia and settled in Calvert County, Maryland. He
transported a number of people to the Province. The members
of his family consisted of his wife, Verlinda Sprigg Stone;
daughters Elizabeth, Mary, and Katharine; sons Richard,
John, Mathew, and Thomas the eldest. In 1649 William Stone
became the first protestant Governor of the Province of
Maryland.

On July 1, 1659, Thomas Stone of Calvert County, son of
Captain William Stone former Governor of the Province, had a
150 acre tract of land surveyed on the east side of Hungar
River (Pat. L4 F160). The tract was called "Stonewick" and
it was the third tract of land that was surveyed in what was
to become Dorchester County.

"Stonewick" was acquired by James Preston of Calvert County
who devised it to his wife, Elizabeth, and daughter,
Rebecca, who on January 4, 1675, sold it to William
Wroughton of Dorchester County, planter (DLR 3 OLD 96); from
William Wroughton originated the name Wroten Island on which
"Stonewick" was located.

The will of Thomas Stone was dated April 24, 1676, and
probated October 5, 1676, (Wills 5, 94) it indicated that
at the time it was made he was a resident of Charles County.
In the will he named his wife, Mary, and two sons, Richard
and William.

## SUDBOROUGH (82)

On September 17, 1665, a 250 acre tract of land was surveyed
for William Sudborough (Pat. L8 F400); the tract was called
"Sudborough's Gift" and it was located on the Eastern Branch
of the Transquaking River.

Rent Roll Record, Liber 10, Folio 451, shows that Sudborough
was dead and no heirs could be found.

## SULIVANE (XX)

In the early 1700's several persons with the name Sulivane
appear in the records: Darby Sulivane and Catherine his

wife; John Sulivane and Rebecca his wife; Owen Sulivane and
Mary his wife; Flowrance Sulivane and Sarah his wife -- all,
appear in, apparently, unconnected branches. However,
according to the will of Flowrance Sulivane (Wills 41, 71)
the names of his children may indicate some relationship:
Daniel, Flowrance, Solomon, Darby, Abraham, and John who
married Denair Cratcher, daughter of Samuel Cratcher and
Mary his wife.

The first Sulivane to surface in the Dorchester County
Records with a continuing family history was Daniel Sulivane
who was born in 1708. He married Sarah Anderton, daughter
of Francis and Mary Anderton his wife. They had the
following children:
    1. James Sulivane (1737- ) married Mary Ennalls.
    2. Daniel Sulivane, Jr. ( - 1798) married Sussannah
Orrick.
    3. Mary Silivane, married Thomas Ennalls.

James Sulivane, son of Daniel and Sarah, and Mary his wife
had the following children:
    1. Daniel Sulivane (1766- ) married Mary Richardson.
    2. Joseph Ennalls Sulivane, married Anne E. (Nancy)
Hooper in 1795.
    3. Henrietta Sullivane (1766- ) married in 1802
Joseph Haskins.
    4. Mary Sulivane (1773- ) married in 1794 Dr. John
(J. H.) Eccleston.

Daniel Sulivane, Jr., son of Daniel and Sarah, and Susannah
had the following children:
    1. Dr. James Sulivane (1773-1818) married in 1795
Elizabeth Ennalls.
    2. Robert Sulivane.
    3. Elizabeth Sulivane, married in 1797 James
Birckhead.
    4. Clement Sulivane (1784-1813).

Mary Sulivane, daughter of Daniel and Sarah, and her husband
Thomas Ennalls had one daughter, Sarah Ennalls (1761-1842)
who married Henry Waggaman (1753-1809).

TALL (155)

Patent Liber 7, Folio 493, shows that Anthony Tall I was
transported in 1662 with his wife, Elizabeth, and son,
Philip. Later records show that Anthony Tall I also had a
second son named Anthony II, and a daughter, Elizabeth.

Anthony Tall, merchant of Bristol, apparently, first
immigrated to Virginia with his wife the former Elizabeth
Coward before they came to Maryland.

On October 28, 1669, Anthony Tall I purchased 50 acres of
"Hudson's Desire" (DLR 1 OLD 40). Anthony I died in 1678.

On November 4, 1672, Anthony Tall II, couper, acquired 50 acres of "Wrights Lott" which was located on Wright's Creek (now called Philips Creek) of the Little Choptank River (DLR 3 OLD 259). On October 9, 1693, he sold it to Richard Owen (DLR 5 OLD 37).

Anthony Tall II made a will dated December 8, 1710, which was probated October 24, 1712 (Wills 13, 462); in the will he devised a tract of land called "Rosses Chance" to his sons-in-law, Charles Ross and Peter Ross. He acquired "Rosses Chance" thru his marriage with Mabella, the widow of John Ross; Mabella's first husband was a Harrington. No record has been found of any children of Anthony Tall II.

Philip Tall, son of Anthony I and Elizabeth Tall, acquired a number of tracts of land; and some of those were located on the Transquaking River. He married Hannah (last name unknown but thought to be Hill, daughter of Agatha Hill - see Will 20, 150) and on February 11, 1705, he made a will which was probated February 28, 1705/6. In his will he named wife, Hannah; sons Anthony and Philip; daughters Mary, Sarah, Agatha and Elizabeth.

TAYLOR (16)

On April 17, 1662, a 400 acre tract of land was surveyed, on what became known as Taylors Island, for John Taylor I of Calvert County (Pat. L5 F362). The tract was called "Taylor's Folly." John's will was dated October 10, 1667, and was probated September 22, 1668 (Wills 1, 324). His will indicated that he was still an inhabitant of Calvert County when it was made. "Taylor's Folly" was devised to his son, John II, and "Armstrong's Quarter" was devised to his daughter, Elizabeth; John II and Elizabeth were his only children.

John Taylor II married Priscilla Pattison, the daughter of Thomas and Ann Pattison of James Island, Dorchester County, Maryland (DLR 1 OLD 192). In his will dated August 4, 1683, John Taylor II mentions his cousin, Thomas Travers, and his aunt, Elizabeth Travers (Wills 4, 223). After the death of John Taylor II his widow, Priscilla, married Nathaniel Manning (see Will of Ann Pattison 11, 301 dated January 21, 1701, in which she mentions her daughter Priscilla Manning).

The will of John Taylor III dated November 29, 1710, lists as his brothers: Richard Manning and Nathaniel Manning and it lists as his sisters, Grace and Sarah Manning, and it also lists his uncle, James Pattison (Wills 13, 251).

No record of the marriage of John Taylor III has been found and since he showed no children in his will it would seem that the male lineage of the branch of the Taylor family ended with his death. However, no positive proof of that fact has been found.

There is a possibility that there still exists in Dorchester County a monument to John Taylor of Calvert County who patented "Taylor's Folly" in 1662. For there is a "school of thought" that Taylors Island was named after him. Some credence is given this thought by a study of some of the early patents for land on Taylors Island. For example: the patent for "Robson's Delight" gives the location as: "In an Island called John Taylors Island."

TAYLOR (50)

Jane Eltonhead was born in 1617 (Arch. of Md., vol. 10, page 560) and the records indicate that her maiden name was Fenwick, a sister of Cuthbert Fenwick (Arch. of Md., vol. 10, page 496). Her first husband was Thomas Smith (Arch. of Md., vol. 4, page 527) who was Captain of one of Claiborne's ships in the battle of 1635. Three years later he was arrested at Kent Island by the forces of Lord Baltimore; taken to St. Mary's; tried; convicted and hung. Jane and Thomas Smith had two daughters, Gertrude and Jane (Arch. of Md., vol. 4, Page 507).

Jane's second husband was Philip Taylor (Arch. of Md., vol. 4, page 527) and they had two children, Thomas and Sarah Taylor as shown by the record of September 29, 1649 (Arch. of Md., vol. 4, page 507) at which time they were inhabitants of Kent Island. Captain Philip Taylor was Claiborne's chief lieutenant (Arch. of Md., vol. 5, pages 220-225) and was originally an inhabitant of Virginia. He was, in 1642, a justice of Northampton County and in 1643 was sheriff of that county.

After the death of Captain Philip Taylor, Jane, his widow married William Eltonhead.

William Eltonhead was Lord of "Eltonhead Manor" and at one time a secretary of the Council. He was captured by the Puritans in the March 24, 1655 battle of the Severn; court-martialed and summarily shot.

After the death of her third husband Jane Eltonhead continued to live at "Little Eltonhead Manor" until her death in 1659.

In her will (Wills 1, 94) which was probated February 28, 1659, she named her eldest son, Thomas Taylor; daughter Sarah; grandchild Roger Anderton; and an Edward Eltonhead who was not otherwise identified in the will but other records show him as an uncle of William Eltonhead.

The records disclose that William Eltonhead had been a staunch and close friend of the Calverts. It is not surprising, therefore, to find that the records show that Philip Calvert became the guardian of Thomas Taylor after the death of his mother, Jane Eltonhead in 1639 (Arch. of

<u>Md</u>., vol. XLI, page 99). Thomas Taylor was about 16 when his mother died (<u>Arch. of Md</u>., vol. XLI, page 345).

Thomas Taylor probably spent the years between 1659 and 1664 in England furthering his education and while there married Frances. The records show that he brought into the Province his son, John, and wife, Frances, and four others.

On March 29, 1664, Thomas Taylor recorded an assignment of part of "Little Eltonhead" to his brother-in-law, Thomas Courtney. Thomas Courtney after a tumultuous love affair with Sarah Taylor, sister of Thomas Taylor (<u>Arch. of Md</u>., vol. XLI, pages 550-551) married her. Sarah's identity is proven by the records on page 507 of volume 4 of the <u>Maryland Archives</u> and page 425 of volume 49 of the <u>Archives</u>.

On May 11, 1668, Thomas and Frances Taylor sold "Little Eltonhead Manor" which they then occupied and which consisted of 600 acres lying in Calvert County to Charles Calvert for 15,000 pounds of tobacco (<u>Arch. of Md</u>., vol. LVII, pages 294-296).

At this point it should be pointed out that some writers have identified Thomas Taylor, son of Jane Eltonhead, as the husband of Elizabeth Marsh and that the pair eventually became residents of the Chapel District in Talbot County. Those writers are mistaken. The Thomas Taylor of Talbot County moved to Talbot from Kent County (see page 107 of vol. 1 of <u>The History of Talbot County</u>) and no relationship is shown in the records of this Thomas Taylor to Jane Eltonhead.

Thomas Taylor, son of Jane Eltonhead is positively identified as the husband of Frances in the transfer of "Little Eltonhead Manor" to Charles Calvert. The records also show that Thomas Taylor and his wife, Frances, remained husband and wife throughout their lifetime as proved by DLR 5 OLD 85 dated October 2, 1696.

At the age of 23, on October 1, 1666, Thomas Taylor of Calvert County was appointed Deputy Surveyor of the Province under Jerome White (<u>Arch. of Md</u>., vol. 57, page 116).

One year earlier, on February 23, 1665, he had had a 700 acre tract of land surveyed in what eventually became Dorchester County (Pat. L8 F507). The tract was called "Handsell" and it was located on the Nanticoke River and Taylor's Creek (known today as Chicone Creek). Four hundred acres of that tract was from an assignment by his mother, Jane Eltonhead, and three hundred acres for transporting John Taylor, his son; Frances Taylor, Samuel Minor, Margaret Vanmersse, Arthur Nuthall, and Mary a servant.

On May 29, 1668, Thomas Taylor was granted "Taylor's Inheritance" containing over 200 acres on Taylors Island

(Pat. L11 F456). In the next few years he obtained, literally, dozens of tracts of land, some large, some small; and in locations from one end of Dorchester County to the other. In addition to those tracts which he obtained by patent he acquired some additional ones by purchase. He acquired by patent on August 14, 1675, a 1000 acre tract located at the head of Secretary Creek called "Bath." On November 19, 1678, he acquired another 1000 acre tract, by patent, called "Taylor's Neglect" located on the south east side of the Chicamacomico River. He became one of the largest land-owners of the County.

Thomas Taylor was appointed Sheriff to succeed Raymond Staplefort and the land records of the County show that he was acting in that capacity in January 1669/70 (DLR 1 OLD 9). He served as sheriff until 1677. He was appointed a commissioner of Dorchester County in 1679 and served for a number of years.

In 1678 he was a Captain in the Militia of Dorchester County (Arch. of Md., vol. 7, page 92). He was later promoted to Major and placed in charge of all the Militia in Dorchester (Arch. of Md., vol. 5, page 554). In 1683 he was named on the "Commission to Purchase Land and Lay Out Towns in Dorchester County" (Arch. of Md., vol. 7, page 612). In March of 1686 he was appointed Examiner and Deputy Surveyor General for Maryland under Col. Vincent Lowe, Surveyor General of the State (Arch. of Md., vol. 17, page 466). In September of 1686 Mayor Taylor was appointed officer for the Town of Cambridge (Arch. of Md., vol. 5, page 503).

On October 2, 1696, Thomas Taylor made a deed (DLR 5 OLD 85) that was tantamount to a will, following is an abstract of that deed:

"Thomas Taylor of Dorchester County, Gent., to his four sons John Taylor, Thomas Taylor, Phillip Taylor, and Peter Taylor: All his property, said four sons to provide maintenance for their father and mother Thomas and Frances Taylor for their lifetime and also for Frances and Mary Taylor their two youngest sisters until they are married and to make over to their sister Aloysia Taylor 400 acres of land on Hunting Creek when she shall require it."

John Taylor, son of Thomas and Frances Taylor, made his will November 17, 1705, and it was probated February 4, 1705/6 (Wills 3, 736). In it he named: sons Thomas and William, daughters Dorothy, Elizabeth, Jane, Frances and Ellinor; wife Dorothy.

Thomas Taylor, son of Thomas and Frances Taylor, made his will April 5, 1709, and it was probated in June of that year (Wills Part 2-12, 113). In it he named: son Bartholomew and an unborn child; wife Jane; and he also named nieces Frances Teate and Dorothy Taylor.

Phillip Taylor, son of Thomas and Frances Taylor, made his will February 10, 1705, and it was probated June 6, 1705 (Wills 12, 75). In it he named no children nor did he name a wife.

## TENCH (112)

Liber 12, Folio 412, and 413, of the Patent Records shows that John Tench, mariner, of Talbot County, immigrated in 1669. In that same year a 200 acre tract of land was surveyed for him. It was called "Tench's Hope" and it was located on Tripp's Creek. Also in that same year a 50 acre tract called "Bridge North" was surveyed for him. It was located on Hudson Creek. Liber 12, Folio 396, shows that John Tench transported to the Province of Maryland John Conney, Hugh Jones, Richard Meekin and Edward Pinder.

The Land Records of Dorchester County show that John Tench's wife was named Elizabeth.

Dorchester Land Record 3 OLD 201 dated January 28, 1679, shows the transfer of "Tench's Hope" to Thomas Taylor and it also shows that John Tench was from the City of Bristol. He sold "Bridge North" to William Willoughby (DLR 4OLD 48).

Dorchester Land Record 5 OLD 113 dated January 10, 1695, shows John Tench, deceased, and named Edward Tench, planter of Dorchester County, as the son of John. It also names the wife of Edward as Katherine.

## THOMAS (X)

On March 4, 1667, Stephen Gary sold to Jacob Waymacke and William Thomas a 100 acre tract of land called "Spring Garden" (TLR L1 F33). The tract was located on Fishing Creek of the Little Choptank. When Jacob Waymacke died he devised his interest in "Spring Garden" to William Thomas.

In Dorchester Land Record 6 OLD 82 of 1705 Joseph Thomas and Jane, his wife, transferred "Spring Garden" to William Thomas (this William was probably a son of the original William).

No record has been found which would disclose the relationship of Joseph Thomas to the original William Thomas.

On November 12, 1714, William Thomas, planter, of Dorchester County, made a will (Wills 14, 180) which was probated December 6, 1715. In that will appears the following: "To son, John, upper part of "Spring Garden" given testator by his father...to son, William, plantation part of "Spring Garden." The will also named daughters Mary and Catherine as well as wife, Mary.

The will of Henry Beckwith II dated January 4, 1755 shows that his son, Nehemiah Beckwith, married Mary Thomas, daughter of William Thomas.

THOMPSON (X)

On August 20, 1681, a 136 acre tract of land was surveyed for Anthony Thompson; the tract was called "Westphalia" and it was located on the northwest side of a branch of a creek called Thompson's Creek that issued out of the north side of the Northwest Branch of the Blackwater River. In the ensuing months several other tracts in the same general area were surveyed for him.

On August 10, 1684, Anthony Thompson was granted a 50 acre tract called "White Haven" which was located on the northeast side of the waterway that is now called Church Creek. This tract later became the site for the Town of Church Creek.

Anthony Thompson made a will dated January 2, 1701, which was probated June 4, 1707 (Wills 12, 178). He willed "White Haven" to his son, Henry. He devised "Westphalia" to his son, Richard. Named, also, in his will were sons Anthony and Thomas as well as daughter, Ellinor.

The land records of Dorchester County show that Absalom Thompson had a resurvey made of "White Haven" in 1764, it is assumed, therefore, that he was the grandson of Anthony and son of Henry. Later still, in 1786, Thomas Thompson sold a number of lots from "White Haven" and it is assumed that he was the son of Absalom.

It should be clearly understood, however, that nothing has been found in the records to prove the relationship of Absalom and Thomas to Anthony.

THOMPSON (George)

On August 23, 1672, a 500 acre tract of land was surveyed for George Thompson; the tract was called "Thompson's Island" (Pat. L17 F302). That Island was later known as Goldsborough Island and still later as Bloodsworth Island.

George Thompson, with his wife, Jane Staplefort, came into the Province of Maryland in 1664 from Northunberland County, Virginia. He was the son of Peter Thompson of England; he married Jane Staplefort, sister of Raymond Staplefort. George and Jane Thompson settled in Calvert County, Maryland.

George Thompson, according to his will of March 7, 1714 (Wills 14, 73) died in Calvert County. In his will he named a son, George; two daughters, Elizabeth and Margaret; and wife, Johanna (he must have married a second time). There is nothing in the records to indicate that George Thompson or any of his children were ever inhabitants of Dorchester County.

NOTE: The will of Raymond Staplefort dated August 11, 1684, and probated September 3, 1687 (Wills 4, 265) refers to George Thompson as "brother."

THOMPSON (X)

On June 8, 1671, John Rawling had a 150 acre tract of land surveyed called "The Friendship." That tract was located on the western side of the Transquaking River. Rent Roll Record, Liber 10, Folio 388, shows this tract in the possession of Charles Thompson who married Rawling's daughter.

The will of Joseph Thompson (Wills 14, 373) which was probated in 1717 designated Charles Thompson, brother of Joseph, as executor of the will.

Joseph Thompson first appears in Dorchester records on April 1, 1673, when he had a 100 acre tract of land patented called "Thompson's Lott." That tract was on the Nanticoke River just south of the tract called "Weston." On June 2, 1684 (DLR 4 OLD 128), Joseph purchased a 200 acre tract on Chicone Creek called "The Forest of Delaware."

Joseph Thompson married Elizabeth Fisher, daughter of Frances Fisher. In his will Joseph Thompson named his wife, Elizabeth; and six children: Joseph, John, Frances, Ann (Ann married John Harrison), Elizabeth and Sarah. Records indicate that there was also a son named Charles.

Elizabeth Thompson, widow of Joseph Thompson, married John Harris. In her will (Wills 21, 290) which was probated November 27, 1734, she mentioned her daughter, Sarah Thompson. After she made her will and before it was probated Elizabeth married again (someone by the name of Richardson - see 8 OLD 154 dated April 3, 1727).

John Thompson, son of Joseph and Elizabeth (Fisher) Thompson made a will on January 10, 1734, which was probated February 20, 1734 (Wills 21, 288). In his will he named his wife, Jane; his brother, Charles, and several other relatives.

No information has been found on the family of Charles Thompson but it would appear that those two brothers, Charles and Joseph, were two of the progenitors of the Thompson line of Upper Dorchester County.

THURSTON (53)

On March 4, 1665, a 350 acre tract of land was surveyed for Thomas Thurston called "Tilberton" (Elberton). The tract was located at the mouth of Watts Creek and on the southside of the Creek. That location was in what is now Caroline County.

On June 24, 1671, Thomas Thurston of Baltimore County sold "Tilberton" to Thomas Hooker; on December 21, 1692, he made a will which was probated April 13, 1693 (Wills 6, 31). His will indicated that he was living in Baltimore County when it was made. He named in his will his son, Thomas; daughters Elizabeth, wife of Charles Rumsey, Sarah, daughter Elizabeth, wife of George Skipwith; wife, Mary.

There is nothing in the records to indicate that Thomas Thurston or any of his family were ever inhabitants of Dorchester County.

TICK (X)

On January 12, 1679, a 50 acre tract of land was surveyed for William Tick; it was called "Tickson/Teverton Addition" and was located in Fishing Creek of the Little Choptank River adjoining the tract of land called "Teverton" (Cert. of Survey, L15 F188). Rent Roll Record, Liber 10, Folio 401, showed the tract in the possession of Joshua Kennerly.

There is a legend that William Tick hung himself and that a "headless ghost" could often be seen in the dim shadows of Tick's Path which wound its way thru the woods from his plantation. In view of that legend it is of interest to note the following record which appears in Probate Liber 4, Folios 294-295, under date of January 12, 1687.

"This is a true and faithful account of the last will and testament of William Tick of Dorchester County, planter, whillest he was alive and had health and sound memory he did in our hearing declare that: First, it was his mind to will and he gave to William Kennelly (Kennerly) of the same County, planter, or his heirs forever all that plantation where he then lived known by the name of "Differton" (Teverton) and all appurtenances to the same belonging.

Secondly he gave to the said William Kanelly (Kennerly) in like manner after his decease to his wife all his personal estate..."

| | | |
|---|---|---|
| John Pitt | Nathaniell Clive | Wm. Sharp |
| John Edmondson | Wm. Dixon | Wm. Stevens |
| Wm. Berry | John Ashdell | Tho. Taylor |
| Wm. Lokwell | James Ridley | John Woodward |

The above record would indicate that the death of William Tick was at least sudden and most likely unusual.

Another record, Volume V, page 37, Archives of Maryland,

shows that William Tick was born in Amsterdam, Holland, and that he was naturalized by an Act of the Assembly in April of 1668.

## TODD (XX)

Captain Thomas Todd, who may have been an uncle of Michael Todd, is recorded to have come first to Maryland in 1640; in 1669 he brought his wife, Ann Gorsuch, and children: Ann, Frances, Johannah, John and Robert. It is possible that Thomas may have been a son of Robert (Robert came over in the Hopewell in 1622 and settled in Virginia) and been married in England and then brought his family over in 1669. He brought over with him on various trips others of the Todd family as follows: Cornelius in 1654; Francis in 1658; David in 1659; Robert and Elizabeth in 1665; Alexander in 1666; Thomas and Francis in 1670; Richard in 1671; John and Jane in 1674 -- all, these appear to have settled in Virginia.

In his will (Wills 5, 227) Captain Thomas Todd names only one son, Thomas, besides his daughters. He also mentions a brother, Christopher. Whether this Christopher is the same Christopher who settled in New Haven, Conn., in 1639 is not certain. Michael Todd of Dorchester was probably descended from the New Haven Christopher Todd.

Captain Thomas Todd was an inhabitant of Baltimore County when he made his will in 1675. While he owned a tract of land on Todds Point in Dorchester County adjoining a tract called "Sarke" (Arch. of Md., vol. 49, page 249) in 1664 no record has been found to show that he was actually an inhabitant of Dorchester County even though Todds Point derived its name from him. But it should be noted that Captain Thomas Todd married Ann Gorsuch and that Lovelace Gorsuch married Rebecca Preston and Lovelace and Rebecca owned at one time part of the adjoining property called "Horne." Most likely Lovelace and Ann were related.

Michael Todd is mentioned in the Dorchester Land Records as early as 1690 (DLR 1 OLD 110) and in 5 OLD dated November 19, 1698, the following abstracted information is disclosed:

"Andrew Insley and Elizabeth Insley, his wife, of Dorchester County, planter, to their son-in-law, Michael Todd, cordwayner alias shoemaker, and their daughter, Margaret Todd, his wife: "Stannaway Forrest" at the head of the northeast branch of Fox Creek which issues out of the east side of Hungar River, containing 50 acres more or less. Also "Andrews Fortune" adjoining the aforesaid land, quantity unknown.
Witnesses: Wm. Lee, Dennis Denawan.

Acknowledged November 22, 1698, by Joseph Goutey, son-in-law and Atty. of grantors. Hu. Eccleston, Clk."

As shown in the above abstract Michael Todd married Margaret Insley, daughter of Andrew Insley and Margaret Jones (Andrew was married twice). Michael was a cordwayner alias shoemaker by trade and he early formed a partnership with John Gootee (see DLR 4 OLD 75 dated May 1, 1690).

Michael Todd made a will dated October 17, 1730, and it was probated August 6, 1731. In it he named the following children: Michael, Benjamin, James, Elizabeth Dean, Dorothy Cole, and Ruth.

Michael II married Mary (last name unknown) and they had the following children: Michael III, Levin born June 24, 1743, William born May 4, 1746, and David.

Benjamin, son of Michael and Margaret Insley, married Betsey Elliott and they had John, Joseph, Job, and Jacob born December 22, 1756, Benjamin, Abraham born April 3, 1754, Sarah, Mary, Jane Phillips, Kessiah Elliott born February 23, 1743, married John Elliott, Jr., and Margaret.

James, son of Michael and Margaret Insley, married Alice Insley and they had: Michael, Jonathan, James, Jabin, Stephen, Althea and Dolly.

Jonathan, son of James and Alice Insley, married Leah (last name unknown) and they had Spencer, George, Cis, Sophia and Phoebe.

Michael Todd III, called Michael of the Fresh Water, left Lower Dorchester County, Md., soon after his father's death and sailed up the Choptank River to a point called Potter's Landing. He settled on a 361 acre tract which he acquired and which was located about seven miles from Federalsburg.

Michael Todd III married Mary, daughter of Harmon Johnson, and they had the following children: Levin, William, David, Michael, Nathan, James, Benjamin, Mary, Phoebe and Rhoda.

TRAVERS (X)

Elizabeth Chapline, daughter of William and Mary Chapline of Calvert County, was born in 1651 (Colonial Families of U. S. A. by MacKenzie, Vol. 2, page 175). She married William Travers of that County. Dorchester Land Record 3 OLD 172, dated August 18, 1679, shows William Travers, of Patuxent, as the purchaser of "Shapleigh's Chance" on Hoopers Island. This tract adjoined the tract called "Chaplin's Holme" which had been devised to Elizabeth by her father, William Chapline.

The records do not disclose when William Travers moved from Calvert to Dorchester County; his will dated November 20, 1700, which was probated October 24, 1701 (Wills 11, 180), shows that he was an inhabitant of Dorchester at that time.

His will named his wife, Elizabeth, as his executrix and it named the following children: Matthew, William, Thomas, Elizabeth, Mary and Sarah.

On June 9, 1712, Elizabeth and Matthew transferred part of "Taylor's Folly" on Taylors Island (DLR 6 OLD 194) to sons and brothers, Thomas and William.

The will of William II was dated March 1, 1728, and probated June 6, 1730 (Wills 20, 30). In it he named sons: William, Matthew and daughters: Rebecca Ferguson and daughter Mary. Son, William, was devised the dwelling plantation while son, Matthew, was devised "Taylor's Folly" on Taylors Island.

Matthew Travers I (1672-1742), son of William and Elizabeth (Chapline) Travers and brother of William II, married Elizabeth Hooper, daughter of Henry Hooper II. The will (Wills 22, 502) of Matthew I was dated November 17, 1741, and it was probated June 9, 1742. In his will Matthew I devised part of "Taylor's Folly" on Taylors Island to his son, William, and son, Henry. He also named sons Matthew and John, and daughters, Priscilla and Ann.

Thus, as shown by the above records, the primary location of the Travers family was changed from Hoopers Island to Taylors Island.

Matthew Travers II married Ann Brome, daughter of John Brome of Calvert County. The will (Wills 29, 421) of Matthew II was dated November 15, 1754, and in it he named the following children: William, Thomas, Matthew, John, Mary, Elizabeth, Nancy, and an unborn child. His wife (unnamed in the will) and his brother, Henry, were made executors.

Few families in the annals of Dorchester County have produced such a remarkable array of leaders in such varied endeavors as have the descendants of William and Elizabeth (Chapline) Travers. Legislators, jurists, military officers, merchants, ship builders, sea captains, physicians -- all, and many more are represented in the Travers line.

Like the Hooper family the Travers family had so many large branches that there are few native Dorchester Countians that cannot trace their lineage back to some branch of the Travers family.

The tax list of 1783 for Dorchester County, Lower District, contains many property owners named Travers, following are just three:

Captain Henry Travers of Col. "Taylors Folly" 50 acres and "Ferry Point" with 1 dwelling house, 1 kitchen, 1 corn house, and 3 other houses; "Neighbors Neglect" 75 acres, "Howard Outlett" 12 acres, "Lower Island Point" 124 acres with a house and 2 other houses for a total of 274 acres.

He also had 11 slaves, 2 horses, and 12 cattle.

Captain Matthew Travers, had 10 small tracts with a total of 342 acres, 1 dwelling house, 1 kitchen, 2 barns, 12 slaves, 2 horses, and 7 cattle.

John Ascom Travers had 5 tracts with 1 dwelling house, 1 kitchen, and 3 other houses.  He also had 14 slaves, 6 horses and 6 cattle.

TREVALLION (XX)

On April 25, 1668, Robert Custis of the Parish and County of York, Virginia, purchased from Isaac Abraham the 150 acre tract called "Ashburne" (TLR L1 F37).  On December 18, 1699 (DLR 5 OLD 152) Robert Custis deeded "Ashburne" to his son-in-law John Trevallion of Charles Parish in York County, Virginia, who had married his daughter, Jane.  That was the second marriage for John and by his first wife, Elizabeth, he had two daughters both of whom died before his second marriage in 1693 to Jane Custis.

John and Jane Trevallion had the following children:
    1.   John Trevallion, born August 8, 1694; died 1723; did not marry.
    2.   Samuel Trevallion, born May 18, 1696; died May 26, 1696.
    3.   Elizabeth Trevallion, born December 16, 1697; married John Stewart III.
    4.   Jane Trevallion, married Richard Manning.

TRIPPE (54)

Henry Trippe (1632-1698) of Canterbury, England, came to the Province of Maryland in 1663.  He transported himself and three soldiers who had served with him in Flanders:  Edward Hich, Cuthbert Browne and John Foster.

On March 20, 1665, he had a 150 acre tract surveyed at the head of Trippe's Creek (later called Brook's Creek) on the Little Choptank River in Dorchester County.  The tract was called "Trippe's Ridge" and it adjoined the land which had been surveyed for Michael Brooke.

Henry Trippe was one of the original commissioners of peace appointed for Dorchester County on May 6, 1669.  He served in that capacity for several years.  He represented Dorchester County at the Maryland Assembly and he became a Major in the militia.  In 1694 Major Henry Trippe returned to England for a visit and on October 9th of that year the Governor and Council of Maryland made the following appointments to the Dorchester County Militia:  Colonel Charles Hutchins, Lt. Colonel John MacKeel, Major John Ennalls, but if it should please God that Major Trippe should return into the Country he is to be Lt. Colonel (Arch. of Md., vol. XX, page 153).

The manner and wording of the appointment would indicate that Col. Trippe was regarded with a great deal of esteem by the Governor and Council of Maryland. He did, of course, return to the Province and spent four years more in Dorchester County before he died.

Henry Trippe married Frances Brooke, widow of Michael Brooke in 1665. He married a second time and according to his will the name of his second wife was Elizabeth. According to his will dated September 12, 1693, which was probated March 21, 1697 (Wills 7, 324), in addition to his widow, Elizabeth, Henry I was survived by the following five children:
1. Henry II, eldest son ( - 1723), married Susannah Heron.
2. John, who immigrated to Kentucky.
3. Edward, married Susan Hambleton, widow of Philemon Hambleton. Susan was the daughter of Hugh and Mary Sherwood.
4. Henrietta, married John Carslake on November 25, 1746.
5. William, married Jean Tate. William died April 24, 1770.

Henry Trippe I acquired numerous tracts of land as indicated by his will including "Sarke," "Trippe's Neglect," "Nemcock," "Trippelows Forest," "Apperley," "Dale's Delight," "Exchange," "Dales Addition," etc.

Brooks Creek on the north side of the Little Choptank River was originally known as Trippe's Creek after the Indian Trader, Henry Trippe I whose first land in Dorchester County was located at the head of that Creek. Trippe Bay, located south of Cook Point, still retains the name it acquired from Henry Trippe, a man who devoted much of his life in the interests of early Dorchester County, and, the man who was the progenitor of the Trippe line in Dorchester and Talbot Counties and much of the Trippe line throughout the Country.

Henry Trippe II married Susannah Heron and they had the following:
1. Henry, who married Elizabeth Emerson.
2. Sarah, who married Henry Callister.
3. Mary Emmerson Trippe, who married on September 22, 1768, Robert Goldsborough.
4. John, who married Ann Ennalls and they had Elizabeth, who married Hugh Eccleston; and Ann, who married John Dickinson.
5. Elizabeth, who married in 1734 Bartholomew Ennalls and they had Henry Ennalls who married Sarah Goldsborough, daughter of Robert Goldsborough and Sarah Yerber of London.
6. Edward, who married Margaret Murray, Edward died in 1772.
7. Sarah, who married Philip Emerson.
8. Mary, who married on January 29, 1739, Jacob Hinderman and they had James Hinderman, John Hinderman,

William Hinderman. Jacob Hinderman died in 1766.

Henry Trippe II made a will dated September 19, 1723, and it was probated January 17, 1723 (Wills 18, 214). In his will he made a bequest for the purchase of a silver plate for the Parish of Great Choptank. He also devised to his son, Henry, land at the head of Secretary Creek called "Bath" and "Addition to Bath."

Henry Trippe III, son of Henry II and Susannah (Heron) Trippe, married Elizabeth Emerson and they had the following:
    1. Henry IV, died unmarried in 1770.
    2. Elizabeth, who married George Maxwell of St. Mary's County and they had three daughters.

Henry Trippe IV made two wills, the first dated May 5, 1763 (Wills 38, 198) in which he named his mother, Elizabeth, as one of the executors and, apparently, she died prior to February 1, 1768 on which date he made a second one (Wills 38, 312). The contents of both wills were about the same. In both wills his nephew, Henry Dickinson, son of John Dickinson, was devised "Carthagena" at the head of Secretary Creek. He also named his sister, Mary Emerson Trippe, and others.

William Trippe, son of Henry Trippe I and Elizabeth, married Jean Tate and they had the following:
    1. Henrietta, married (first name unknown) Hughes.
    2. Elizabeth, who married Edward Noel of Castle Haven and they had Elizabeth Noel, who married James Kempt, Prot. Epis. Bishop of Maryland; and Sarah Noel, who married Capt. Cox, USN
    3. William, who married (1) Elizabeth Gibson, widow of Jacob Gibson, (2) Elizabeth Skinner of Talbot County. William Trippe died June 1, 1777. His children were: James, who married (1) Ann Dawson, (2) Elizabeth Skinner; Richard, born June 30, 1763 died January 16, 1849, married (1) Harriet Edmonson, (2) May 5, 1799, Mary Ennalls, daughter of Col. Joseph and Sarah Ennalls.
    4. Edward Trippe, who married Sarah (Noel) Byus, daughter of Edward Noel of Castle Haven, and widow of Joseph Byus.
    5. John Trippe, born April 17, 1711, married Elizabeth Noel.
    6. Jean MacKallin.
    7. Henry Trippe -- This Henry Trippe was not named in the will of his father, William Trippe, nor is he named in several genealogies that show the children of William Trippe, but he is readily identified by his will dated February 9, 1761 (Wills 31, 442).

NOTE: All of the grandchildren of William Trippe have not been named in the above listing.

Like Henry Trippe I some of his descendants have distinguished themselves in a variety of fields.

Captain Edward Trippe, born in 1771 at "Trippe's Regulation" (now Todds Point) built and was Captain of the first steamboat to be operated on the Chesapeake Bay.

Lieutenant Commander John Trippe, nephew of Captain Edward Trippe, was born in 1785. At the age of 16 he entered the United States Navy as Midshipman. Three years later, now Lieutenant, he acquitted himself with such bravery and gallantry that he was awarded the Congressional Medal of Honor by Congress and was presented with a gold sword and belt by the Maryland Legislature of 1806. In addition to the Congressional Medal of Honor and gold sword, Lieutenant Commander Trippe has had three vessels of the United States Navy to bear his name. A navy sloop was commissioned in 1812 and took part in the Battle of Lake Erie that same year. In 1910 the destroyer "Trippe" was commissioned and took part in World War I. In 1938 another destroyer "Trippe" was commissioned.

Another Trippe who distinguished himself was Captain Edward Trippe's brother, Levin Trippe. He commanded the privateer "Isabella" and was killed on her while in a Naval engagement in the Revolutionary War.

John Trippe, the 5th child of William, who married Elizabeth Noel, distinguished himself in another manner - he had 21 children.

TUBMAN (X)

Patent Record L14, F233, dated September 30, 1670, shows that William Jones received an assignment from Richard Tubman for 50 acres of land for his (Tubman) time of service. On May 21, 1672, William Jones and Richard Tubman had surveyed a 50 acre tract of land at the head of Hungar River on the south west side which tract was called "Saint Giles Field." Rent Roll Record, Liber 10, Folio 370, shows the tract in the possession of Richard Tubman. Tubman also acquired from William Jones tracts called "Jones Orchard" and "Jones Chance" as well as several additional tracts from others. He also had patented in his own name a 50 acre tract called "Tubman's Point."

Richard Tubman served as a commissioner of Dorchester County for several years. He married Eleanor Staplefort, the daughter of Raymond Staplefort (DLR 8 OLD 227).

The will of Richard Tubman was dated April 6, 1719, and it was probated January 13, 1727 (Wills 19, 183). In his will he named his wife, Eleanor, and his son, Richard II.

Richard Tubman II married Sarah Keene, daughter of Benjamin

Keene and Mary (Stevens) Keene. Mary (Stevens) Keene was the daughter of John and Priscilla (Hooper) Stevens. Priscilla was the daughter of Henry Hooper II and his wife, Mary (Woolford) Hooper.

Richard Tubman II and Sarah (Keene) Tubman had the following children:
1. Mary, born 1742, married Thomas Keene, son of Richard and Susannah (Pollard) Keene.
2. Sarah, born 1743, married Henry Cornwell.
3. John, born 1745, married Rachel Brooke of Calvert County.
4. Dorothy, born 1748, married Charles Staplefort.
5. Richard III, born 1752, married 1st Nancy Travers 2nd Mary Keene.

Richard Tubman II died January 27, 1786, aged 69 years. He was buried in St. Gile's Field, otherwise known as Cedar Point.

Richard III and Mary (Keene) Tubman had the following children:
1. Richard IV, born 1782, married Zaporya Wallis.
2. Ann, born 1784, married Major Samuel Keene.
3. Susan, born 1786, married John McMullen.
4. John, born 1788, married Nancy Nunan.
5. Charles, born 1789, married 1st Emily Barnes 2nd Susan Keene.
6. Dr. Robert, born 1791, married 1st Dorothy Staplefort 2nd Mary Gaithers Keene.

TURNER (157)

On August 2, 166, Daniel Clarke sold to William Merchant, planter, and Henry Turner, carpenter, 100 acres of "Clark's Outlett" which was located on Salt Marsh Creek (DLR 1 OLD 61).

Dorchester Land Record 4 1/2 OLD 21 dated September 3, 1679, shows Henry Turner as deceased and Abigail as his widow.

Dorchester Land Record 6 OLD 181 dated August 10, 1710, names Thomas as the son of Henry and Abigail and it also names Henry Turner as the son and heir of the said Thomas. That record also shows that Abigail took a second husband named Adams.

Other records show that the wife of Thomas Turner was named Elizabeth.

WAGGAMAN (XX)

Captain Henry Waggaman I was born in England; his parents were Jonathan Waggaman and Margaret Elliott; by 1745 he had married in Somerset County, Maryland, Mary Woolford, daughter of Levin Woolford and Sarah Jones; Sarah Jones was the daughter of Captain Thomas Jones and wife, Martha Davis; Martha Davis was the daughter of William Davis and wife, Anne Hooper.

Captain Henry Waggaman I and Mary (Woolford) Waggaman had a son named Henry II born in 1753.

On May 3, 1780, Henry Waggaman II married Sarah Ennalls, daughter of Thomas Ennals and Mary Sulivane; Mary Sulivane was the daughter of Daniel Sulivane (1708-1783) and Sarah Anderton (see DLR 7 OLD 57, 7 OLD 79, 8 OLD 447 and 10 OLD 27). Thomas Ennalls, son of Joseph and Mary (Brooke) Ennalls, married a 2nd time, Mary Anne Hayward.

Henry Waggaman II and Sarah (Ennalls) Waggaman had the following children:
1. Henry Waggaman, died young.
2. Thomas Ennalls Waggaman, born February 20, 1782, married Martha Jefferson Tyler, died 1832 and was buried at "Greenway" Tyler plantation burial ground, Williamsburg, Virginia. Martha was the daughter of Gov. John Tyler and sister of President Tyler.
3. Eliza Waggaman born 1784, did not marry and died July 6, 1866, buried Christ Church Cemetery, Cambridge.
4. Henry Pierpoint Waggaman born 1785, married Elizabeth Cropper.
5. John Waggaman, twin died infancy.
6. Mary Waggaman, twin died infancy.
7. George Augustus Waggaman, born 1790, married Marie Camille Arnoult.

Henry Waggaman II and his wife Sarah (Ennalls) Waggaman lived at "Fairview" their Choptank waterfront home located on Whitehall Creek.

Henry II was an attorney and on April 6, 1799, he was appointed by the officials of the State of Maryland as one of the Commissioners to acquire and make disposition of the Choptank Indian Lands. He also served as a delegate to the Maryland Assembly.

Henry Waggaman II died May 26, 1809, at age 58; Sarah, his wife, died October 16, 1842, at age 81; both were buried in Christ Church Cemetery, Cambridge.

WALL (153)

On October 28, 1669, Richard Webb of Calvert County, planter, sold to Thomas Wall of Dorchester County, planter, 100 acres of land and the tract was called "Snake Point." It was located on the east side of Fishing Creek of the Little Choptank River.

Thomas Wall and Alice his wife sold the tract to William

Worgin and Alice his wife on November 3, 1674.

Dorchester Land Record 4 OLD 107 dated June 2, 1684, identifies Thomas Wall as an innholder and in 4 OLD 234 he is further identified as Thomas Wall, Sr.

Dorchester Land Record 4 1/2 OLD 31 dated April 2, 1687, shows that George Martin married a daughter of Thomas and Alice Wall and also that they had a son named Andrew Wall who was characterized as their youngest son.

Thomas Wall made a will dated January 14, 1701, which was probated March 3, 1701 (Wills 11, 179). In the will he named sons Andrew, Joshua, Joseph and Alexander; wife, Mary (apparently he had married a second time). Son, Thomas Wall, was not named in the will.

Alexander Wall, son of Thomas, Sr., married Mary Merchant, daughter of William and Mary Merchant.

WAYMACKE (135)

On March 4, 1667, Stephen Gary sold a 100 acre tract of land called "Spring Garden" to Jacob Waymacke and William Thomas (TLR L1 F33). The tract was located at the head of Fishing Creek of the Little Choptank River.

Jacob Waymacke made a will dated March 22, 1670, which was probated May 26, 1673. In his will he devised "Spring Garden" and all personal estate to William Thomas.

WEBB (67)

On May 24, 1665, a 100 acre tract of land was surveyed for Richard Webb. The tract was called "Snake Point" and it was located on the east side of Fishing Creek of the Little Choptank.

Richard Webb of Calvert County, planter, sold "Snake Point" to Thomas Wall of Dorchester County on October 28, 1669 (DLR 1 OLD 79). Other records show that Richard Webb, eventually, became an inhabitant of Talbot County. Dorchester Land Record 6 OLD 131 dated March 2, 1708 shows that a Richard Webb married Rebecca Parrot, the daughter of William Parrot; that Richard Webb could have been a son of the Richard Webb who acquired "Snake Point;" in any event there is nothing in the records to indicate that Richard Webb ever became an inhabitant of Dorchester County.

WEINFIELD (18)

On April 28, 1662, John Weinfield had a 200 acre tract surveyed which was called "Weinfield" (Pat. L10 F413). It was located on what is known today as Hooper Point.

Rent Roll Record, Liber 10, Folio 344, shows the tract in the possession of William Pollard and the Debt Book of 1734 shows that it was still in his possession as of that year.

Dorchester Land Record 4 OLD 49 dated February 16, 1680, refers to the will of John Weinfield of Calvert County dated February 20, 1678/9 but this writer has not been able to locate said will and no other information has been located in the records about John Weinfield.

## WHEELER (X)

Dorchester Land Record 5 OLD 68 dated January 7, 1695, deeds 50 acres of "Skinners Neglect" on the northwest side of the Blackwater River near the head thereof from William Skinner of Dorchester County, carpenter, to Henry Wheeler, Sr., cordwainer. On the same date, Henry Wheeler also purchased from William Skinner an adjoining tract of 50 acres called "Beckwith's Addition" (DLR 5 OLD 67). In Dorchester Land Record 5 OLD 93 dated June 1, 1697, the wife of Henry Wheeler is identified as Alice. The records indicate that Henry Wheeler was also known as John Wheeler and it was under the latter name that his will was made on June 22, 1697, and probated October 7, 1697 (Wills 7, 333).

In his will he devised both "Skinners Neglect" and "Beckwith's Addition" to his son John (He states in his will that he, John, purchased the two tracts from William Skinner). He also named in his will sons Henry and Charles; daughters Jane Reed, wife of William Reed (Jane married Timothy MacNamara II after the death of William Reed), Ann wife of Christopher Short, Mary, wife of John Stewart; wife, Alice.

Dorchester Land Record 7 OLD 17 dated November 24, 1716, shows that John Wheeler II married Sarah (last name unknown).

John Wheeler II made a will on November 11, 1727, which was probated March 25, 1730 (Wills 19, 898). In his will he named his wife, Sarah; and sons Henry, James, John and Solomon.

## WHITE (63)

Jerome White, Surveyor General of Maryland, had a 1000 acre tract of land surveyed on April 7, 1665 (Pat. L7 F592); the tract was named "Weston" and it was located on the north side of the Nanticoke River.

On March 31, 1671, Charles Calvert commissioned Baker Brooke as Surveyor General and in the Commission he noted that Jerome White had been in England for some time and, apparently, Jerome White died there for his brother, George White of England, inherited his property.

There is nothing in the records to indicate that Jerome White was ever an inhabitant of Dorchester County.

WHITELEY (XX)

Some previously published accounts of the lineage of Arthur Whiteley are deficient in some aspects. According to those accounts he was born March 6, 1652, in Northamptonshire, England, and that he immigrated to Dorchester County in 1676; and further, that he married, in 1705, Elizabeth Rich, widow of William Rich (Colonial Families of U.S.A. by MacKenzie, vol. 1, paged 581).

The above account of his purported first marriage overlooks a number of Dorchester County Land Records.

On June 25, 1687, Arthur Whiteley acquired 150 acres of "Harwoods Choice," a tract of land located near the head of Fishing Creek (DLR 4 OLD 206). Then, on June 1, 1693, a tract of land called "Orphans Relief" was divided between Arthur Whiteley, innkeeper, and Charles Wheeler who had married the Worgan sisters (DLR 5 OLD 36 dated June 1, 1693). Those sisters were the orphans of William Worgan who had on October 6, 1674, furnished the building for a courthouse at Dorchester Town. The courthouse building was on property adjoining the property that had been acquired by Arthur Whiteley. William Worgan was also identified as an innkeeper. Thus, the Dorchester Land Records show that Arthur Whiteley first married a Worgan.

On August 2, 1699, Arthur Whiteley, planter of Dorchester County, transferred to his son-in-law, John Miller, a 50 acre tract of land with the proviso that if John Miller died without issue the land was to go to Arthur Whiteley's two daughters, Adling and Ann Whiteley (DLR 5 OLD 130).

Dorchester Land Record 6 OLD 123 shows the transfer of several tracts to William Hatfield, Jr., and Adling his wife, natural daughter of Arthur Whiteley.

Thus, the Dorchester Land Records show that Arthur Whiteley was not only married and had children by 1699 but, that one of the children was married by that time, and, that was six years before Arthur Whiteley married Elizabeth Rich. It is also very possible that he had other children by that date.

The only information that has been found about Arthur Whiteley's first wife is that her name was Mary. That fact is disclosed in the will of Thomas Preistly (Wills 11, 76) dated September 8, 1700. In the will Preistly refers to Mary Whiteley, the wife of Arthur Whiteley, as his cousin.

On July 30, 1730, Arthur Whiteley made two depositions that showed that he was 78 at that time. His will was dated January 20, 1729, and probated March 12, 1735 (Wills L21

F532). In his will he named the following children:  Arthur
Rich, Anthony, Alexander, Augustus, Abraham and Bing.

Arthur Rich, the oldest son, was born March 2, 1706, and
died November 4, 1771.  He was buried in the Whiteley
graveyard on the plantation called "Arthur's Seat" which was
located on the Dailesville Road at the head of Fishing
Creek.  His wife, Katherine, as well as several other
members of the Whiteley family were also buried there.

Arthur Rich Whiteley (1706-1771) and Katherine, whom he
married on July 30, 1730, had the following children:
    1.   Arthur, born June 10, 1731.
    2.   Betty, born December 10, 1732, married Colonel
Stevens Woolford.
    3.   Mary, born March 18, 1735, died May 1737.
    4.   Mary, born December 28, 1737, died October 24,
1781, married December 1, 1760, Matthew Travers of William.
    5.   Sarah, born March 12, 1740, married April 9, 1757,
John Stevens.
    6.   Arthur, born May 26, 1741, died March 20, 1784,
married July 13, 1768, Nancy Conway.
    7.   Nancy, born February 28, 1747, married October 16,
1769, Rev. Thomas McCracken.
    8.   Anthony, born January 1, 1749.
    9.   William Rich, born August 27, 1752.

Augustus Whiteley, son of Arthur and Elizabeth Rich, married
Elizabeth Hubbard before March 19, 1743, proved by deed from
Daniel Hubbard to Elizabeth Whiteley (DLR 13 OLD 18) which
states in part, "For the natural love and affection which I
have and do bear to my beloved only daughter Elizabeth
Whiteley, wife to Augustus Whiteley..."

Augustus and Elizabeth (Hubbard) Whiteley had the following
children (Chancery Papers No. 7397 - Hall of Records):
    1.   Augustus.
    2.   John.
    3.   Arthur.
    4.   Nehemiah, who married Rosanna Stewart August 17,
1785, Nehemiah died in 1814.
    5.   Mary, who married John Mitchell II.
    6.   Elizabeth, who married (?) Wheeler.
    7.   Sarah, who married John Wheeler.
    8.   Catherine, who married (?) Jenkins.
    9.   Ann, who married Thomas Dell.

Augustus, son of Augustus and Elizabeth (Hubbard) Whiteley
had the following children (Chancery Papers No. 7397 - Hall
of Records):  Henry, Mary, Nancy, William, Arthur, and Rose
Ann Whiteley.

Descendants of the Whiteleys intermarried with the
Woolfords, Travers, Stevens, Conways, and other well-known
Dorchester families.

The descendants of Arthur Whiteley who migrated to the adjoining County of Caroline and to the State of Delaware became politically and militarily active in those governmental entities.

Lt. Col. William Rich Whiteley was with the 4th Maryland Battalion of the "Flying Camp" in the Revolution and later became the head of the militia of Caroline County. In 1811 he represented Caroline County in the Maryland Senate.

The Colonel's son, William Stevens Whiteley, was a member of the Delaware State Legislature and later was a Senator representing Caroline County in the Maryland Senate. Still later he became a judge of the orphans court of Caroline County.

Some members of the Dorchester branch of the family became wealthy landowners. An example is shown by the 1783 Dorchester Tax List (Lower District) which shows Captain (Militia) Arthur Whiteley as the possessor of 1355 acres of land with 4 dwellings, 3 kitchens, 3 barns, and 11 other buildings; also, 20 slaves, 13 horses, and 50 cattle.

WILLIS (XX)

The first person with the surname Willis to appear in the records of Dorchester County was John Willis. He appeared as a witness on two deeds in the Dorchester Land Records in the year 1680. He could have been the same John Willis who made a will on September 18, 1712, which was probated November 24, 1714 (Wills 14, 12). In his will he named sons William and John; daughters Elizabeth and Grace. An addendum to the will indicated that there were two other sons that were not named in the will.

Dorchester Land Record 2 OLD 161 dated March 13, 1722, notes that Andrew Willis lived at Shoal Creek as of that time. Another record, 8 OLD 404, dated September 30, 1730, shows that Andrew was 40 years old as of that date. Andrew Willis made a will dated May 24, 1733, which was probated August 23, 1738 (Wills 21, 918). In his will he devised "New Town" to his sons Richard and George. He also mentioned sons John, William, Andrew and Thomas; daughter Sarah; wife, Rebecca.

Another Willis appearing briefly in the records of Dorchester County in the early 1700's was Thomas Willis and his wife, Lidia.

No record has been found that shows any relationship between Andrew, John and Thomas Willis mentioned in the preceding paragraphs nor has any record been found that would connect either of those three with the Richard Willis who is discussed in the following paragraphs; but in all probability a relationship did exist.

Dorchester Land Record 4 1/2 OLD 1 dated October 21, 1689, is actually the last will and testament of Richard Willis I; it reads, in part, as follows: To two sons Richard and John, dwelling plantation of 300 acres called "Rondly" when they attain age of 21 years; it also named daughter, Frances, and wife, Frances. The records of Third Haven Meeting show the births of the aforesaid children as: Richard August 13, 1684; John July 7, 1686; and Frances August 7, 1688.

The records of Third Haven Meeting show that the widow of Richard Willis, Frances, married Edward Fisher, planter, on January 8, 1699, at a meeting house near Tuckaho Creek.

On July 26, 1718 (DLR 7 OLD 63) Frances Fisher deeded certain lands to her sons Richard and John Willis with the proviso that they in turn convey "Rondly" to John Dawson.

On February 29, 1723/4, Frances Fisher, widow, of Edward Fisher, made a will which was probated May 7, 1729 (Wills 19, 679). In the will she named sons Richard Willis and John Willis; daughter, Frances Newton and Edward Newton the husband of Frances; granddaughters Frances and Mary, children of Frances and Edward; granddaughter, Elizabeth Thompson.

Richard Willis II, son of Richard and Frances, made a will dated November 6, 1741, which was probated January 20, 1741/2 (Wills 22, 439). In his will he named wife, Mary; granddaughter, Elizabeth Jolley.

Richard Willis III, wheelwright, made a will dated May 11, 1737, which was probated November 19, 1737 (Wills 21, 814). In his will he named sister Mary; cousin John Newton; Margaret, daughter of Edward Newton.

WILLOUGHBY (XX)

Archives of Md., vol. 10, page 237, shows that William Willoughby was an inhabitant of Virginia in 1652.

On March 16, 1670, a 100 acre tract of land was surveyed for him; the tract was named "Willoughby's Purchase" and it was located on John's Creek on the southside of the Great Choptank River adjoining Steven's land. In the next few years he acquired several additional tracts, some of patent and some by purchase.

Dorchester County Land Record 3 OLD 20 dated November 4, 1672, identifies William Willoughby as a "playsterer" and it named his wife as Hannah.

Dorchester County Land Record 6 OLD 221 dated March 22, 1709/10, shows in a deposition of William Willoughby that he was 86 years old as of that date.

The last mention of Hannah in the land records was in 5 OLD
33 dated June 5, 1693.  In Dorchester Land Record 6 OLD 172
dated March 26, 1711, William Willoughby is identified as a
"mason" and his wife is Anne.

On September 13, 1712, a William Willoughby made a will
which was probated in 1713 (Wills 13, 538).  In his will he
named his wife, Anne; young daughter, Sarah Willoughby; and
three sons Andrew, Samuel and Edward.

Samuel Willoughby, son of William, married Elizabeth
Skinner, daughter of Thomas Skinner, and they had a son
named Martin Willoughby (See DLR 10 OLD 85 and 10 OLD 152).

Martin Willoughby made a will dated January 2, 1750, (Wills
31, 311).  In his will he named wife, Rebecca; sons Titus
and Samuel; brother Job Willoughby.

WILSON (XX)

The Third Haven Meeting Records show James and Sarah Wilson
as parents of the following:  James b. 11/10/1693; Joseph b.
12/16/1695; Sarah b. 3/5/1698; Mary b. 8/19/1699; George b.
1/3/1701; William b. 6/3/1703/ and Thomas b. 10/8/1706.

James Wilson who was born on November 10, 1693, married Mary
Berry on October 10, 1716.  He must have married a second
time since later Land Records show his wife as Elizabeth.
He was the father of a son, also named James who married
Lilly Newton and they settled in Dorchester County in the
Fork District.

James and Lilly acquired a property called "Wilson's Plain
Dealing" which was located at the eleventh milestone of the
Maryland-Delaware Line and at what was then called "Wilson's
Cross-Roads."

James Wilson and Lilly his wife of Dorchester County on July
14, 1821, sold to Joseph Johnson of Sussex County, Delaware,
for the sum of $150.00 116 square perches of "Wilson's Plain
Dealing."  The 116 square perches were located in Maryland
in the fork of what was then known as "Wilson's
Cross-Roads," adjoining the Maryland-Delaware Line.

Johnson erected on his newly acquired plot a tavern which
became known as "Johnson's Crossroads Tavern."  The
Crossroads became known as "Johnson's Crossroads" and much
later as "Reliance."

James Wilson died December 19, 1840 at 94 years of age and
Lilly Newton, his wife, died October 29, 1840, at 85 years
of her age; both were buried on a farm located on the north
side of what is now Maryland Route 392 in the Fork District
(in 1968 the farm was owned by Jerome Frampton and occupied
by Olin Taylor).

WINGATE (XX)

Patent Record L16 F308 shows that Thomas Wingate immigrated from Virginia in 1671 with Elizabeth, his wife.

In 1683 both he and his wife, Elizabeth, are shown in DLR 4 OLD 129.

In 1684 and 1685 he is shown as a partner with John Spicer in several land acquisitions.

In 1688 John Spicer and his wife, Norah, sold a parcel of land and only Elizabeth Wingate signed the deed which would indicate that Thomas, her husband, was dead by that date.

Dorchester Land Record 6 OLD 109 dated February 10, 1699, shows "Jane" as the wife of Thomas Wingate. This was probably Thomas Wingate the second. Henry and Philip Wingate are also mentioned in this record and they are in all probability the children of Thomas the first. In a later record Philip is shown as a carpenter.

In DLR 8 OLD 325 dated December 31, 1729, Robert Wingate is shown as the son-in-law of William Evans and his wife, Alice. The wife of Robert is shown as "Hanah."

John Wingate is also mentioned in the Dorchester Land records several times in the 1720's.

A Philip Wingate is shown as a shoemaker in the 1723 records. Whether or not this was the same Philip Wingate that was shown as a carpenter in 1705 is not clear. The 1744 records show the age of a Philip Wingate as 65 years old (DLR 12 OLD 228).

The records, in summary, indicate that Thomas Wingate, the immigrant to Dorchester, had the following sons: Thomas, Henry, Philip, Robert, and John.

The Wingates had such a bountiful number of offspring that the order of descent has not been determined. However, following is the record of Wingate wills on file at the Hall of Records in Annapolis. No doubt, some are the will records of the children of the immigrant Thomas Wingate. A quick study of these will records will help one understand why the community of Wingate was named after that family.

Will of John Wingate dated July 15, 1747, in L25, F139, of the Will Records at the Hall of Records in Annapolis, Maryland, shows the following children: Sons: Thomas, John, Henry and James. Daughters: Rachel Scott, Lucy Parks, Priscilla Sanders, Rebecca Wingate, Mary Wingate, Comfort Wingate, Elizabeth Harper, Hanner Meredith, and Ann Pritchett. Wife: Rachel.

Will of Philip Wingate dated November 19, 1757, in L30 F660 in the above mentioned records shows the following children: Sons: Thomas, John, Philip. Daughters: Tabitha, Rachel, Disinah, Leah, and Sous. Wife: Sarah.

Will of Philip Wingate dated April 13, 1764, in L33 F8 in the above mentioned records shows the following children: Sons: Robert, William, Angelo, Lster (?), Hezekiah, John, Philip, and Thomas. Daughters: Elizabeth Willey, and Rachel Willey.

Will of Henry Wingate dated October 2, 1764, in L33 F2 in the above mentioned records shows the following children: Sons: John, Thomas, Zebulon, and Levin. Daughters: Mary Woolon, Elizabeth Wingate, Rebecca Wingate, Rachel Rumbley, Ann Wingate, Priscilla Wingate, and Mary Wingate.

Will of Thomas Wingate dated May 23, 1767, in L35, F414 in the above mentioned records shows the following: Son: Philip Wingate. Daughter: Juda Pritchett. Granddaughters: Delia Adams and Sarah Adams.

WINSMORE (135)

On October 30, 1667, Daniel Clarke sold to Robert Winsmore a 300-acre tract on Sharp's Creek called "Daniel's Choice." Sharp's Creek is known today as Lee Creek and it is located at the head of the Little Choptank River.

Patent Record, L12 F232 shows that Dr. Winsmore was a resident of what became Dorchester County as early as 1668. He was a commissioner of Dorchester in 1671 and he served several terms.

Dr. Winsmore proved his "head rights" on June 8, 1672 (Pat. L 16 F522). He transported from Virginia to Dorchester County: himself, Ann his wife, John and Robert his sons; Elizabeth, Judith and Ann his daughters; and seven other persons.

Dr. Robert Winsmore made his will on October 23, 1676. It was probated January 20, 1676/7. In his will he named his daughter, Elizabeth who married Alexander Fisher. He also mentioned daughters Judith, Sarah and Anne. He named two sons, Robert and John. He also named his wife, Katherine, apparently, he had married a second time.

Anne, the daughter of Dr. Robert Winsmore, married John LeCompte, eldest son of Anthony and Hester LeCompte.

John Winsmore married Elizabeth, the daughter of William and Sarah Mishew, and they had a daughter named Sarah but no sons.

Robert Winsmore II, son of Dr. Robert Winsmore, married Mary

(Wheeler) Hayward the widow of John Hayward who had died in 1692. Robert II lived only one year after he married Mary and they had one son named Robert. Mary married John Stewart after Robert's death and when John died she married John Hambrook.

There is no mention of any member of the Winsmore family in the Dorchester records after 1693. So, the name Dr. Robert Winsmore, that ardent Quaker whom George Fox visited on his tour thru Dorchester, and the man after whom Winsmore's Bridge was named, passed into oblivion.

WOOLFORD (XX)

Roger Woolford I was in Northampton County, Virginia, March 1660/1, when he married Mary Denwood. Mary Denwood was the daughter of Levin Denwood of Northampton and Accomack Counties, Virginia, and sister of Levin Denwood of Somerset. Roger Woolford came to Manokin in 1664 and settled on the north side of the Manokin River, east of Goose Creek; he was a surveyor of highways, a justice of the peace 1676-1697; member of the Maryland Assembly 1671, 1674, and 1682. He died in 1702. Roger and Mary (Denwood) Woolford had the following children:
    1. Mary Woolford, born prior to February 4, 1663, married Henry Hooper II after his 1st wife, Elizabeth Denwood, died.
    2. Elizabeth Woolford, born February 8, 1664, married Thomas Ennalls and when he died she married William Holland.
    3. Rosanna Woolford, born March 1, 1666.
    4. Roger Woolford II, born July 20, 1670 (see further).
    5. Sarah Woolford, born March 8, 1672, married Govert Loockerman.
    6. Ann Woolford, born August 26, 1675.
    7. James Woolford, born September 9, 1677 (see further).
    8. Levin Woolford, born September 20, 1683.

James Woolford (1677-1758), son of Roger Woolford I and Mary (Denwood) Woolford, was born September 9, 1677, and he married Grace Stevens, daughter of John Stevens and Dorothy (Preston) Stevens, on March 9, 1698 (see Records of Third Haven Meeting). James Woolford and Grace (Stevens) Woolford had the following children according to the will of James which was dated October 8, 1756 (Pro. 30, 672): James, Thomas, John, Roger, Levin and Rosanna Gray, wife of Joseph Cox Gray. The will indicated that there were other children not named in the will and other records show the children not named were Elizabeth, Ann, Sarah, David and William.

Roger Woolford II had moved to Dorchester County by 1696 when he became a justice of the County. He represented Dorchester County in the Maryland Assembly several terms.

He married Elizabeth, the daughter of Bartholomew Ennalls.
When Bartholomew died he devised "John's Point" and "John's
Point Addition" to Elizabeth. The two tracts remained in
the Woolford family for many generations.

Historians say that the original home on "John's Point" was
the site of the first court in Dorchester County.

Roger II and Elizabeth (Ennalls) Woolford had the following
children:
    1.  Mary Woolford (twin), born February 29, 1691,
married John Pitts and had Roger Pitts and Mary Pitts.
    2.  Elizabeth Woolford (twin), born February 29, 1691,
married Thomas Hicks.
    3.  John Woolford, died in 1750, married Mary Brown.
    4.  Thomas Woolford (1700-1751) -- see further.
    5.  Rosannah Woolford, married Jacob Loockerman.
    6.  Sarah Woolford, married John Jones.

Thomas Woolford (1700-1751), son of Roger II and Elizabeth
(Ennalls) Woolford, married Sarah, daughter of John Stevens.
    Thomas made a will dated October 29, 1750 (Pro. 28,
180). In the will he named the following children:
    1.  Thomas, who married Mollie Taylor.
    2.  Roger III, who married Elizabeth Jones (see
further).
    3.  Stephen, who married Elizabeth, daughter of Arthur
Rich Whiteley and his wife Katherine.
    4.  Bartholomew, who married Mollie Keene.
    5.  Levin, who married Mollie the widow of Bartholomew.
    6.  James, who married Nancy Pattison.
    7.  John Woolford.
    8.  Nancy, who married (1) Robert Mills, (2) (?)
Eskridge.

Roger Woolford III was born in 1727; he married Elizabeth
Jones. They had a son named Thomas Woolford who was born in
1755 and died in 1841. Thomas married Elizabeth (Betsy)
Woolford in 1781 and they had four sons and two daughters:
    1.  John Woolford.
    2.  William Woolford.
    3.  Roger Woolford.
    4.  Isabelle Woolford, who was born in 1785 and married
(1) in 1807, George Applegarth (2) in 1812 Thomas Byus.
    5.  Elizabeth Woolford.
    6.  Thomas Woolford, who married in 1814 Priscilla
Jones.

For those persons with further interest in the Woolford
family it is suggested that they examine File R Md 920 K of
the Maryland Room of the Dorchester County Library which
contains a lengthy genealogy of that family by James A.
McAllister, Jr. Perhaps the article which follows entitled
"A Captain Woolford is wrongly identified as a Colonel
Woolford" may also be of interest.

"A CAPTAIN WOOLFORD IS WRONGLY IDENTIFIED AS A COLONEL WOOLFORD"

In 1909, seven years after the "History of Dorchester County, Maryland" by Elias Jones was published, a suggestion was made in writing to the author by Judge James Gay Gordon of Philadelphia that the genealogy of Colonel Thomas Woolford, the Revolutionary War hero, which was contained therein should be corrected in any future issues of that history. No corrections were made, and as a result, the wrong grave has been designated by the DAR as that of Colonel Thomas Woolford; and the wrong genealogy still appears in the original and later issues of that publication.

The records show that there were two Thomas Woolfords who served in the Revolutionary War from Dorchester County. For purposes of clarification the two will be discussed separately in this article.

The Thomas Woolford who is wrongly credited by Jones as being the Revolutionary War hero is discussed first, and since he did serve both as a Lieutenant in the Revolutionary War and as a Captain in the Dorchester Militia in the War of 1812, the title Captain is used in this article to properly identify him.

Captain Thomas Woolford, son of Roger Woolford and Elizabeth (Jones) Woolford, was born January 10, 1755 and he died October 8, 1841. He married Elizabeth (Betsy) Woolford in 1781 and they had four sons and two daughters.

The Revolutionary War record of Captain Thomas Woolford is disclosed in Pension Claim S 14882 and Pension Application No. 33178 of October 10, 1837. He was commissioned a Lieutenant on April 1, 1777 in Captain Edward Noel's Company. The Company was attached to Colonel William Richardson's Fifth Maryland Regiment. He served for a period of eight months in that War. The pension file shows his date of birth, January 10, 1755, and the file mentions his wife, Elizabeth; his son Thomas; and his daughter Isabella Byus. The file also shows that he served as a Captain in the Dorchester County Militia in the War of 1812.

The grave of Captain Thomas Woolford was moved from "John's Point" to Gethsemane Church Graveyard in Madison, Maryland and an S. A R. marker was placed on it. It is unfortunate that the grave of Captain Thomas Woolford has been mistakenly identified as the grave of Colonel Thomas Woolford.

The Pension Records prove the correct identity of Captain Thomas Woolford and show that an incorrect genealogy is contained in Jones' History. However, there is another method of clearly identifying Captain Thomas Woolford.

The 1756 Debt Book (Liber 20) shows that Roger Woolford, father of Captain Thomas Woolford, owned "John's Point" in that year of 1756. "John's Point" descended to Captain Thomas Woolford and Dorchester Land Record 18 ER 116 dated September 10, 1840 shows that he, Captain Thomas Woolford, Sr., deeded "John's Point" to his grandchildren: Roger L. Woolford, Lewis Woolford and William Woolford. The title Captain is shown in two locations in the deed. Captain Thomas Woolford died one year after making that deed, and without doubt, he was buried on his dwelling plantation, "John's Point."

Since the Revolutionary War hero, Thomas Woolford, was in fact a Colonel in the discussions about him which follow, he will be referred to as Colonel Thomas Woolford. The actual facts concerning Colonel Thomas Woolford were not easy to find, probably because since 1902 writers and researchers have repeated the erroneous information contained in Jones' History. The parents of Colonel Thomas Woolford were James and Grace (Stevens) Woolford.

James Woolford of Somerset County was born in 1677 and was the son of Roger and Mary (Denwood) Woolford. He married Grace Stevens, the daughter of John and Dorothy (Preston) Stevens of Dorchester County on March 9, 1698 (see Records of Third Haven Meeting).

James Woolford made a will (Wills 30, 672) dated October 8, 1756, and in his will he devised his dwelling plantation and all of his lands to his sons James and Thomas Woolford. He did not name those lands in his will, but the Debt Book of 1756 (Liber 20, Folio 147) shows that he owned the following tracts: "Hydes Chance," "Barron Ridge," "Barron Addition," "Winfields Trouble," and "Stevens Chance." He had acquired two of those tracts from Thomas Brannock on June 5, 1747 (14 OLD 144). In his will James also named sons John, Roger and Levin; daughter Rosanna Gray, wife of Joseph Cox Gray; and he indicated that there were other children. Other records show that the other children not named in the will were Elizabeth, Ann, Sarah, David and William. Dorchester Land Record 2 NH 504 of June 11, 1782 - March 10, 1784 shows that Roger, the son of James, was born in 1716 while James, the son of James, was born in 1734. A DAR publication shows the birth date of Colonel Thomas Woolford to be 1735; the origin of this date is not shown but based on the information in DLR 2 NH 504 it could very well be the correct date of the birth of Colonel Thomas Woolford.

On September 8, 1795, Colonel Thomas Woolford and his wife, Priscilla, transferred to Roger Woolford, merchant, (DLR 8 HD 540) the several tracts which had been owned by his father, James Woolford, and which tracts had descended to him. Roger was the son of James and the Colonel's brother.

One year prior to the time that he transferred the several

tracts of land to his brother, Roger, Colonel Thomas
Woolford acquired approximately 600 acres of land on Fishing
Creek of the Little Choptank River (DLR 8 HD 134 dated
December 24, 1794). The 600 acres was of a tract called
"Teverton." Another Dorchester Land Record 12 HD 601 dated
March 26, 1798, shows that the Colonel was living at
"Teverton" as of 1798. Those two records specifically
identify Thomas Woolford as Colonel Thomas Woolford.

Records at the Dorchester County Courthouse show that
Colonel Thomas Woolford and Priscilla Stevens obtained a
marriage license on December 29, 1783. They had at least
three children: Thomas Woolford (Dr.) born October 10,
1793, died January 27, 1853; Kitty Woolford born April 16,
1797; James Woolford the youngest son who died prior to
1832.

Priscilla, the Colonel's wife, died June 8, 1802 (see
Records of Dorchester Parish).

Dorchester Land Record 4 ER 604 of March 21, 1817, shows
that (Dr.) Thomas Woolford made a petition for a division of
the lands of his father (Colonel) Thomas Woolford, deceased,
between the petitioner and his brother, James Woolford, a
minor. A Commission was appointed and the lands were
divided. The Commission specifically identified the
deceased in its report as "Colonel" Thomas Woolford. James
Woolford, son of Colonel Thomas Woolford, died prior to 1832
for in that year Dr. Thomas Woolford, the other son of
Colonel Thomas Woolford, acquired the property of the
deceased James Woolford (see Chancery Record B145 F403 of
1832).

Dr. Thomas Woolford, son of Colonel Thomas and Priscilla
(Stevens) Woolford, married Margaret Lecompte January 6,
1818, (see _Maryland Gazette_ of January 15, 1818). Dr.
Thomas Woolford and his wife, Margaret, had the following
children:
1.  Thomas Augustus Woolford (1818-    ).
2.  Benjamin LeCompte Woolford (1821-    ).
3.  James Alexander Hamilton Woolford (1823-    )
married and had issue:
    Kate Lecompte Woolford, who married Judge James Gay
Gordon of Philadelphia and had issue. They were the
grandparents of Elizabeth G. Knight. A second child was
Mrs. Dr. William P. Chunn.
4.  Thomas Edward Woolford (1825-    ).
5.  Catherine P. Woolford (1827-1884) married Robert H.
Pattison (1825-1875) and had issue:
    Robert E. Pattison, Governor of Pennsylvania; Kate
Pattison who married Benjamin Carlin.
6.  Emily E. Woolford (1829-    ) who married John B.
Smoot, Mayor of Alexandria, Virginia, in the 1880's.

Dr. Thomas Woolford died January 27, 1853, and was buried in

Christ Church Cemetery, Cambridge, Maryland. The records show that his widow, Margaret, and her surviving children sold part of "Teverton," the Colonel's home plantation on Fishing Creek in 1853 to Amos Bowdle (DLR 2 FJH 405 of October 6, 1853) and part in 1856 to Thomas Willis (3 FJH 578 of July 15, 1856).

Margaret (LeCompte) Woolford, widow of Dr. Thomas Woolford, died July 7, 1871, and she was buried beside her husband.

The service record of Colonel Thomas Woolford is scattered in several publications.

Volume 18 of the Archives of Maryland, pages 25-28, show that he was commissioned Captain of the 6th Independent Maryland Company on January 5, 1776. Volume 18 of the Archives also contains the muster roll of the original Company.

Historical Register of Officers of the Continental Army During War of Revolution, April 1775 to December 1783, by F. B. Heitman contains a sketch of the service record of Colonel Woolford.

A History of the Maryland Line in the Revolutionary War 1775-1783, by Reiman Stewart also contains some facts about the service activities of the Colonel.

In summary, the records show that he was commissioned Captain of the 6th Independent Maryland Company on January 5, 1776; December 10, 1776, Captain in the 1st Maryland; Major on 20th February 1777; Lieutenant Colonel 2nd Maryland April 17, 1777; Lieutenant-Colonel Commandant 5th Maryland October 22, 1779; taken prisoner at Camden August 16, 1780; exchanged December 20, 1780; transferred to 4th Maryland January 1, 1781; retired January 1, 1783.

For more detailed information concerning the service activities and exploits of Colonel Thomas Woolford during his seven years of duty in the Revolutionary War it is suggested that the above mentioned publications be examined and it is also suggested that reference be made to McSherry's History of Maryland.

The Index of Revolutionary War Pension Application (Hoyt Index) shows that Colonel Thomas Woolford was issued 500 acres of land on February 20, 1794, on Bounty Land Warrant No. 2404. No supporting papers were contained in the file, apparently they were lost when the War Office burned in 1800. Another publication shows that the 500 acre warrant was combined with a number of other warrants to total 4000 acres which were surveyed in Ohio for a land agent named James Johnson. Records have not been checked to ascertain if Colonel Woolford obtained a deed for the 500 acres or if he just sold the rights.

History of Maryland, by James McSherry shows that Colonel
Thomas Woolford was one of the original members of "The
Cincinnati Society of Maryland." Records of the Society
show that he was succeeded by his son, Dr. Thomas Woolford,
who in turn was succeeded by his son, James.

Research of the genealogy and activities of Colonel Thomas
Woolford has not turned up an obituary nor has the location
of his grave been found. The "Republican Star" of Easton,
Maryland, on March 6, 1804, carried a notice dated February
25, 1804, showing Roger Woolford as the executor of Col.
Thomas Woolford's estate (this Roger Woolford was the
brother of Col. Thomas Woolford). That notice established
the fact that the Colonel died sometime prior to February
25, 1804.

WORGEN (X)

On October 6, 1670, Robert Harwood of Miles River, Talbot
County, deeded to William Worgan and Alice his wife of
Fishing Creek, Little Choptank River, 150 acres of a tract
of land called "Harwood's Choice." The 150 acres was
located at the head of Fishing Creek adjoining the land of
Stephen Gray.

Later Worgan's land was designated by the Maryland Assembly
as the site for Dorchester Town and it was here that the
second court of Dorchester County was held. In fact, it was
held in a dwelling owned by William Worgan.

The records show that William Worgan was an innkeeper who
had a daughter named Mary who married Arthur Whiteley.
Whiteley was also an innkeeper. Another daughter of William
Worgan, Sarah, married Charles Wheeler.

WRIGHT (81)

Patent Liber ABH, Folio 204, shows that Arthur Wright
demanded 100 acres of land for transporting himself into the
Province of Maryland in 1651 and a warrant was issued to lay
out 100 acres for him on the Patuxent. (NOTE: Ishmael
Wright also transported himself into the Province of
Maryland in 1651).

Archives of Md., vol. 10, page 317, shows Arthur Wright to
be a planter of Patuxent in 1656.

On September 10, 1665, a 100-acre tract of land called
"Hodson's Point" was surveyed for Arthur Wright; the tract
was located on the north side of the Little Choptank River
at the mouth of Stewart's Creek (now known as Beckwith
Creek). In the years that followed a number of tracts were
patented in Dorchester County by Arthur Wright: "Taylor's
Chance" on the Chicamacomico; "Wright's Lott" on Wrights
Creek (now known as Phillips Creek); "Crick" on the north

side of Little Choptank; "Wright's Hope" on Todds Bay and Wrights Creek; "Five Pines" on Castle Haven Bay -- all, were surveyed for Arthur Wright. He also acquired other land by purchase.

Dorchester Land Record 1 OLD 58 dated August 3, 1670, shows that he was sub-sheriff of Dorchester County at that time.

On November 4, 1672, Arthur Wright sold "Wright's Lott" (3 OLD 259). Sometime after that time and prior to September 29, 1679, Arthur Wright died, for on that date Abigail, his widow, deeded livestock to her children (4 OLD 6). Her children listed in that record were: Grace Wright, Absalem Wright, Edward Williams, Arthur Wright and Naomi Wright.

The records of Third Haven Meeting show that Naomi Wright and Joseph Adkinson were married February 2, 1699 at a meeting house near Fishing Creek, Dorchester County.

NOTE: See sketch on Edward Wright.

WRIGHT (68)

Patent Liber ABH, Folio 141, shows that Ishmael Wright demanded 300 acres of land for transporting himself, Ann his wife, and Ishmael his son into the Province of Maryland in 1651. NOTE: Arthur Wright also transported himself into the Province of Maryland in 1651.

Archives of Md., vol. 10, page 410, shows that Ishmael Wright was appointed constable for the southside of Patuxent in December of 1654. He was aged 40 at that time. On page 317 of that volume he was characterized as a planter of Patuxent; and page 448 also of that volume identifies Joseph Wright to be the younger son of Ishmael the elder and page 455 and 456 identifies in September of 1656 an Ishmael Wright, Sr., and an Ishmael Wright, Jr.

On May 26, 1665, a 200 acre tract of land was surveyed for Ishmael Wright; it was called "Wright's Choice" and it was located on the west side of the Transquaking River.

"Wright's Choice" was acquired by John Brannock who sold it to Thomas Ennalls who in turn sold it to Edward Stephens. The tract was resurveyed for Stephens and included in "Presburys Composition."

There is nothing in the records to connect Ishmael Wright with any other Dorchester County branch of the Wright family although he could very well be the brother of Arthur Wright. In any event there is nothing in the records to indicate that Ishmael Wright ever became an inhabitant of Dorchester County.

WRIGHT (XX)

There were several Edward Wrights appearing in early
Maryland Records. An Edward Wright represented Kent County
at the Maryland Assembly in the early years of that county.

An Edward Wright is shown in the Somerset County records
when he married Katherine Covington who was baptized June
10, 1661, and who died August 1681. He was also listed in
the deed records of Somerset County.

Rent Roll Record Liber 10, Folio 385 on the tract of land
called "Crick" shows that the tract of land was given by
Morris Mathews to Elinor Wright and that it was in the
possession of her father, Edward Wright. In the will of
Morris Mathews he devised "Crick" to Elinor, daughter of
Edward Wright, and he noted in his will that Edward Wright
lived there when the will was made on September 3, 1705
(Wills 12, 298).

It has not been proven that any of the above Edward Wrights
were in any way related to the Edward Wright who had a 64
acre tract of land patented on December 10, 1714, which
tract was called "Whites Chapel" and it was located on the
west side of Chicone Creek. This Edward Wright married
Martha Kennerley, daughter of Joshua and Martha Kennerley.
It was probably this Edward Wright who was commissioned by
the Governor and Council in 1698 to make the survey for the
Nanticoke Indian Reservation.

The Edward Wright who married Martha Kennerley made a will
on March 31, 1747, and it was probated August 12, 1747
(Wills 25, 138). It shows that he owned land in Baltimore
County as well as in Dorchester County. The will indicated
that he was an inhabitant of Dorchester County when it was
made. It named his wife, Martha; sons Joshua, William,
Edward, Levin, Jacob and Lemuel; no daughters were named but
the will indicated that there were three.

Joshua Wright, son of Edward and Martha Wright, married 1st
Esther (last name unknown) and they had one son, Constantine
Wright, and 2nd, Sarah Turpin on February 19, 1781. No
record of any children by the 2nd marriage has been found.

Constantine Wright, son of Joshua and Esther Wright, was
born about 1755. He married 1st Bethaney Wroten and they
had the following children:
    1.  Euphamia Wright, married 1st John Pattison
September 23, 1807; 2nd Nimrod Andrew.
    2.  Joshua Wright, married Mary C. Hutchinson.
    3.  Elizabeth Wright (Bethaney), married Thomas
Connolly, March 14, 1816.
    4.  Levitia Wright, married William Corkran, October
28, 1823.
    5.  Jesse Wright, married Eliza Willis, January 11,

1819.
    6. Nancy Wright, married Francis Stevens, January 11, 1814.

    7. Kennerly Wright, married 1st Celia Lewis, January 29, 1818, 2nd Nancy (Nichols) Corkran, widow of Elisha Corkran on December 5, 1875.

    8. Cornelious Wright, married Mabel Stevens, November 9, 1824.

    9. Mary Wright, married William Stevens, February 9, 1824.

Constantine Wright, son of Joshua and Esther Wright, married 2nd Nelly Hurst on December 23, 1820, and they had one son, Peter Wright, who married Elizabeth Charles, daughter of Cannon Charles.

WROTEN (X)

When he immigrated to Maryland, William Wroten transported himself, his wife Johanna; son Thomas; daughters Allina, Diana, Elizabeth and Margaret; also James Crosse and William Furman his servants (Pat. Liber 17, Folio 547).

The Land Records of Dorchester County indicate that Wroten was an inhabitant of Dorchester County as early as 1670 for on February 6th of that year he purchased a 100-acre tract of land called "Staplefort's Lott" from Raymond Staplefort; the tract was located on the northeast side of Hungar River (DLR 1 OLD 97).

On October 16, 1671, Charles Calvert appointed William Wroten a Commissioner and Justice of Dorchester County.

On January 4, 1675, he obtained from the heirs of James Preston of Calvert County a 150-acre tract called "Stonewick" (DLR 3 OLD 96). That tract was located on what became known as Wroten Island. William and Johanna, his wife, deeded "Stonewick" to their son, William, Jr. on March 8, 1697/8.

Dorchester Land Record 7 OLD 8 of August 11, 1716, mentions William Wroten, Jr. and Rachel his wife. It also shows John Wingate as their well beloved brother which would indicate that Rachel was the brother of John Wingate.

William Jr. made a will on January 29, 1745 (Wills 24, 419) in which he named a son, Thomas; daughter Rachel Pritchett; and wife Rachel.

Generally personal titles have not been used in this index. It should be noted that only one listing per page is shown in the index whereas an item may actually appear more than once on the page listed.